HENRY FORD COMMUNITY COLLEGE
ESHLEMAN LIBRARY
5101 EVERGREEN
DEARBORN, MICHIGAN 48128

D1175354

WITHDRAWN

Prodigal Son / Elder Brother

Prodigal Son /

Religion and Postmodernism
a series edited by Mark C. Taylor

Elder Brother

Interpretation and Alterity in Augustine,
Petrarch, Kafka, Levinas

Jill Robbins

The University of Chicago Press
Chicago and London

HENRY FORD COMMUNITY COLLEGE
ESHLEMAN LIBRARY   AUG ·
5101 EVERGREEN   1993
DEARBORN, MICHIGAN 48128

JILL ROBBINS is assistant professor of English and comparative literature at
State University of New York, Buffalo.

The University of Chicago Press, Chicago 60637
The University of Chicago Press, Ltd., London
© 1991 by The University of Chicago
All rights reserved. Published 1991
Printed in the United States of America
00 99 98 97 96 95 94 93 92 91   5 4 3 2 1

Library of Congress Cataloging in Publication Data

Robbins, Jill.
   Prodigal son/elder brother : interpretation and alterity in Augustine,
Petrarch, Kafka, Levinas / Jill Robbins.
      p.   cm. — (Religion and postmodernism)
   Includes bibliographical references and index.
   ISBN 0-226-72110-8 (alk. paper)
   1. Prodigal son (Parable) 2. Judaism—Relations—Christianity. 3.
Christianity and other religions—Judaism. 4. Augustine, Saint, Bishop of
Hippo. Confessions. 5. Petrarca, Francesco, 1304–1374. 6. Kafka,
Franz, 1883–1924. 7. Lévinas, Emmanuel.   I. Title.   II. Series.
BT378.P8R63 1991
261.2′6—dc20
                                                                    90-19722
                                                                    CIP

261.2
R634 p   c.1

♾ The paper used in this publication meets the minimum require-
ments of the American National Standard for Information Sciences—Permanence of Paper for Printed Library Materials, Ansi
Z39.48-1984.

Contents

Acknowledgments

It is a pleasure to acknowledge the obligations that I have incurred during the writing of this book. A much condensed version of chapter 1 first appeared in *Genre* 16, no. 4 (Winter 1983): 317–33, and a slightly different version of chapter 2 in *Philological Quarterly* 64, no. 4 (Fall 1985): 533–53. Permission to reprint is gratefully acknowledged. A slightly different version of chapter 3 first appeared in Geoffrey H. Hartman and Sanford Budick, eds., *Midrash and Literature* (New Haven, Conn.: Yale University Press, 1986). I thank the editors of Yale University Press for permission to reprint. A Resident Georges Lurcy Fellowship at the Whitney Humanities Center, Yale University, in 1984-85 and a Faculty Research Development Grant at the State University of New York at Buffalo in 1986 gave me free time and financial assistance.

Paul de Man and Karsten Harries guided this work in its earliest stages. I benefited greatly from the advice of Harold Bloom, J. Hillis Miller, and Elie Wiesel. Daniel Boyarin shared his knowledge of midrash with me. I am grateful to Roy Roussel and William Warner, who read and criticized an earlier version of this book. Other friends and colleagues gave me generous encouragement: Carol Jacobs, Rodolphe Gasché, Stacy Hubbard, Rick Feero, Cathy Caruth, Lang Baker, Deborah Root, Lewis Fried, and especially Amresh Sinha. I owe particular thanks to Henry Sussman and Mark C. Taylor, whose perceptive readings significantly influenced the book's final form. I am

grateful to Gerald L. Bruns and Cynthia Chase, who advised me
on the completed manuscript.

I am most indebted to Geoffrey H. Hartman for his help and
encouragement throughout the course of this project, and for
his intellectual example.

Introduction: Figurations of the Judaic

The question of Christian theological models for literary inter-pretation has long been treated, both practically and theoretically, by literary scholars engaged in particular interpretations of Christian writers.[1] The theoretical end of the question has also been a traditional concern of hermeneutics, which, from its beginnings as a biblical discipline among early Christian writers to its philosophical unfolding in the nineteenth and twentieth centuries, has sought an interpretation *of* interpretation. Yet the corresponding question of Judaic models for literary inter-pretation has been much less treated. Indeed, it has remained in virtual eclipse.

One reason for this eclipse is that the Christian tradition already includes an account of the Judaic in its assertion of the *figural* relationship between the two testaments, namely, the idea that the Old Testament anticipates and is fulfilled by the New. In a work written for the instruction of new converts to Christianity, Augustine proposed the formulation, *In Veteri Testamento est occultatio Novi, in Novo Testamento est manifestatio Veteris:* "In the Old Testament there is a concealment of the New, in the New Testament there is a revelation of the Old."[2] Yet Augustine's formulation itself occults and conceals the truth claim of the Hebrew Bible that would be independent of the Gospel. It excludes consideration of the Hebrew Bible apart from what Harold Bloom calls its "captive" existence as the "Old Testament."[3] Christian hermeneutics, in its very inclusion of the Judaic, also excludes it.

1

This book poses the question of Judaic as well as Christian models for literary interpretation. In so doing, it seeks to include the Judaic otherwise. Yet such an effort must still take the eclipse of the Judaic as its starting point. This eclipse cannot be reduced to a regrettable oversight which needs to be corrected. If it were merely a question of the Judaic sources of philosophical and literary hermeneutics being obscured, then bringing the Judaic "into the light" would suffice. But within the metaphorical logic of figural interpretation, the Judaic is obscured *by* the very light the Gospel relentlessly sheds on it. It is eclipsed by being seen. In short, the eclipse of the Judaic—insofar as the Judaic is concealed in its very "concealing," excluded *as* included—has considerable rhetorical complexity. It has hermeneutical significance as well. For the question of Judaic models for literary interpretation, it determines a mode of access. It determines specifically the necessity of working through the interpretation the Judaic has received within figural interpretation, one that is often negative and privative, before even beginning to ask about Judaic interpretation in its own terms.

What is figural interpretation, and what is its reference to the Judaic? Within Christian hermeneutics, the patterns of fulfillment are rich and varied, both in their theological registers and as modes of literary representation. Augustine's formulation, proposed in a dogmatic and pedagogical context and long since congealed into a formula, cannot cover the entire territory. Yet the formula still proves instructive, for it sets forth terms which are central to the figural discourse: "In the Old Testament there is a concealment of the New, in the New Testament there is a revelation of the Old." The two testaments are related as old to new, hidden to manifest. These temporal and optical oppositions structure the entire discourse of the relationship between the two testaments.

According to Erich Auerbach, figural interpretation denotes primarily a temporal relation of promise to fulfillment. The opposition between hidden and manifest refers most properly to "a meaning first concealed then revealed."[4] The opposition between hidden and manifest provides the figural discourse with a theory of meaning and, ultimately, with a theory of the sign, both based on the distinction between sensible and intelligible sense. It describes *how* an older event signifies a later one. This extends to its variations within the figural discourse as the oppositions between blindness and seeing, shadow and reality, carnal and spiritual, literal and figurative. But the temporal opposition between old and new is foremost. As Mark C. Taylor argues, at stake there is the (theological) concept of the unity of history itself.[5]

In Auerbach's account, being able to understand the vital connection between two concrete historical events separated in time extends to an understanding of historical reality as a whole and ultimately affirms the interpreter in his historicity. Since the figures—persons and events—of the Old Testament are related to their fulfillment in the New by means of an accord or similarity, figural interpretation also affirms and celebrates the interpreter's perception of resemblances. The figural significance of Isaac's birth from a promise, of Isaac's carrying the wood of his own sacrifice, of a father's offering his son and receiving him back can be discovered in their resemblance to the story of Christ.[6] The constant interplay between old and new, past and present, that which in *figura* Auerbach calls "the changing aspect of the permanent,"[7] has a quality of actualization that allows for potential connections to the life of the interpreter as well.

Paul Ricoeur expresses this existential dimension of figural interpretation when he talks about the relationship between *liber* and *speculum*, the invitation to decipher at once the book and the life in the mirror of the book. This double invitation allows personal conversion—the death of an old self and rebirth of the new—to be understood in the light of Christ's passion and resurrection. It also renders hermeneutics, the understanding of meaning, as Ricoeur says, "coextensive with the entire economy of human existence."[8] This book's readings of Augustine and Petrarch investigate the economy of salvation that is implied in Christian hermeneutics. They follow out the tropologic—the logic of twists and turns—of narratives of personal conversion. The (self-)exegetical basis of these narratives is the figural relation between Old and New testaments.

Although Auerbach cautions against a reading of *figura* that would deny the historicity of the first of its two terms, the priority given the second term is undeniable. In fact, priority–specifically metalepsis, the reversal of early and late—is the central trope of figural interpretation. The retrospective view of figural interpretation renders the first "testament" secondary. Against the chronological and logical order, the New Testament asserts its priority over the old. Augustine writes: "For although the Old Testament is prior in time [tempore], the New Testament has precedence in merit [dignitate], since the Old Testament is the herald of the New."9 The reversal of the priority of the two testaments is of the order of value. Promise and fulfillment oppose deferred presence to full presence. The reversal is also of the order of truth. The oppositions hidden and manifest, shadow and reality, imply the epistemological valorization of the second term. In the writings of Saint Paul, from which figural interpretation draws much of its inspiration, the second term fulfills *and* annuls the first.

The New Testament and the early Church often figured the relationship between the Old and New Testaments as a relationship between elder and younger brothers. To assert the reversal of priority of the two testaments, they made use of the biblical paradigm of the reversal of primogeniture—the passing over of the firstborn son in favor of the younger one. Thus the supersession of the elder brother by the younger brother–as in the case of Esau and Jacob—prefigures the supersession of the Jewish people by their younger brother, the Christian people, as in the verse from Genesis cited by Paul: "the elder will serve the younger" (Rom. 9:12).

A related Pauline passage makes use of the rival wives of Abraham—Hagar and Sarah—as well as their sons, the elder and younger brothers Ishmael and Isaac. Paul argues that the servitude of the Old Testament and the freedom of the New were themselves prefigured:

For it is written that Abraham had two sons, one by a slave and one by a free woman. But the son of the slave was born according to the flesh, the son of the free woman through promise. Now this is an allegory: these women are two covenants. One is from Mount Sinai, bearing children for slavery; she is Hagar . . . she corresponds to the present Jerusalem, for she is in slavery with her children. But the Jerusalem above is free, and she is our mother. . . . Now we, brethren, like Isaac, are children of promise. But as at that time he who was born according to the flesh persecuted him who was born according to the Spirit, so it is now. But what does the scripture say? "Cast out the slave and her son; for the son of the slave shall not inherit with the son of the free woman." (Gal. 4:22–30)[10]

Paul contrasts Hagar the slavewoman and her son Ishmael, who was born in the course of nature, with Sarah the freewoman and her son Isaac, born as the result of a promise. The two women—related as carnal to spiritual—and their two sons provide a lineage for the two peoples, the Jews and the Christians. They tell in a figure of the rejection of the Jews and the election of the Christians in their place.[11] Moreover, here, as in the passage from Romans, the text from Genesis is *cited* as proof of the servile status of the Old Testament and of the substitution of the Christian people for their elder brother, the Jewish people. In this interpretive gesture, the Old Testament does not simply prefigure the events of the New. It prefigures the figural relationship itself. The Old Testament prefigures specifically its own supersession by the New Testament. The Old Testament is thus cited as an authority to discredit the Old Testament.

Augustine, in his gloss on the Galatians passage in the *City of God,* makes Hagar and Sarah figure not just the Old Testament's servitude and the New Testament's freedom but two kinds of signification as well. While Sarah is that part of the earthly city which has been made into an "image" of the heavenly city,

Hagar, the servant of Sarah, with her son, represented the image of this image. But the shadows were to pass away with the coming of the light, and Sarah, the free woman, signified the free city, which the shadow, Hagar, in turn, served to signify in another way *[alio modo significandae].* And that is why Sarah said, "Cast out the slavewoman and her son."[12]

Sarah figures the fulfillment; Hagar figures the figuring of the fulfillment. Augustine describes in effect the theory of figural signification that would underlie such a prefiguring that is itself prefigured. Elaborating on the standard figural vocabulary of image and reality, he calls Hagar "an image of an image." While

Paul cited the Genesis verse to authorize the "casting out" of Hagar and her children, the Jewish people, Augustine cites it to "cast out" Hagar, the figure of *figura,* and the "other" mode of signification that she represents as well.

The Pauline and Pauline-based readings of the biblical reversal of fraternal and spousal rank render the Old Testament, as Rosemary Reuther puts it, "a text for anti-Judaism on the one hand, and for ecclesial triumphalism on the other."[13] They posit a violent hierarchy between old and new. The violence of these readings rejoins the "heliopolitics"[14] of the figural discourse associated with the opposition between hidden and manifest. The interpretive obscurity, the "concealment" that characterizes the Old Testament, is no longer salutary; it is interpreted privatively as a blindness.[15]

In Augustine's *Expositions on the Psalms,* these negative attributes of the Old Testament are in turn transferred onto persons, onto those Jews who read the Old Testament without the benefit of figural interpretation. Glossing a verse from Psalm 57, "He hath given unto reproach those that trampled on me" (v. 3), in the context of a Christological reading which interprets "me" as Christ, and "those given unto reproach" as the Jews, Augustine writes:

Therefore in what does the reproach of the Jews consist? The Jew carries a book, from which a Christian may believe. Our librarians are what they have become, just as it is customary for servants to carry books behind their masters, so that those who carry faint and those who read profit. And it is in that that the reproach of the Jews traditionally consists; and that which was so long ago foretold is fulfilled: "He hath given unto reproach those that trampled on me." So what kind of reproach is it, brothers, when they read this verse and they who are themselves blind turn toward their own mirror? The appearance of the Jews in the holy scripture which they carry is just like the face of a blind man in a mirror; he is seen by others, by himself not seen. "He hath given unto reproach those that trampled on me."[16]

The "reproach" unto the Jews, it turns out, consists (1) in their servitude, in their carrying the book which they are unable to read because they fail to read figurally (and thus in a relationship to their own scripture that has been reduced to a custodial function), and (2) also in their self-concealment, their blindness, when they fail to recognize themselves *as* "the reproach" signified in the figural reading of the scriptural verse. As the reproach unto the Jews is, in Augustine's reading, double, so is their blindness, according to a logic which is consistent with the central tropes of figural interpretation.

Figural interpretation proposes a transfer from shadow to light, blindness to seeing. The Old Testament, when it is read with reference to the Gospel, can be illuminated as a source of light. But when it is not read with reference to the Gospel, the Old Testament is a privation of light; it is in eclipse. Then its interpretive obscurity rebounds upon its readers as a blindness, as a Judaism that is blind to the very light it emits. Because it fails to see that it is blind, it is blind *to* its own blindness, like "the face of a blind man in a mirror." Such a Judaism testifies to its own blindness (and to the Gospel's specular relationship to the Old Testament book) with a double blindness, which is the radical self-opacity of the outside.

Saint Augustine's particular anti-Judaic polemic is, according to Bernhard Blumenkranz, part of his attempt to come to terms with the Jewish resistance to the Christian mission. It is also tied up with his antiheretical polemic (proving useful in responding to those pagans who said that the prophetic texts were fabricated), as when Augustine describes the Jews as "librarians," bearing involuntary witness to a text that they themselves do not understand. Many of Augustine's assertions about the figural relationship between the two testaments are part of this antiheretical polemic as well. For example, Augustine's formula, "in the Old Testament there is a concealment of the New, in the New Testament there is a revelation of the Old," which asserts the perfect harmony and interdependence between the two testaments, may have been made in response to those who, following Marcion, wanted to sever the New Testament's bond to the Old. Ironically, many of Augustine's assertions about figural interpretation are part of an attempt to "save" the Old Testament.[17]

But the necessity for the negative and privative interpretation of Judaism in Augustine's work and in early Christian hermeneutics is not just extrinsic; it is intrinsic to the figural claim.

Figural interpretation depends, for its governing oppositions and for its claim to make a transfer from old to new, on understanding Judaism as hidden and as old. It has to suppress the Hebrew Bible, to render it an "Old Testament." For the Hebrew Bible, a scripture read without reference to the New Testament, would not understand itself in opposition to the New Testament. It would not understand itself in terms of the dyadic and hierarchical oppositions which make figural interpretation possible.

In rendering the Hebrew Bible an "Old Testament," figural interpretation has also to suppress the model of language that the possibility of the Hebrew Bible represents, as is the case with Augustine's gloss on Hagar and Sarah. When Augustine proposes to read Sarah as an image of the heavenly city and Hagar as an "image of an image," this "image of an image" turns out to be one "image" too many. Like a "figure of figure," the "image of an image" cannot definitively be said to belong to one of the two poles of figural interpretation, image and reality, figure and fulfillment. Thus Augustine's own reading of Hagar and her "other mode of signification" threatens to destabilize the governing oppositions on which his figural interpretation rests. It disrupts the self-reflexive closure of his interpretation *of* interpretation, of his theory of figural signification. When Augustine "casts out" Hagar, he casts out not just the otherness or alterity of the Judaic but a textual alterity as well. He casts out the threat that Hagar represents, namely, a rhetorical dimension of language unassimilable to the model of language on which the figural discourse depends.[18]

That model of language is phenomenological (i.e., perceptually based). It characterizes *both* the temporal and the optical oppositions, old and new, hidden and manifest. It makes possible the totalizing, chiastic symmetry of Augustine's formulation—"in the Old Testament there is a concealment of the New, in the New Testament there is a revelation of the Old." However, if the "in" does not simply denote a relationship of container and contained, outside and inside, but is the "in" of inscription, then it needs not to be seen but to be read. To understand the figural relationship between the two testaments, then, is not just to make an intelligible transfer between sensible and intelligible, carnal and spiritual, literal and figurative (as Augustine's hermeneutics would assert), it is also necessarily to read this figural relationship *as* a figure in yet another sense, as the figural or rhetorical dimension of the relationship between the two testaments. The necessity of reading the very figurality of the figural relationship between the two testaments (which surfaced for Augustine in the figure of Hagar) disrupts the asserted homology between literal and figurative, and carnal and spiritual. It disrupts the phenomenological oppositions that organize the figural discourse. It disarticulates the figural claim.

In short, in the figural discourse, the form of the suppression of the Judaic is rhetorical, marked by textual instances that are incompatible with the phenomenological model of language on which the figural discourse depends. This is evident in Augustine's reading of Hagar and in all of the projects of excluding the Judaic *as* included. Not only does the suppression of the Judaic take rhetorical form, but also *what* is suppressed in the figure of the Judaic *is* the rhetorical, a dimension of language that escapes and disrupts the phenomenological oppositions governing the figural discourse. Thus, while the suppression of the Judaic makes the figural discourse possible, it also makes it impossible.

Alerted to what he calls the "ambiguities" of the New Testament's hermeneutic detour through the Old, Ricoeur asks: "Would it not have been simpler to proclaim the [Christ] event in its unity? . . . Why has Christian preaching chosen to be hermeneutic by binding itself to a rereading of the Old Testament?" He suggests that the event "receives a temporal density by being inscribed in a signifying relation of 'promise' to 'fulfillment.'" But also,

In taking on time, it takes on meaning. By understanding itself indirectly, in terms of the transfer from the old to the new, the event presents itself as an understanding of relations. Jesus Christ himself, exegesis and exegete of Scripture, is manifested as logos in opening the understanding of the Scriptures.[19]

The *understanding* of the figural relation between the two testaments is what most fundamentally makes Christianity hermeneutic. It allows the Christian proclamation to constitute itself by a detour away from and back to itself. It is what determines the understanding of "hermeneutics" so that it is almost inseparable from "Christianity."[20]

In summary, the polemic associated with the name of Marcion (to which Ricoeur alludes in his question and answer) is internal to Christianity's interpretation of interpretation. Christian hermeneutics has to "save"—in every sense—the Old Testament. Yet it also has to throw out any aspect of it that implies it is not in need of saving. It thus has to posit the Judaic as a lack—insufficient and partial—and as an excess to be cast out, to inscribe it as outside. But by *in*scribing it *as* outside, by thus (in Ricoeur's phrase) "binding itself" to the Judaic, the text of Christian hermeneutics is in a double bind in relation to its excluded condition of (im)possibility.

This book finds an example of such a problematic double bind in the New Testament's inscription of its outside in the figure of the elder brother of the prodigal son. In the parable of the prodigal son in Luke 15, of which I develop a detailed reading in chapter 1, the younger son leaves his home, squanders his fortune, and returns to his father. But when the father graciously welcomes the repentant prodigal and kills the fatted calf to celebrate his return, the elder brother, who has never left the father, does not wish to remain in the father's house. He stands outside, "in the field," angrily reproaching his father: "All these years I have served you, yet you never gave me so much as a calf." He refuses to join the celebration.

As I argue in this book's chapters on Augustine and Petrarch, the prodigal son's journey—a movement of departure from and return to home and self—figures the very detour to the self that constitutes Christian hermeneutics and its economy of salvation. It underwrites all narratives of personal conversion, whether they be exemplary, like Augustine's, or belated, as in the case of Petrarch. So central is the prodigal son's story to the Christian imagination, describing as it does God's mercy toward sinners, that it has been called "the Gospel in the Gospel."[21]

The elder brother's story—if he has a story at all, for he neither departs nor returns—is on the periphery. The "outside" in which he serves his father is a place of complaint and unredemption. Excluded, by what critics call his jealousy, stubbornness, and blindness, from an understanding of the good news, and excluded even from an understanding of himself as excluded, he is at once in excess of the totalities valorized by the parable and indispensable to them.[22]

In giving voice to what readers of the parable have called "a legalistic merit doctrine," the elder brother figures the Jew in, and in relation to, the Gospel. As in the earlier examples of the Christian hermeneutical use of the reversal of primogeniture, the relationship between the prodigal son and his elder brother figures the figural relationship between the two testaments. The anthropological conflict is in fact a conflict of interpretations, for the elder brother who is passed over in favor of the prodigal son figures a Hebrew Bible which has been rendered an elder testament. What critics have identified as the elder brother's fanatical adherence to the letter of the law compares unfavorably to the plenitude of grace the prodigal son's story teaches. Here the earlier-identified interpretive gesture in which the Old Testament is made to yield anti-Judaic readings is completely "internal" to the New Testament discourse. The elder brother testifies to the Old Testament's insufficiency. He is the proof-text for the interpretation of the Old Testament's servitude and blindness.

But, as in all the other cases of this interpretive gesture within the figural discourse, when Christian hermeneutics by necessity suppresses the Judaic, it also exists in uneasy relation to this suppressed possibility. It is as if this unease were the textual form of what Nietzsche calls the "unheard of philological farce in regard to the Old Testament . . . the attempt to withdraw the Old Testament from the Jews by asserting that it contains nothing but Christian doctrine and belongs in truth to the Christians as the true people of Israel . . . a process which cannot possibly have been compatible with a good conscience."[23] For what this interpretive procedure most consistently suppresses is the self-understanding of Judaic exegesis. This is evident in Augustine's image of the Jews carrying the book from which the Christians believe, a book that the Jews themselves are unable to understand. The Jews are related to the Old Testament book physically or carnally: they *carry* it; the

Christians are related to it spiritually: they *believe* from it. This polemic against the "dead letter" (i.e., Jewish literalism), indeed the entire figural discourse, depends above all on suppressing the self-understanding of Judaic exegesis.

For the self-understanding of Judaic exegesis would give the lie to the figural assertion that the Old Testament discredits its own authority and transfers it to the New. It would disrupt the dyadic and hierarchical oppositions such as carnal and spiritual, literal and figurative, that structure every figural claim. It would make it possible to understand this religion of the book and its relation to the letter of language—otherwise. For if the book the Jews carry is not an Old Testament but a Hebrew Bible, then the figural discourse would collapse. Thus Christian hermeneutics has to suppress the self-understanding of Judaic exegesis. But it cannot, as it were, suppress it enough. It cannot suppress the Judaic without leaving a trace, as when it *in*scribes it as outside. Christian hermeneutics is "itself" at every point traced by the self-understanding of Judaic exegesis, namely, midrash.

Midrash, from the root word *darash*, "to seek or search out," denotes both the compilations of rabbinic commentary on scripture produced during the first five centuries of the Christian era and the actual activity of studying scripture, searching out its "non-obvious" meaning. In James Kugel's account,[24] midrash is primarily an attitude toward scripture, rather than a genre: its basic impulse is searching out the Bible for its present relevance, "actualization," "projecting the biblical past onto the present." Kugel points out that, to the extent that midrash or its prototype is an inner-biblical phenomenon, this biblicization of the present is a feature that characterizes not only the genres of apocalyptic and eschatological writings but all the modes of early biblical exegesis, including allegory and typology. (This common feature would be just one of the ways in which historically there can be no simple opposition between Jewish and Christian interpretive modes.) But the important difference between midrash, as an activity of postexilic Judaism, and other interpretive approaches, according to Kugel, concerns its specific "time-sense," or the distinctive nature of the present to which the midrash addresses itself. Whereas for the allegorist "the events of the soul portrayed in scriptural history apply to each man in his own life" and whereas for the apocalyptist "the broad strokes of divine activity in the biblical past are actually reappearing in the present day," for the midrashist there is the sense that, in Daniel Patte's phrase cited by Kugel: "God acted (in the past), will act (in the eschatological future), but is *not* acting in between."[25] The resulting sense of immanence—a radical immanence in which transcendence is nonetheless inscribed—may help to explain how, for the midrashist, the Bible is a point of reference more compelling than the present, a point of reference whose internal connections are inexhaustible.

The starting point for midrash is the scriptural verse, which is cited and then commented upon (often quite obliquely) by cross-reference to another scriptural verse. Such cross-reference, or juxtaposition, of verses is a basic procedure of midrash. The juxtaposed verse only sometimes belongs to the immediate scriptural context. More often, even preferably, it is found as far away from the initial verse as possible.[26] The rabbinic assumption is that anything in scripture can comment on anything else.

Between the scriptural verse and the verse to which it is juxtaposed lies an unstated question, a provocation, a problem. Midrash deals with problems in the scriptural text, philological and logical. These range from unusual or unfamiliar usages to contradictions within scripture, to its real or imagined gaps, to repetitions, redundancies, superfluities, to anything unusual on the textual surface. It is especially in response to scripture's perceived gaps that one finds the imaginative or embellishing function of midrash. Of course discovering a "problem" is sometimes simply a pretext for advancing a particular solution or articulating the urgent issues of a contemporary situation. As Judah Goldin has put it, midrash treats *or* creates problems in scripture.[27] The provocation for a midrashic remark needs in turn to be searched out, to be read.

Other fundamental midrashic procedures would come under the category of wordplay: these include paronomasia, metathe-

sis (transposition of a letter), and revocalization of the (conso-
nantal) biblical text. Finally, the form of the midrash requires
comment. As the transcription of an oral tradition, it presents
itself as a dialogue between rabbis, often over many generations. Within this "dialogue," as it has been redacted, a multiplicity of at times contradictory solutions to a scriptural problem are cited together.

Recently midrash has attracted the attention of literary critics
as a vital form of commentary in its own right and as an alternative source of our interpretive tradition. The midrash's degree of attentiveness to the scriptural text is exemplary. Its
"searching" attitude toward the text is at once rigorous, exact-
ing, and playful. Its meticulous concern with detail, with the
smallest semantic nuances, extends even to the nonsemantic, to
the text's diacritical markers. As a radically text-bound procedure that is not unlike what contemporary critics call reading,
as a form of interpretation whose historical origins and whose
practice suggest that it is not rooted in the presence of the
present, midrash has been seen to herald developments in
poststructuralism in significant ways.[28]

For example, the midrashic way of reading one text by cross-
reference to and commentary on another suggests a radical
openness to the text in its interrelatedness to other texts. It is as
if the perpetual referral of verses, with the multiple interpretations this engenders, were a refusal to give a single, exhaustive
explanation that would close off the reading. In this universe of
radical intertextuality, the implicit theory of language is nonmi-
metic: texts refer not primarily to reality or to a state of affairs
but to other texts. Midrash, as Susan Handelman suggests, is
turned *inward* toward a network of relations *within* scripture.[29]
Its orientation is not referential but intralinguistic.

This may sound surprising in talking about a form of interpretation of scripture, that supremely referential text. Yet despite the rabbinic assumption that everything in scripture is
significant, midrash is not solely oriented toward the determination of the scriptural text's meaning; that is, it is not exclu-
sively hermeneutic. Midrash is at least as much concerned with
how the scriptural text is made, with its poetics, testified to by
the predominance of (intra)linguistic and rhetorical operations,

wordplay, and everything we call plays on the signifier. Moreover, midrash does not simply observe these features of the
scriptural text; it mobilizes them within its own discourse as
modes of argumentation, as solutions to scriptural problems,
resulting in a distinctive interpretive diction.

Compared to the "clarification" we might expect from biblical commentary or exegesis, midrash seems to be a commentary
that does *not* seek to illuminate. The rabbinic commentator
who "searches out" the meaning of a scriptural verse resembles
Franz Kafka as a commentator on his own stories, as Maurice
Blanchot characterizes him: "He does not transpose the narrative onto a level which might make it easier for us to grasp. The
language he uses as commentator buries itself within the fiction
and does not distinguish itself from it."[30] This aptly describes
what appears in the midrash as a certain irreducibility of narra-
tive-commentary, a blend of commentary and creativity.[31] Unlike what we generally know as biblical commentary, the midrash does not "transpose" a scriptural verse into the form of
generality; it "buries itself" within scripture. Like a *literary*
criticism, it produces literature about literature. In midrash,
obscure verses are not brought into the light of intelligibility. If
the hidden remains hidden, that is not because it is ineffable but
perhaps because the underlying theory of language does not
base itself on the opposition between hidden and manifest. The
underlying theory of signification also distinguishes the midrashic from the typological use of intrabiblical correspondences.
In midrash, signification is not conceived as a going beyond the
sensible dimension of the sign to its intelligible signified. As
Geoffrey H. Hartman says, words "fall toward themselves" in
midrash instead of "pointing beyond" themselves as they do in
Christian typology and figural interpretation.[32]

Finally, midrash does share with *figura* the ability to mediate
between past and present. But while figural interpretation allows the interpreter to discover his interpretive temporality in
the temporal mediations that *figura* accomplishes, midrash
does not constitute the interpreter as a subject. As Hartman and
Sanford Budick explain it, this may be due to the midrashic
technique of juxtaposition of scriptural verses, which absorbs
even the interpreter into "a continuum of intertextual supple-

ments."[33] It may also be because midrash is so turned away from the visual. Midrash ignores the relation of *liber* and *speculum*. It is indeed in eclipse but not in a privative sense, not "the face of a blind man in the mirror," with the specter of mutilation that Augustine evokes, but turned away from the light and perhaps from the very solar metaphor itself.

In view of these claims, I would like to qualify my earlier reference to midrash as the "self-understanding" of Judaic exegesis. Midrash privileges neither a controlling interpretive self, nor is it necessarily oriented toward the (hermeneutic) task of understanding. Such a designation was part of an examination of the place of the Judaic *within* the Christian tradition and an attempt to detach the Judaic from the negative determination it has received there. All of my references to midrash in this book should be understood within the context of this attempt. My designation of midrash is thus not primarily historical, although it depends for its significance on the historical phenomenon of early rabbinic interpretation and takes off from it. As with my use of the term *Hebrew Bible,* it is hermeneutical, for it refers to a mode of *access* to the Judaic scripture that would be independent of the Gospel, a mode of access that includes the exegetical possibility and the distinctive mode of figuration proper to the Judaic. (My designation of midrash is also hermeneutical insofar as I focus on the recovery and reception of this ancient form of interpretation in the contemporary literary critical field. My aim is not to provide a historical explication of midrash but to make explicit the historically situated assumptions of those doing the recovering.)[34]

Hence, when midrash is invoked in this book (as in "midrash traces Christian hermeneutics"), it is part of a double operation of reading *and* unreading the determination of Judaic exegesis in the Christian tradition. (This is one reason why I generally do not define midrash in terms of what it is but in terms of what it is not.) For example, in my readings of Augustine and Petrarch, midrash intervenes as that which disrupts a totalizing figural poetics. It emerges as the locus of an awareness of the rhetorical dimension of language, the very dimension of language that prevents Christian hermeneutics from entirely suppressing the figure of the Judaic. Midrash traces Christian hermeneutics, in the sense that the figuration of the Judaic in Christian hermeneutics (as Old Testament, for example) and everything that would be part of the activity of a subject in this figuration, is inhabited by an unassimilable rhetorical alterity, "outside" the control of a subject. What shelters this unassimilable rhetorical alterity and this different understanding of the letter in its rhetoricity or materiality is the figuration *of* the Judaic, or proper to it.

My reading of Kafka in this book's third chapter is concerned with the possibility of identifying a specifically Judaic mode of figuration. What Martin Buber calls Kafka's "Paulinism of the unredeemed"[35] or the way in which Kafka positions himself as a Jew in relation to the Gospel and in relation to words which "point beyond themselves" (positioning himself as an "elder brother," in effect) prompts an exploration of midrash as a model for literary diction that could be an alternative to New Testament parable. Midrash does provide a model, albeit obliquely, for the Kafkan exegesis and mode of figuration, particularly in the case of what Jean-Francois Lyotard calls the Bible's "humor in relation to commands."[36]

While Kafka's work seems to call out for a Judaic interpretive model, the work of Emmanuel Levinas invokes it explicitly. Levinas needs some introduction here. Although this French Jewish philosopher of ethics is one of the most important voices in contemporary philosophy, he is little known on the American scene. (To the extent that he is known, it is largely thanks to Jacques Derrida's important essay, "Violence and Metaphysics.")[37] Levinas was born in 1906 in Lithuania. He studied in Strasbourg from 1923 to 1930 and was naturalized as a French citizen in 1930. He was a student of Husserl and Heidegger in Freiburg in 1928–29. His biography, as he puts it, "is dominated by the presentiment and the memory of the Nazi horror."[38] Both this "presentiment" and this "memory" take the form of an unwavering concern to render ethics, the imperative to be responsible to the other, a first philosophy.

Levinas's discussions of the priority of ethics are conducted within the traditions of phenomenology and ontology and against those traditions, which he claims ignore the other. He claims that the basis of his critique of phenomenology and ontology—his ethical thought—is inherited from the Hebrew tradition, specifically the Hebrew Bible read in conjunction with Talmud and midrash. Levinas is important to this book as a whole, because his work suggests new possibilities of reading the Judaic in its opposition to the "Greek" or "Christian." My chapter on Levinas tries to think through the tentative equation between the alterity of the other and the alterity of the Judaic that emerges in the chapters that precede it, and that is a central question for the reading and the reception of Levinas's work.

Thus the notion of the Judaic which guides much of this study opens other perspectives. It suggests an alterity that is in turn textual and intersubjective. The first part of this book examines the figuration of the Judaic within Christian hermeneutics and is particularly concerned with the interplay between a textual alterity and the alterity of the Judaic. The second part, which turns to a figuration proper to the Judaic, seeks to make explicit the links between Judaic, textual, and intersubjective alterity. As the book proceeds, it focuses increasingly on the question of the alterity of the other. The question is no longer simply how to read the suppression of the other but also how to write with an awareness of the other, how to write in a way that is not a suppression and appropriation of the other. What model of "dialogue" would suffice, what model of the other would respect his alterity? The book's concluding section, entitled "Versions of the Other," surveys the possible answers to these questions this book has traversed.

The status of the turn *to* the Judaic within this book requires comment. It is part of an effort, as it were, to ask about the discourse of the elder brother of the prodigal son, the discourse of the "dead letter." Such an effort imposes the question: what kind of return to the Judaic is possible? To ask what language the elder son can speak is to encounter a problem of speaking: how to speak the language of the "outside." The problem lies in the necessity of speaking about the Judaic in a language and a conceptuality that leans toward the hermeneutical. It lies in the necessity of invoking midrash in a literary critical language whose legacy is in figural interpretation. What kind of presentation can do justice to midrash's radical textual principles? How not to bring the Judaic "into the light?" The book's section entitled "Toward the Outside" tries to set these inquiries in motion. This section not only turns thematically to the Judaic, it enacts this turn.

Thus, in turning to a figuration that would be proper to the Judaic, the oppositional structure in which the Judaic is figured within Christian hermeneutics is not left behind. The question of the figuration of the Judaic retains two senses. How is the Judaic figured or imaged in Christian hermeneutics, and what is the figuration proper to the Judaic? These two senses of the question are not consecutive; they inhabit each other. This is borne out in the chapters on Kafka and Levinas. Both writers are oriented toward two traditions at once; they write in the margins of the dominant tradition, both toward and away from it. Kafka's midrashic diction goes by way of New Testament parable. In order to articulate a Hebrew ethics, Levinas speaks a philosophical language that he calls "Greek." When both these writers read the Hebrew Bible, they have to, as it were, read the New Testament first.

The sense of "first" here differs from the metaleptic reversals of early and late discussed earlier. When the New Testament asserts its priority over the Old, it overturns mere chronological succession in the name of value. But the sense in which reading the Hebrew Bible necessitates first reading the New Testament describes an immersion in a Christian conceptuality that is *pre*-supposed when one tries to gain access to the Judaic and that necessitates the detour through the Christian. The Christian conceptuality is *pre*supposed, even if one seeks (as in Levinas's case) to recover the Judaic as something ontologically prior or conditioning of the (Greco-)Christian conceptuality. One of the efforts of this book is to negotiate these different senses in which "the first will be last."

In summary, this book's turn to the Judaic is not simply a turn from new to old. Since even the figuration proper to the Judaic must be read within an oppositional structure, or read via the Christian, this return is neither nostalgic nor immediate. Moreover, the continuance of this oppositional structure, which is also a hierarchical one, underscores the sense in which the conflict of interpretations between midrash and hermeneutics (or between midrash and figural interpretation), as this book understands it, is not primarily historical.[39] At stake is the discursive asymmetry between the two, speaking about midrash in the language of hermeneutics. Because of this discursive asymmetry and because, in this book, midrash is a name for the eclipsed other of hermeneutics, for an alterity within hermeneutics, midrash cannot, finally, be called an "alternative" to hermeneutics. Hermeneutics and midrash are not two possibilities that appear in the same light. One is (in) the light; the other appears in a certain nonlight.[40]

Within the attempt to pose the (eclipsed) question of Judaic models for literary interpretation, the Judaic was found to *be* the eclipse. But as the eclipse of the Judaic can also be understood otherwise, the negative and privative interpretation of the Judaic is reinscribed. This reinscription is not simply the result of an interpretive intervention. To a certain extent, it is a possibility already liberated when Christian hermeneutics attempts to suppress the Judaic and remains in uneasy relation to this suppressed possibility. But the very possibility of this reinscription is also the impossibility of any return to the Judaic "in its own terms." This book attempts not a solution to but a deepening of this problem.

1 /

Prodigal Son and Elder Brother:
The Example of Augustine's *Confessions*

In book VIII.3, of the *Confessions*, Augustine's narrator digresses from the story of his life to meditate on how God and man rejoice more in the conversion of a great sinner than in uninterrupted piety.

Oh good God, what is it in men that makes them rejoice more when a soul that has been despaired of and is in very great danger is saved than when there has always been hope and the danger has not been so serious? For you too, merciful father, dost *more rejoice over one penitent than over ninety-nine just persons, that need no repentance*. We too are filled with joy whenever we hear the story of how the sheep which had strayed was brought back *[reportetur]* on the exultant shoulders of the shepherd and of how the coin was put back *[referatur]* into your treasury with all the neighbors of the woman who found it rejoicing. And the joy we feel in the solemn service of your house brings tears to our eyes, when in your house we hear read the story of your *younger son, that he had been dead and has come back to life; that he had been lost and has been found [quoniam mortuus erat et revixit, perierat et inventus est]*.[1]

The three parables from Luke 15 alluded to here have particular import for Augustine's narrator, who himself tells the story of a great sinner—one who has mistresses and an illegitimate child—who renounces his fleshly nature. In fact, the parable of the prodigal son is supremely pertinent to the narrator's story, because the prodigal son's story is the story of the death and resurrection of the self, the story of a conversion. All conversion

21

narratives necessarily understand themselves in terms of the parable of the prodigal son: death and rebirth, sin and grace, departure and return, self-alienation and self-recovery. The scriptural theme of the prodigal son in Augustine's *Confessions* is not merely a theme; it is the ground of its intelligibility.[2]

Augustine's narrator's reference to the prodigal son in book VIII.3 is not an isolated instance. The numerous allusions to the parable which precede the excursus in book VIII demonstrate the narrator's implicit self-understanding as the prodigal son. In book I, for example, Augustine's narrator compares his former estrangement from God to the prodigal son's departure from home. But since that estrangement from God is the result of being caught up in lustful affections, the narrator suggests that the sense of the prodigal son's journey be interiorized: "We do not go away from you [God] or return to you on foot or by spatial measurement. Nor did that younger son in the Gospel get horses for himself or chariots or ships; he did not fly away on any visible wings or travel by any motion of the limbs that in a far country he might waste in riotous living what you gave him at his departure" (I.18). Augustine combines here the Plotinian theme of the flight toward the divine country with the parable of the prodigal son in order to show that man's distance from God is spiritual.[3]

Another moment of the prodigal son's story is addressed when, in book II, the narrator sums up the episode of the robbing of the pear tree. He says that he strayed so far from God that he became "a wasteland" *(regio egestatis)* to himself (II.10). This region of *egestas*—hunger, lack, or destitution—has been compared to the famine in the distant country *(regio longinqua)* where the prodigal son resides when he begins to be "in want" *(egere)*.[4] Like the prodigal son, Augustine's sinner abandons a state of satiety, even superabundance, and exchanges it for a lack: "For I stole something of which I had plenty myself, and much better than what I stole" (II.4).

Three more allusions to the prodigal son in the *Confessions* explore this condition of satiety and its transformation into a lack. At home the prodigal son enjoys a plenitude of gifts from his father; when he takes his inheritance away from home, he squanders it. Augustine's narrator laments the similar way in which as a youth he squandered the gifts that God the Father gave him—intelligence and quickness of understanding—on the art of rhetoric, at which he excels to the point of becoming a professor of rhetoric, a "word-seller" *(venditor verborum)*. He also squandered his gifts on fruitless reading of texts such as Aristotle's *Categories,* which he understood but which did not help him to understand God. Of other unwholesome texts, such as the Manichaean writings, the narrator says that he "fed on" their doctrine but instead of being nourished he became weaker: "Far indeed was I straying from you, debarred even from the husks of the swine whom I fed with husks" (III.6). One of Augustine's editors glosses the line: "He lost interest even in the literature which he fed his pupils."[5] Like the prodigal son, Augustine's sinner finds himself in a repugnant situation indeed.

Finally, the prodigal son's distant country is again at issue when the narrator recounts his attempt at Plotinian ecstasy. The sinner glimpses "an unchangeable light," but because he does not yet know Christ, he cannot sustain his gaze and instead finds himself in a "region of total unlikeness" *(regio dissimilitudinis)* (VII.10). This quasi-mystical reference has been connected with the prodigal son's *regio longinqua,* understood not merely as an ethical distance from God in sin but as a radical ontological difference between man and God.[6]

All the allusions to the prodigal son in the *Confessions* emphasize the negative moment in the prodigal son's story, that is, his departure from home and his residence in a distant country, or (in the terms of the parable) his death. But in the *Confessions,* as in the parable of the prodigal son, this negative moment or death has its symmetrical counterpart in a subsequent moment of rebirth. These two moments take place within an economy— a loss and gain in a system of exchanges—of salvation. For example, when the prodigal/Augustine squanders his inheritance, an initial plenitude is lost. But yet another gift from the father (grace or mercy) transforms this loss into a far greater gain (salvation). This transformation effects an inversion of the values of loss and gain and an exchange of their properties that transcends their opposition in a "profitable loss." This is the interest of "the coin put back in God's treasury" (VIII.3).

This economic relationship between a negative and a recuperative moment in the parable of the prodigal son structures the entire *Confessions*. The economy of salvation is figured by the metaphors of death and rebirth, departure and return, sin and grace, blindness and sight, and—very prominently—aversion and conversion.

The doubleness of these metaphors is important because, as a narrative of conversion, the *Confessions* already has a built-in doubleness: it distinguishes between Augustine the already converted narrator and Augustine the subject of the narrative (the great sinner on his way to conversion). At the moment of conversion the sinner becomes the converted narrator, an "I" who is able to tell the story of its self-loss and self-recovery. This kind of division of the self, the possibility of losing or finding oneself in a succession of "moments," is the condition of possibility of personal history and the writing of that history. In this way, the conversion experience makes possible the first-person narrative; conversely, a formal requirement of a first-person narrative is a conversion experience. Moreover, the "I" that writes the story of its self-loss and self-recovery necessarily writes the story of its own coming into being as a story. Every story of a conversion is the story of "how I came to write a narrative of conversion," or "how I was a great sinner, then grace intervened, making it possible for me to write the story of how I was a great sinner," or even "how I was a tabula rasa, then grace intervened" and so on.

Every narrative of conversion, which reviews a life from the vantage point of its ending and endows it with retrospective coherence, also demands a dual viewpoint. The partial view of the experiencing subject, blinded by sin, is contrasted with the totalizing viewpoint of the converted narrator, for whom every sinful moment prior to conversion can be understood *as* sin prior to grace. This totalizing viewpoint depends on the prodigal son's death and rebirth, since it amounts to a survival of one's own death, a vantage point "beyond the grave." Augustine's converted narrator can retrospectively interpret all his former errings and detours as instances of the wrong kind of turning (*a*version or *per*version), which negatively anticipate the right kind of turning (*con*version), the turn to God.[7]

The quintessential wrong turn in the *Confessions* is the robbing of the pear tree in book II. The sinner and his unsavory companions steal some pears, the narrator says, "not to feed ourselves, but to throw to the pigs" *(non ad nostras epulas, sed vel proicienda porcis)* (II.4). The gratuitousness of the crime is emphasized by the fact that the sinner was not hungry *(nulla conpulsus egestate)*, rather, he was "stuffed with iniquity" *(sagina iniquitatis)* (II.4). But his appetite was insatiable: "I burned to gorge myself on hell" *(exarsi enim aliquando satiari inferis)* (II.1). The theft is performed solely for its own sake: "I loved nothing other than the act of theft itself and it too was nothing" *(ipsum furtum amavi, nihil aliud, cum et ipsum esset nihil)* (II.8). The narrator then qualifies this: "In the act of theft I must have loved something else too, namely the company *[consortium]* of those with whom I committed it" (II.8). In fact, the converted narrator extensively interprets this nothing (which he identifies as a sin of pride): "So all men who put themselves far from you [God] and set themselves against you *[adversum te]* are in fact attempting perversely to imitate you *[perverse te imitantur]*" (II.6).

The scene is not just an aversion (turning away) but a perversion (an overturning, a turning askew). The narrator calls this perverse attempt at playing God a "darkened likeness *[tenebrosa similitudine]* of omnipotence" (II.6). This scene of perversion has a perverse resemblance to the conversion scene as well if, following Kenneth Burke, one notes that insofar as the act of theft was gratuitously evil *(gratis)*, it is a parody of God's equally gratuitous act of grace *(gratia)* whereby Augustine had become converted.[8] Moreover, the unwholesome influence of the company of sinners would be "a perfect parody of Brotherhood within the Church."[9] A. Solignac also notes the "correspondence" of conversion and perversion here, namely, the salutary influence of individual examples of saintliness (book VIII) and this "contagion of a group of friends for evil."[10]

These "correspondences" are not surprising, given that within the economy of the *Confessions* this scene of perversion is the sinner's representative fall into Original Sin. As William

Spengemann suggests, "a conversion that is preceded by a sinful life is more interesting, even more valuable than uninterrupted grace."[11] This would mean in effect that a sinful life is a narrative exigency. The sinner's fall into perversion or aversion is logically prior to his conversion: in order to balance the books, there must be something to redeem, or buy back. Given Augustine's understanding of predestination, the conversion cannot be said to follow—that is, to result from—the errancy of his youth in the (theo)logical sense, any more than the gratuitousness of the Incarnation can be said to result from Original Sin. However, by another logic, which we might call "narrative," Augustine's conversion indeed follows from his aversion and recuperates it. Burke asks with reference to book II as a whole: "In the very thick of his concern with his 'perversity,' does he not here in effect announce to his readers (via a 'confession' to God) that the charges against him have been 'dismissed' [dimissa]?"[12]

Finally, we might remark the presence of the pigs in this episode, functioning as a metonymy for the greatest distance from God. Feeding them or having contact with unclean animals is a biblical *topos* for a culminating indignity, a degradation. They are always on the receiving end of something loathsome (like the pagan literature that the sinner feeds them while he gorges himself on Manichaean doctrine). Here pigs again receive the fruits of the sinner's labor, swallowing up the nothingness *(nihil)* of his theft.

All the sinner's activities prior to his conversion (the definitive turn in the right direction) can be interpreted, conveniently enough, as versions of the wrong kind of turning, from -*vert* words such as *pervertere, avertere, advertere, vertere,* which allegorize the sinner's proximity to conversion, to turns such as *volvere* and *versare,* which have not even a negative direction, but which imply a more general de-viation, a departure from the straight path onto "crooked ways" *(vias pravas)* and the "winding path of error" *(circuitus erroris).* Any activity of turning or viation without God as its direction is characterized by dispersal (many ways), error (circling), and falsity. One example of such a false turn, even a "false conversion," is the sinner's attempt at Plotinian ecstasy in book VII. Yet this example proves less convenient for the totalizing figural approach to the *Confessions*. Looking back on the episode, Augustine's narrator contrasts the self-sufficiency and pride of the Plotinian attempt at transcendence *(praesumptio)* with the humility of sinful man in confession *(confessio)* (VII.20). However, the false conversion is convincing enough to have left many of Augustine's readers wondering if what seems to be a simulacrum is the real conversion or if his conversion was a gradual process.[13] These suggestions upset the premise upon which the *Confessions* rests, namely, that a single moment (the *Tolle, lege* of book VIII) was capable of coherently structuring an entire life and its pious recounting. One can indeed argue, following John Freccero in a reading of Dante, that if the Augustinian distinction between *praesumptio* and *confessio* is taken seriously enough, the false conversion of book VII may be read as a figure that has its fulfillment in the true conversion of book VIII.[14] Then the false conversion would be yet another example of how Augustine's narrative reflects on itself by means of internal symmetries and correspondences. But the question perhaps remains: Can the turns which precede Augustine's conversion be said with certainty to prefigure it (as its symmetrical negative) in a fully controlled way, or do they undermine the uniqueness of that turn?

Augustine's narrator in the *Confessions* is adamant about the inadequacy of a merely philosophical conversion. True conversion, the conversion to Christ, happens not in intellectual isolation but in relation to others, in what Pierre de Labriolle has called "the contagion of example."[15] Romano Guardini writes that the truth of God's revelation as a theoretical abstraction is "impotent," whereas "the same thoughts, once they are embodied in specific persons, . . . summon the yet hesitant soul to come into its own."[16] Such a summoning of Augustine's sinner comes from three exemplary stories of conversion that are told to him—those of Victorinus, Anthony, and the *agentes in rebus*. Augustine's conversion in book VIII is explicitly a gloss on these anterior stories. He skillfully extracts elements from them—most prominently the importance of reading for conversion—and reconstructs them in his own intensely personal account. This relationship to prior examples allows Augustine to situate himself in terms of a paradigm of salvation history.

In book VIII, the narrator recounts that Simplicianus told him the story of Victorinus, a translator of Plato, an idol worshiper *(venerator idolorum)*, and a professor of rhetoric who runs a "talking shop" *(loquacem scholam)*, and who by sustained reading of the Holy Scriptures became a converted Christian. The narrator says: "I burned to imitate him, and this, of course, was why he [Simplicianus] had told me the story" (VIII.5). The narrator then recounts that one day a certain Ponticianus visited Alypius and him at home. Ponticianus spies a book lying on the table: "He took it up, opened it, and found *[tulit, aperuit, invenit]* the apostle Paul" (VIII.6). (Here we may remark the triadic figure that will be so important in Augustine's sinner's conversion: *arripui, aperui et legi.)* This discovery prompts Ponticianus to tell a story (which the narrator doesn't actually disclose until his own conversion) about Anthony the monk, who entered a church while the Gospel was being read—"Go, sell all that thou hast, and give to the poor, and thou shalt have treasure in heaven, and come and follow me"—and "as though the words read were spoken directly to himself" *(tamquam sibi diceretur quod legebatur)* was converted. (Augustine's sinner also converts by way of a scriptural verse, but he reads "in silence.")

Ponticianus begins yet another story about himself and three companions at Treves, who were out taking a walk. The party splits *(digressos)* into two and proceeds in two different directions. One of the groups, consisting of two *agentes in rebus* (administrative spies), wanders into a house, and finds a book in which the life of Anthony is recounted. One of the men begins to read, "and as he read, he began to think of how he himself could lead a life like this" (VIII.6). He grows angry with himself (just as Augustine's sinner does in VIII.7), and "he read on, and his heart, where you [God] saw it, was changed *[mutabatur intus]* and, as soon appeared, his mind shook off the burden of the world. While he was reading and the waves of his heart rose and fell, there were times when he cried out against himself, and then he distinguished the better course and chose it for his own" (VIII.6). He tells his story to his friend, who converts. The two of them tell their stories to their fiancées, who convert. But surprisingly enough, Ponticianus and *his* friend, arriving late, as it were, are not changed at all *(nihil mutati)* (VIII.6). They weep and congratulate, but they are not infected with the "contagion of example." This little immunity is the only exception to these rapidly multiplying examples, whose number will soon include Augustine's sinner.

The stories Ponticianus tells have such a decisive effect on Augustine's sinner that they provoke in him a dramatic scene of self-confrontation that ultimately propels him into the garden of his conversion. The narrator says:

Ponticianus narrated these things. But you, Lord, during his words [literally "in between his words"], were turning me back toward me myself, bearing me away from behind my back, where I had put myself, while I did not wish to turn toward myself; and you set me before my face, that I might see how filthy, how distorted and sordid, spotted and ulcerous I was. And I saw, and I was horrified, and there was no place where I might flee from myself. And if I tried to turn my gaze away from myself, he narrated that which he narrated; and you opposed me back to myself, and you thrust me into my eyes, that I might find iniquity and hate it. I had known it, but I dissimulated it, I overlooked it, and I forgot it.

Narrabat haec Ponticianus. Tu autem, domine, inter verba eius retorquebas me ad me ipsum, auferens me a dorso meo, ubi me posueram, dum nollem me adtendere, et constituebas me ante faciem meam, ut viderem, quam turpis essem, quam distortus et sordidus, maculosus et ulcerosus. Et videbam et horrebam, et quo a me fugerem non erat. Et si conabar a me avertere aspectum, narrabat ille quod narrabat, et tu me rursus opponebas mihi et inpingebas me in oculos meos, ut invenirem iniquitatem meam et odissem. Noveram eam, sed dissimulabam et cohibebam et obliviscebar. (VIII.7)

The peculiarity of the passage has to do with its two grammatical selves: the self as subject and object, *locus* and direction of its own activity. The resulting syntactical oddity—the number of first-person reflexive pronouns plus the intensive *ipse,* the constant iteration of the first person—gives the impression, not inappropriately, of one "me" too many. The strategy of the passage can perhaps be explained by analogy to the division between sinner and converted narrator: here that division is internalized. Or it can be explained by analogy to the Augustinian psychology of the will divided between proleptic adherence to the spiritual life and nostalgia for fleshly pleasures: one self has a moral overview of the sinner's conduct, while the other turns away from that view. This moral indetermination on the part of the sinner is dramatized by an excess of partial turnings. (We have translated the passage as literally as possible to point to this tropological agitation.) The sinner's moral indetermination has also a singularly savage quality. In his turning toward and away from himself, the sinner turns on himself, both in the sense of self-reproach (*retorquere*, "to turn, twist, or bend back," has from *torquere* overtones of torture and contortion) and in the sense of troping on the self.

"You, Lord . . . were turning me back *[retorquebas]* toward me myself, bearing me away from behind my back, where I had put myself, while I did not wish to turn toward myself, and you set me before my face, that I might see . . ." The sinner had turned away from himself; God turns the sinner back to himself. The systematic interdependence of the notions of turning away from and turning toward the self should be evident. *Retorquere*, "to turn *back*," already contains a history of self-loss and self-recovery in the ambiguity between its spatial and temporal senses. But the figure that organizes the entire passage is that of self-seeing: what the sinner turns toward and away from himself is his gaze. "You, Lord, were turning me back . . . that I might see . . . and I saw . . . and if I tried to turn my gaze away from myself . . . you thrust me into my eyes." It can be shown that in Augustine, seeing is a figure for a capacity to know. There is Augustine's narrator's demand to see God's face: "Hide not your face from me: let me die, lest I die, that I may see it" *(noli abscondere a me faciem tuam: moriar, ne moriar, ut eam videam)* (I.5). In this we might recognize Moses' demand to see God's glory (or face) in Exodus 33, a demand to know God in his eternal essence. But Moses sees only God's back—if that, according to some commentators.[17] In book X.5, Augustine paraphrases Paul's "now we see through a glass darkly, but then face to face" while speaking about the possibility of self-knowledge. Spengemann points out that while Paul "leaves the object undesignated, Augustine interpolates 'myself.'"[18] At stake then, when Augustine's narrator says "you set me before my face that I might see," is the possibility of the self's knowledge of itself as object, a totalizing symmetry between knower and known, "face to face."

But how can one be "before one's face" or "behind one's back?" How, for that matter, can one "turn on oneself" or "see oneself?" It is evident that, short of total self-dismemberment, none of these activities is possible on the physical, or one might say literal, level. They are figures based on a transfer from physical to spiritual sense. (In this same kind of transfer, physical self-seeing became intelligible, became self-knowing.) All of the physical contortions described in this passage have to be taken in this spiritual sense. However, there is one figural activity, "you thrust me into my eyes," that causes some trouble even to this sense. This figure produces two incompatible meanings, namely, (1) you made me see myself and (2) you made me blind myself. The first meaning is arrived at through a transfer from physical to spiritual seeing. The second meaning is arrived at by taking this figure at what seems to be its grotesque literal level. But is this so? The distinction between the two levels may, in fact, be impossible to maintain. The figural transfer that produced the first meaning, "you made me see myself," is based on physical seeing's being "blinded" so as to be understood as spiritual seeing. The second meaning, "you made me blind myself," is based on an equally figurative transfer: being thrust into one's eyes is still impossible on the physical level. The first figural transfer was a "blinding" of physical seeing so as to be understood as spiritual seeing; the second transfer entails a blinding of *that* blinding. How is this double blinding to be understood? Has the system of spiritual seeing/blinding been blinded again? If so, this blinding of blinding is a transfer no longer based on a distinction between physical and spiritual, literal and figurative. (It could be said to be a figure for the passage from literal to figurative, a figure for figuration, a figure of figure.) In this way the double blinding places in question the figurative logic upon which the entire "self-confrontation" scene is based. For the figural logic which dominates the "self-confrontation"—the transfer from physical to spiritual—would then contain a blind spot, a bit of excess which cannot quite be accounted for, that the text cannot reflect on. This blind spot is not just a blindness *to* but a blindness *in* language. We cannot read the phrase according to the first meaning without the second meaning's intruding. Perhaps there is always a blind spot, not only to "self-confrontation" but to self-seeing and to the self-knowing it would enable.

The simultaneity of self-seeing and self-blinding in the phrase "you thrust me into my eyes" produces a similar disruption of the *Confessions'* narrative logic as well. In the conversion of Paul (which depends on a chiastic relationship between blindness and seeing, physical and spiritual), the two moments are sequential: I was blind (spiritually, when I saw physically) and now I see (spiritually, now that I am blind physically). Conversion, the passing from the first to the second moment, is what guarantees the intelligibility of the story and makes possible the totalizing retrospective view: now I see that I was blind, and I see that I see (as when Paul regains his physical sight, which is now spiritual as well). When Augustine's narrator says "you thrust me into my eyes," namely, that in the same moment, he both blinded and saw himself, it is as though a nonconverted narrator tried to tell his story. But such a story, when it is not narrativized, is unintelligible. Yet he has to tell it. Immediately following the passage, the narrator explains that he deferred *(differre)* to follow God, lest God cure him "too soon" from the disease of a lust which he "preferred to be satisfied rather than extinguished" (VIII.7). This deferral of his conversion is the deferral of the possibility of telling the story of the conversion. But as he defers the story, he has to tell the story of the deferral of the story, which is, as we have shown, either no story at all or a very peculiar story indeed. This story of "no story" may be read as yet another "false conversion" or as another "immunity" to the contagion of example to which Augustine's own conversion is not quite immune. It is to the conversion scene as the blind spot is to self-seeing.

We shall be seeking the imperfect reflection of this blind spot and this peculiar story of "no story" in Augustine's use of the parable of the prodigal son (as a means of self-understanding) and in the conversion scene (the quintessential moment of self-seeing, or illumination). But before we discuss Augustine's use of the parable, let us first see what is usable in it and what is not.

He also said: A man had two sons. The younger said to his father, "Father, give me *[da mihi]* the share of the inheritance that would come to me." So the father divided the inheritance between them. A few days later, the younger son got together everything he had and left for a distant country *[regionem longinquam]* where he squandered his inheritance on a life of debauchery *[dissipavit substantiam suam vivendo luxuriose]*. When he had spent it all, that country experienced a severe famine, and he began to be in want *[egere]*, so he hired himself out *[adhaesit]* to one of the local inhabitants who put him on his farm to feed the pigs. And he would willingly have filled *[implere]* his belly with the husks the pigs were eating, but no one gave him anything *[nemo illi dabat]*. Thus having returned in himself *[in se autem reversus]*, he said, "How many of my father's paid servants abound in bread, and here I am dying of hunger! I will rise up *[surgam]* from this place and go to my father and say: 'Father, I have sinned against heaven and against you; I no longer deserve to be called your son; treat me as one of your paid servants.'" So he rose up from the place and went back *[surgens venit]* to his father. When he was still a long way off, his father saw him and was moved with compassion. He ran to the boy, clasped him in his arms, and kissed him tenderly. Then his son said, "Father, I have sinned against heaven and against you. I no longer deserve to be called your son." But the father said to his servants, "Quick! Bring out the best robe and put it on him; put a ring on his finger and sandals on his feet. Bring the calf we have been fattening, and kill it; we are going to have a feast, a celebration, because this son of mine was dead and has come back to life; he was lost and is found" *[quia hic filius meus mortuus erat, et revixit; perierat, et inventus est]*. And they began to celebrate.

Now his elder son was out in the field, and as he came and drew near the house *[Erat autem filius eius senior in agro: et cum veniret, et appropinquaret domui]*, he could hear music and dancing. Calling one of the servants, he asked what this might mean. "Your brother has come" *[venit]*, replied the servant, "and your father has killed the calf we had fattened because he has got him back safe and sound *[salvus]*." He was angry then and refused to go in *[introire]*, and his father, having come out *[egressus]*, began to plead with him; but he answered his father, "Look, all these years I have served you and I never transgressed your commandment *[nunquam mandatum tuum praeterivi]*, yet you never gave me *[nunquam dedisti mihi]* so much as a kid that I might celebrate with my friends. But as for this son of yours, when he comes back *[venit]* after devouring your property with harlots, you kill the calf we had been fattening." The father said, "My son, you are always with me *[tu semper mecum es]* and all that I have is yours. But it was fitting that we should celebrate and rejoice, because this brother of yours was dead and has come back to life; he was lost and is found" *[quia frater tuus hic mortuus erat, et revixit; perierat, et inventus est]*. (Luke 15:11–32)[19]

The prodigal son's story is a drama of self-alienation and self-recovery. He leaves his home (falling action, sin, aversion, loss); then, at the extremity of his suffering, he "returns in himself" and literally "rises up" to return to his father (rising action, grace, conversion, recovery). His father kills the fatted calf and rejoices: "My son was dead and has come back to life; he was lost and is found." In the terms of the father's interpretation, the prodigal son's itinerary is dialectical. Following the figure of Christ, he is home (life), away from home (death), and home on a higher level (afterlife?). In the economy of the prodigal son's career, loss brings about a greater restoration.

The parable is generally understood as an illustration of God's mercy. The father, in his love, is an image of God, whose joy is in forgiving.[20] The occasion for the parable in Luke is the criticism that Jesus received for dining with publicans and sinners. This parable, along with the parable of the lost sheep and the lost drachma, is Jesus' vindication of the Gospel. A structuralist study of Luke 15 that discusses the interrelationship between the three parables notes that the first two parables (the lost sheep and the lost drachma) thematize the economic order. The coin is a monetary unit and the sheep a farm product: both are used in the exchange of goods. Both parables insist on "the decrease in value of the large quantity and the great increase in value of the small quantity,"[21] namely, the value of the one lost sheep over the ninety-nine who have not strayed and the one lost drachma over the nine in the woman's possession. "Likewise," Jesus says, "there is more rejoicing in heaven over one repentant sinner than over ninety-nine virtuous men who need no repentance" (Luke 15:7). The same study then insists on a "transformation" from economic to human values in the parable of the prodigal son: the joy in relation to the repentant prodigal "loses all connotation of possession or property," for "it is no longer the object, whether lost or found, which needs to be counted and evaluated but the performance of a subject in transforming his own state."[22] This "performance of a subject," we argue, is precisely economic: the prodigal son's self-loss ensures his self-recovery, his redemption. The result of this "performance" is not the possession of an object but the possession of the self as subject-object. And this performance depends on the symmetry of self-dispossession and self-possession: "My son was lost and is found."

Augustine's reading of the parable of the prodigal son in the *Quaestiones Evangeliorum* (a fragmentary collection of replies sent to a pious reader) is, following the allusive reading of the parable in the *Confessions,* entirely predictable. Augustine's reading emphasizes the dialectical structure of the prodigal son's itinerary. This may be schematized in four ways.

The first schema is gifts, gifts squandered, better gifts. The prodigal son requests his share of the inheritance, just as, Augustine says, the soul delights in its own powers (to live, to know, to remember), which are divine gifts. The prodigal son takes these gifts, with the idea of enjoying the creation at the expense of the Creator, and squanders them. Hence he finds himself in a situation of no gifts: "no one gave him any" *(nemo illi dabat).* Upon his return home, the prodigal is given a robe, a ring, and sandals, which are, according to Joachim Jeremias, "the manifest tokens of reinstatement."[23]

In the gastronomic realm, the itinerary is satiety, famine, feast. He leaves his home (a situation of plenty) and plunges into a situation of total deprivation, signified by feeding the ubiquitous pigs. *"The hunger in that region,"* says Augustine, "is a lack of the word of truth; *one of the citizens of that region,* a certain airy chief belonging to the service of the devil; *the pigs,* the unclean spirits who were under him; *the pods on which the pigs fed,* the secular doctrines sounding with sterile vanity."[24] The prodigal returns to a feast, and the calf that feeds the "hungering son" is "the selfsame Lord himself, but according to the flesh, satiated with reproaches" (line 95).

In theological terms, the prodigal's itinerary is equivalent to paradise, fall, redemption. Augustine likens the prodigal's perverse enjoyment of God's creation to the sin of pride in the fall of mankind, "overconfident with reference to its powers" (line 20). When the father *runs* to meet his returning son (a voluntary descent in status),[25] it is God descending in Christ, "reconciling the world to himself" (line 76). The robe which the father presents to the son is "the dignity which Adam lost" (lines 90–91).

Last, in a philosophical sense, the prodigal life means living in what is "exterior" and relinquishing "him who is interior" (lines 23–24) (a threat, we might recall from the *Confessions*, inherent in any activity that is not God-directed). The distant region is "the forgetting of God" (line 25). The prodigal son's recollective return in himself is, for Augustine, a miracle (how could he remember that which he had forgotten?) and marks a remembering of Christ and a return to what is interior.

The prodigal son departs, returns, and reposes in the father. And so the joy is complete. Or is it? The parable continues: "Now his elder son was out in the field." The elder son does not go away and return; he merely obeys his father. (In Hegelian terms, he is an empty thesis, mere immediacy.) When he learns of his younger brother's return, he is angry, refuses to enter the house, and reproaches his father: "Look, all these years I have served you . . . yet you never gave me so much as a kid." His father replies: "My son, you are always with me . . . but . . . this brother of yours was dead and has come back to life." The prodigal son, in his death and resurrection, has a history, but the elder brother seems to exist in a dreary present which, as one critic puts it, is a "meticulous observance of a series of 'thou shalt nots.'"[26] Within the parable, the elder brother undergoes no conversion (death and rebirth) and has, therefore, no temporal destiny and in a sense "no story." Angry and unredeemed, he is outside "in the field" *(in agro)*. If the elder brother has a story, that story is "outside," *is* the story *of* the "outside."

The elder brother's complaint concerns the lack of proportion between merit and reward. How can one be greater than ninety-nine? Why is wasting the inheritance privileged over conserving it? According to one critic, to ask these questions is to miss the point: precisely such a "legalistic understanding of the divine-human relationship is shattered by the unexpected event of forgiveness which comes to man from beyond himself."[27] When the prodigal son resolves first to become one of his father's paid servants and then discovers that all he has squandered has been redeemed (bought back), he goes beyond the legalistic terms of the elder brother's relationship to the father, which is based on an economy of reciprocal exchange, to a new economy, where less is more and more is less. The elder brother's anger in the face of this new economy not only reveals to his critics the "self-righteousness"[28] and the "blind self-complacency" of one "trusting in his scrupulous observance of the letter of the law"[29] but indicates further that his obedient relationship to his father has been "based on a misunderstanding."[30] In the critical tradition surrounding the parable, the old economy to which the elder brother adheres is rendered increasingly suspect. The elder brother's relationship to the father is not only "legalistic" but "servile."[31] Moreover, although the elder brother may keep "the letter of the law," he breaks "all its spirit."[32]

In the parable, the angry elder brother is outside "in the field" *(in agro)*, like Cain about to kill his brother: "And it came to pass, when they were in the field, that Cain rose up against Abel his brother, and slew him" *(Cumque essent in agro, consurrexit Cain adversus fratrem suum Abel, et interfecit eum)* (Genesis 4:8).[33] The elder brother is not only literally outside, he is "outside" the story's spiritual significance. While the whole house rejoices, he alone is insensate to a story so significant that it has been called "the Gospel in the Gospel" *(Evangelium in Evangelio)* "because of the number of gracious truths which it illustrates."[34] Over and against his brother's self-recognition and his father's joy, he refuses to understand the edifying nature of the story. The father (principle of intelligibility, in the image of God) understands both sons. The prodigal understands himself in an itinerary of death and rebirth (or at least understands that his understanding has been shattered). But the elder brother understands nothing, neither himself nor his brother nor his father. He is a figure for non-self-understanding or misunderstanding. The elder brother is "outside" in the sense that he is excluded from those "to whom it is given *[datum est]* to know the mystery of the kingdom of God"

(Mark 4:11). The parable of the prodigal son contains, like all parables, the distinction between the parabolic and the non-parabolic, here in the figures of the younger and elder brothers.[35] The reader who does not understand the parable is then inscribed as the elder brother. As Jeremias reminds us: "The parable was addressed to men, who, like the elder brother, were offended at the Gospel"[36]—that is, the Pharisees and the scribes. The elder brother is indeed a Cain, a letter that kills.

Not only does the elder brother not understand but he cannot be profitably understood. For this reason, he is often excluded from critical discussions of the parable. John Ruskin remarks this exclusion of the elder brother in the *Praeterita,* when, during a "fashionable seance of Evangelical doctrine," Ruskin's protagonist asks what might be learned "from the example of the *other* son?" This wicked question horrifies the company, and finally someone explains "that the home-staying son was merely a picturesque figure introduced to fill the background of the parable agreeably, and contained no instruction or example for the well-disposed scriptural student."[37] From here it is only a short step to those critics who want the elder brother out of the parable altogether. Julius Wellhausen argues that the elder brother section is an addition to the original text of the parable: "The comparison of the two brothers which is presented in 15:25f. [the parable of the prodigal son] expresses a motif on which no stress is laid in 15:11–24 [the parables of the lost sheep and the lost drachma]. There, there is no comparison, and we ask as little about the attitude of the elder brother as we do about the attitude of the ninety-nine sheep and the nine drachmae."[38] The elder brother (who is getting more insensate by the minute) is the victim of a mathematical principle in which ninety-nine is less than one. He is a bit of excess that spoils the good feeling attendant upon his brother's return. Dan Via, Jr., concedes that the elder brother may be part of the original text. But, as Via puts it, "the parable is aesthetically satisfactory without him."[39] The elder brother is outside the parable's aesthetic integrity, even outside the aesthetic.

Augustine's gloss on the elder brother in the *Quaestiones Evangeliorum* makes explicit what is often just implied in the history of the parable's interpretation: the elder brother is a figure for the Jew, specifically the Jew in and in relation to the Gospel. The Lukean text invites this reading because of the structural position and image of the Pharisees in relation to Jesus' parables, namely, as an audience whose alleged self-righteousness the parable criticizes and reproaches.[40] In Augustine's gloss, the real problem of the elder brother/Jew is his exegetical stance:

While meanwhile his elder son, the people Israel following the flesh *[secundum carnem],* has not in fact departed into a distant region, but nevertheless is not in the house, *however he is in the field,* namely, he is toiling with reference to earthly things *[terrena],* in the rich legacy itself of the law and the prophets, and in all Israelite considerations. . . . Coming in from the field, he began to approach the house, that is, servile *[servilis]* to works, he rejected his labor, and considered the freedom of the Church from these same scriptures *[ex isdem scripturis].*[41]

In Augustine's reading, the elder brother is "in the field," studying the Hebrew Bible (a primary act of Jewish piety). But as he is "in the field," caught up in earthly things, his is a labor of carnal understanding, namely, he reads his scripture without reference to the Gospel. (In *Contra Faustum Manichaeum,* Augustine writes that the Jews, like Cain, work the earth and observe the law in a carnal manner, because when they read the Old Testament, a veil *[velamen]* covers their eyes.)[42] The elder brother's earthly toil involves observance as well as exegesis (what Augustine calls "Israelite considerations"). Coming in from his servile interpretive labor in the field, the elder brother considers the liberty that a spiritual or allegorical interpretation of these same scriptures would offer. The scenario that follows establishes the proselytizing theme which pervades the history of the parable's interpretation. When the elder brother discovers from the servant (of God) that the rejoicing is on account of Christ, he grows angry and refuses to enter the house. The father's going out to the elder brother is interpreted as an appeal to the Jews to enter the Church, "so that all Israel—to whom to an extent blindness has occurred, just as to the one absent in the field—may become saved."[43] Augustine explains away the troublesome fact of the elder brother's observance ("I never transgressed your commandment") by saying (1) the elder brother met only the first commandment ("thou shalt have no other gods before me") and (2) even in this the elder brother is clearly an exception among the Israelites.

The point Augustine makes here in the *Quaestiones Evangeliorum* and also in the *Tractatus adversus Judaeos* is that not only do the Jews not understand the Gospel they read, they do not understand their own scripture. It is instructive to see how Augustine, in the *Tractatus,* radicalizes the elder brother's nonunderstanding. He begins by quoting Paul: "*Behold Israel according to the flesh* (1 Cor. 10:18). This we know to be the carnal Israel; but the Jews do not grasp this meaning and as a result they prove themselves indisputably carnal."[44] The Jews cannot understand themselves *as* carnal because their understanding *is* carnal. He who does not understand certainly does not understand that he does not understand (otherwise he would understand). He can only misunderstand himself misunderstanding. Similarly, Augustine formulates this in terms of blindness. He exhorts the Jews to recognize themselves in the psalmist's phrase: "*Let their eyes be darkened that they see not* (Ps. 69:23) . . . but you are so blind that you do not recognize yourselves for what you really are."[45] If the Jews could see that they were blind, then they would be saved. But blindness (whether physical or spiritual) cannot see that it is blind without a chiastic exchange between blindness and sight, physical and spiritual—without a Pauline conversion. He who is blind is blind to his blindness; that is, he has a radical self-opacity. So too the elder brother has to be outside an understanding of himself *as* outside (this is precisely the logic of the outside).

But this outside is a necessary outside. Just as Christian conversion depends on the death of an old self and the rebirth of the new, so too that conversion depends on an exegetical conversion, from a dead letter (old) to the living spirit (new). The parable depends precisely on the elder brother for its distinctions (letter versus spirit, legalism versus faith) and for its claim to tell the story of the passage from death (the letter of the old law) to life (the spirit of the new faith). The dead letter, the old law, has to be there as something to pass through, to go beyond.

The personal itinerary from death to life is also an interpretive itinerary from carnal to spiritual understanding. The same dead letter, read spiritually, bears witness "to the prophecies which were given beforehand concerning Christ."[46] The parable, then, can neither get rid of the elder brother nor do without him. He has to be inside the parable, inscribed *as* its outside, as a trace of the rejected alternative—insensate, deaf, blind, unable to understand—yet he makes the spiritual understanding of the parable possible. He is, to borrow a remark from Bernhard Blumenkranz about the image of the Jew in patristic literature, "like a blind man with a lantern who shows the way to others but doesn't see it himself."[47]

Hence Augustine's exclusion of the elder brother (when he reads him, as in the *Quaestiones Evangeliorum,* or when he does not, in the *Confessions)* is necessary if the parable is to be intelligible. Augustine's narrator in the *Confessions* needs the parable of the prodigal son in order to recapture himself retrospectively in an itinerary of death and resurrection. In the quotation with which we began this essay, the narrator cites the father: "My son was dead and has come back to life." But the applicability of the quotation is of course to the sinner who became the converted narrator. Augustine uses the parable of the prodigal son as the model for his specular self-understanding: he is able to be the one who understands (the father) and the one who is understood (the younger son). Augustine, to understand himself, inscribes himself in the parable as both father and son. Yet if Augustine is to understand himself, the elder brother must also misunderstand, and misunderstand himself misunderstanding, or else the intelligibility of the discourse of conversion would collapse.

But what if this figure for misunderstanding is himself misunderstood? What if the elder brother is not a Cain at all but an Abraham, whose itinerary is not a departure and return but, to follow a suggestion of Emmanuel Levinas, "a departure without return"?[48] When, in Genesis 12, Abraham is commanded to leave his country, his kindred, and his father's house, this triple specification can be read to mean that there is no going back. For Levinas, Abraham's departure without return names a journey from the self(same) to what is radically other, or a negative that is not recuperable. The prodigal son's prodigality is recuperable. He departs, returns, and reposes in the father. But the elder brother finds no repose. Perhaps his is another kind of returning, an always returning, characterized by incompleteness. The elder brother is blind, but what if his blindness is not the opposite of seeing but a turning away from the light? In other words, perhaps the patristic and Pauline metaphors for the elder brother can be reread, or unread. If the elder brother does not understand, perhaps his is a different way of understanding nothing.

There are then at least two ways of interpreting the elder brother, or, let us say, the text of Judaism. The first is as a Cain—angry, murderous, and servile. The second is as an Abraham—teacher of righteousness. Mistaking Abraham for Cain may be the most systematic "mistake" in patristic literature. In the *City of God,* for example, Cain, not Abraham, is said to be the father of the Jews; the Jews are symbolized by Cain because they killed Christ, and so on.[49]

Mistaking Abraham for Cain is, above all, an exegetical quid pro quo: a quid pro quo on the part of the exegete and a quid pro quo of exege*ses*. If the elder brother is a Cain, he is a dead or killing letter to be transcended; if the elder brother is an Abraham, he is a letter but not dead—a letter, say, to be studied midrashically. In short, if Abraham has been mistaken for Cain, it may be all the more necessary that he remain outside. For the exegetical conversion from Old Testament to New Testament is also a conversion from the Hebrew Bible to the "Old Testament"—from a scripture that does "not" understand itself in terms of the Gospel to one which is in every way in the service of it. The "mistake" is indeed a necessary one.

The consequences of this mistake for Augustine's *Confessions* are as follows. Augustine, in excluding the elder brother, inaugurates a critical tradition that does not read the elder brother or reads him as outside. The intelligibility of the parable depends on such an exclusion. Augustine's specular self-understanding (understanding himself as the prodigal son) depends on the exclusion of the figure for misunderstanding (the elder brother). But if Abraham has been mistaken for Cain, then Augustine's self-understanding (understanding himself as the prodigal son) depends on misunderstanding the elder brother (the figure for misunderstanding). Augustine's self-understanding depends on misunderstanding the figure for misunderstanding. But in misunderstanding the elder brother, Augustine is, in a sense, an elder brother (that is, the one who misunderstands). Augustine, in order to understand himself (be the prodigal son), has to misunderstand the elder brother (be the elder brother)—which amounts to not understanding himself. In other words, Augustine's self-understanding depends on a misunderstanding so radical that it disarticulates that understanding. Yet the misunderstanding of misunderstanding is constitutive of understanding. The reader (including the present one) who would claim to understand the elder brother cannot recognize himself there because, in understanding, the reader inscribes himself not as elder brother but as prodigal son.

This question of the reader is important because of the proselytizing motive of all narratives of conversion. We recall that whenever Augustine's sinner hears or reads the story of a conversion, the *example* of others produces in him a fever of imitation. Similarly, there is no question that the intended effect of Augustine's narrator's story on *his* reader is precisely this "contagion of example."[50] If Augustine's reader does not benefit from his example, he is an elder brother—and he cannot recognize himself. If he does benefit from the example, recognizes himself as the prodigal son and converts, he still has not disposed of the elder brother.

Another consequence of mistaking Abraham for Cain should be mentioned. A consequence for conversion in general, it would be the disarticulation of its terms—blindness and sight, death and rebirth, sin and grace, departure and return—which all belong to a phenomenology (i.e., ultimately based on a perceptual model) of the self. If personal conversion depends on an exegetical conversion not just from Old Testament to New (still in terms of dead and living, carnal and spiritual, blind and seeing) but from Hebrew Bible to "Old Testament"—namely, the translation of a proper name—then that "passage" upon which all conversion depends is not phenomenological but in-tralinguistic. There are traces of this in Augustine's text. In VIII.12, immediately after the sinner's reading of the scriptural verse which converts him, Augustine's narrator describes the change in himself: "it was as if *[quasi]* a light of confidence filled my heart." With this *quasi* ("as it were") the narrator marks a figural shift to phenomenological terms. In the excursus of VIII.3 (how God rejoices more at the conversion of a great sinner), Augustine's narrator gives six examples to illustrate the principle: "the more pain there is first, the more joy there is after." All the examples but one are taken from sense experience: the victorious general after a dangerous battle, the calm that follows a treacherous storm during a sea voyage, the recovery of a friend who was gravely ill, the pleasure of drinking after eating salty foods, and the giving over of a young woman to her bridegroom after a delay. Then follows the example of Paul's great humility after his prideful persecution of the Christian sect: "When . . . the pride of Paulus the proconsul was so beaten down that he came under the light yoke of your Christ and became a simple subject of the great king, the apostle, to mark the glory of such a victory, wished, from the former Saul, to be called Paul" *(ipse quoque ex priore Saulo Paulus vocari amavit ob tam magnae insigne victoriae)* (VIII.4). Paul's conversion from blindness to sight is "marked" by the translation of a proper name. Such a conversion is not a substitutive relationship between blindness and seeing, old and new, carnal and spiritual, but a change of name on the level of the letter (a change of name perhaps not unlike mistaking the name of Cain for Abraham). The figure that best describes such a conversion is not metaphor but metonymy, which means, literally, "change of name."[51]

If we are right about the elder brother's necessary inscription as excluded in all scenes of self-understanding, then he should be inscribed in Augustine's own exemplary conversion scene, the scene in which he gains the "face-to-face" knowledge of himself that makes it possible for him to tell his story.

In book VIII.12, the sinner—who has been propelled into a neighboring garden under the influence of Ponticianus' stories—is under a certain fig tree, weeping. The narrator recounts:

Suddenly a voice reaches my ears from a nearby house *[de vicina domo]*. It is the voice of a boy or a girl (I don't know which) and in a kind of singsong the words are constantly repeated: "Take up, read. Take up, read" *[Tolle lege, tolle lege]*. I began to think carefully of whether the singing of words like these came into any kind of game which children play, and I could not remember that I had ever heard anything like it before. I checked the force of my tears and rose to my feet *[surrexi]*, interpreting nothing other than myself to be commanded divinely to open the book and read the first passage which I should come upon *[nihil aliud interpretans divinitus mihi iuberi, nisi ut aperirem codicem et legerem quod primum caput invenissem]*.

The sinner first considers the possibility of a naturalistic explanation, rejects the idea, and rises up *(surrexi . . . resurrexi?)*, divinely commanded to interpret "nothing other." The sole interpretation *(nihil aliud interpretans)* is that the voice is a divine command to open the book and read . . . himself. The divine command is nothing other than himself commanded to interpret himself. Interpretation here is nothing other than self-interpretation. This is, of course, the whole interpretive effort of a conversion narrative.

So I went eagerly back to the place where Alypius was sitting, since it was there that I had left the book of the Apostle when I rose to my feet. I seized the book, opened it, and read in silence the passage upon which my eyes first fell *[arripui, aperui et legi in silentio capitulum, quo primum coniecti sunt oculi mei]: Not in rioting and drunkenness, not in chambering and wantonness, not in strife and envying: but put ye on the Lord Jesus Christ, and make not provision for the flesh in concupiscence.* I had no wish to read further; there was no need to *[nec ultra volui legere nec opus erat]*. For immediately as I had reached the end of this sentence, it was as though my heart was filled with a light of confidence *[quasi luce securitatis infusa cordi meo]* and all the shadows of my doubt were swept away.

The sinner seizes, opens, and reads *(arripui, aperui et legi)* the book and recognizes himself in a quotation from St. Paul. In this moment, a life history of reading—pagan literature,

Aristotle, Plotinus—culminates, and an entire tradition of reading-for-conversion is incorporated and surpassed. This moment of self-recognition, this self-reading, is a reading to end all reading, is the end of reading ("I had no wish to read further; there was no need to"). He buries the old man and becomes the new, gaining an inner sight ("a light of confidence") that renders all his former blindness visible. He tells his friend Alypius what has happened, and the effect is predictably contagious. Alypius, following Augustine, receives the following scriptural verse as *his* oracle and is converted.

However, in this scene of self-reading, there is, on the level of the letter, a philological trace of an excluded other figure—Abraham. "And he [Abraham] stretched forth his hand and seized the knife to slay his son" *(Extenditque manum et arripuit gladium ut immolaret filium suum)* (Gen. 22:10).[52] Augustine's sinner seizes the book; Abraham seizes the knife.[53] Both are moments of peripety. Augustine picks up the book and reads; he turns finally and is turned. Abraham picks up the knife; "and the angel of the Lord called unto him out of heaven . . . Lay not thine hand upon the lad." All the same, one can hardly imagine a greater contrast than Augustine's being commanded to interpret himself and Abraham's being commanded to slay his beloved son. The Christian reading of the *Akedah* has Isaac, of course, as a type of Christ and Abraham as God sacrificing his only son: the Old Testament passage finds its fulfillment in Christ's death and resurrection. But we do not need Christian typology here to show that this *arripere*, at the moment Augustine quotes it, is already being suppressed and rewritten, that the dead letter is being spiritualized, that the new law is superseding the old. Where Abraham picks up the knife (the killing letter), Augustine picks up the letters of St. Paul (the spirit that giveth life). At the moment Augustine quotes the *arripere*, he turns the Hebrew Bible into the Old Testament.

Yet Augustine cannot pick up the book without picking up the knife as well. He cannot pick up St. Paul without picking up the dead letter. In fact, he cannot pick up St. Paul without, *on the level of the dead letter*, picking up the dead letter. He cannot convert, understand himself, or tell his story without allegorizing the Old Testament; and in order to allegorize it, he has to quote it. Yet, in quoting the Old Testament, there is always the danger of being quoted by the Old Testament, understood no longer as Old Testament but as Hebrew Bible.[54]

Afterword

Augustine, in the *Confessions*, has a "real" elder brother, who makes a single appearance in book IX at his mother's deathbed. There he makes an unfortunate remark "to the effect that he hoped she would have the good fortune to die in her own country and not abroad." Augustine recounts: "On hearing this an anxious expression came over her face, and she gave him a reproachful look for still savoring of such earthly things. Then she looked into my face and said, 'See what he is saying!'" (IX.11).

Another exceedingly rare appearance of Augustine's elder brother occurs in *De beata vita*, where we find out his name—Navigius. There Augustine uses the metaphor of the philosophical life as a sea voyage and considers the difficulty of returning to one's native land. A dialogue follows, and Navigius is the only one of the group who persistently refuses to understand what his younger brother is saying. (We should note that it is impossible to decide whether the strife between Augustine and his elder brother is instrumental in the psychological and biographical sense or merely the inevitable result of his exegetical strategy.) Augustine begins the discussion:

"Does it seem obvious to you that we are composed of soul and body?" Although all the others agreed, Navigius replied that he did not know *[Navigius se ignorare respondit]*. "Do you really know nothing, nothing at all," I said to him, "or is this to be counted among the things that you do not know?" *[Nihil, nihilne omnino scis, inquam, an inter aliqua quae ignoras etiam hoc numerandum est?]* He replied, "I do not think I know nothing at all" *[Non puto me, inquit, omnia nescire]*. "Can you tell us some of the things about which you know?" "I can," he said. "If it is not too much trouble," I continued, "mention some one of them." Since he hesitated, I suggested, "You know, at least, that you are alive?" "I know," he declared. "You know therefore that you have life, since no one can live except by life." "This also," he declared, "I know." "You know also that you have a body?" He replied affirmatively. "Well then, you already know that you consist of body and life." "That much I know, but I am not certain whether there are only these two." "Therefore you are not in doubt," I said, "about these two, body and soul, but you are not sure whether there is something other *[aliud]* which is necessary to make up and complete a human being." "Yes," he replied. "We shall investigate, if possible, at another time, what this something other might be," I said.[55]

2 /

Petrarch Reading Augustine:
"The Ascent of Mont Ventoux"

Rare is the reading free from danger, unless the light of divine
truth shines upon the reader, teaching him what is to be pursued and
what is to be avoided.
Petrarch, *Rerum Familiarium* II.9

At the summit of Mont Ventoux, Petrarch opens his copy of
Augustine's *Confessions*, reads the first passage his eyes fall upon, and recognizes himself in Augustine's text. Like Augustine,
Petrarch undergoes a conversion by reading. Conversion—the
death of an old self and rebirth of the new, a *turn* from old to
new—ensures the dual perspective of sinner and converted narrator that makes possible the telling of the story, a story that is
presented as it unfolds, yet has a retrospective structure. At the
moment of conversion, when the sinner becomes the converted
narrator, the story comes into being as a story. In other words,
the experience of personal conversion is also the conversion of
and to the story. At the close of "The Ascent of Mont Ventoux,"
a letter addressed to Dionigi da Borgo San Sepolcro, Petrarch's
father confessor, Petrarch exemplifies this conversion of the
story when he marks the passage from reading to writing:

I returned late at night to the little rustic inn from which I had set out
before dawn. . . . While the servants were busy preparing our meal, I
withdrew quite alone into a remote part of the house to write this letter

49

to you in all haste and on the spur of the moment *[raptim et ex tempore]*.[1]

By inscribing the time of writing in his letter, Petrarch seeks to show that his text is organically connected to his spiritual experience and thus to authenticate both text and experience. However, this apparent attempt to ground the letter is precisely what first attracted attention to its artifice, leading scholars to the discovery of the letter's late date of composition. In 1932, Vittorio Rossi argued that the letter, a carefully designed piece of art, could not possibly have been written in the evening of the day of the ascent. The letter's contrast between the detours of Petrarch and the straight path of his brother Gherardo implied further that it could not have been written in 1336 as claimed: Gherardo became a monk in a Carthusian monastery only in 1342. Giuseppe Billanovich noted that the letter's alleged addressee was in Avignon in 1336 and there was no reason for trying to make it appear as though Dionigi were in Italy at the time. Billanovich suggested that the date of the letter, which would have made Petrarch (like Augustine) thirty-two at the time of his conversion, was freely chosen for its symbolic meaning and, since the letter was not found in the collection of the alleged addressee at the time (a collection to which Giovanni Boccaccio had access), finally dated the letter at 1353, almost twenty years after its alleged date of composition.[2] Dionigi, who died in 1342, probably never received the letter at all.[3]

In the wake of this discovery, Petrarch's "conversion narrative" has undergone something of a reevaluation. Many critics now consider it a "mere fiction," a view that was held long before the discovery of Petrarch's deception, by critics who found the conversion "a spectacle," "a scene that he played with his own soul."[4] Others insist that while the letter may be fictitious, the ascent is not necessarily so: "For unless this story had some kernel of truth, can we believe that Petrarch would have dared to affirm: 'I invoke God as my witness'?"[5] One critic asserts that fiction is the best means for Petrarch to arrive at the truth (of self, of experience, of tradition) that he is seeking.[6]

Nevertheless, these verdicts still move within a horizon that belongs to conversion narrative and maintain its assumptions. The concerns about the truth of "The Ascent of Mont Ventoux" are raised in terms of text and experience, which is precisely what conversion by reading proposes to mediate. The question of the letter's fictionality is posed in the theatrical terms of self-representation and thus leaves intact the claim to specular self-representation (recognizing oneself in a text) that conversion by reading makes. Critics, in fact, seem intent on not giving up the redemption claimed in Petrarch's text: they now redeem Petrarch *or* his text. In short, although Petrarch's conversion is in doubt, the necessity of reading his letter as a narrative of conversion is not. What still remains to be read in Petrarch's text is precisely reading, conversion by reading. But before attempting to read reading, we should first establish what it means for Petrarch to read Augustine.

Petrarch begins his letter: "Today I ascended the highest mountain in this region . . . led solely by the desire to see *[cupiditas videndi]* its conspicuous height" (p. 36). While Petrarch's desire to see the view from the mountain's peak has earned him acclaim as a precursor of the modern alpinist,[7] this desire to see is, in Augustinian terms, not so laudable, being a prime instance of the "concupiscence of the eyes" condemned in book X of the *Confessions.* Seeing (a synecdoche for all sense experience, according to Augustine) attaches itself to visible creation at the expense of the invisible creator. Such physical seeing is, in effect, a spiritual blindness. Augustine says, in a synesthetic comparison: "Corporeal light . . . is a tempting and dangerous sweetness, like a sauce spread over the life of this world for its blind lovers."[8] Petrarch's explanation of his motivation for the ascent is, in other words, a self-indictment. The ascent is in fact a descent, for when he begins it he is in concupiscence, blindness, and sin.

This is an auspicious beginning for a narrative of conversion, which recounts the passage from sin to salvation. In an economy that is both theological and aesthetic, Petrarch needs to establish himself as a sinner in order that there be (1) something to redeem and (2) a story to tell. For this reason, the reading of Livy, which Petrarch explains was the impetus for the climb, is also implicitly criticized. Reading Livy directs Petrarch to what is outside, visible, available to the senses, and is thus the negative counterpart of the reading of Augustine at the summit and the inner-directedness it inspires. The Livy reading is not necessarily bad in itself, just partial and incomplete: it anticipates and is fulfilled by the reading at the summit.[9] For, after reading Augustine, Petrarch will say: "I turned my inner eye toward myself" *(in me ipsum interiores oculos reflexi)*. Physical seeing is to the reading of Livy as spiritual seeing is to the reading of Augustine. The overall pattern of Petrarch's letter may be summarized thus: it is the story of a desire to see followed by a renunciation of seeing, or, in Pauline terms, the story of the passage from spiritual blindness to a spiritual sight that "sees" that it was blind. It is also the story of learning how to read, of the passage from partial to totalizing reading.

Petrarch's choice of his younger brother Gherardo as a companion for the ascent and the comparison of the two brothers that follows emphasize further Petrarch's sinfulness and distance from salvation. He recounts:

My brother endeavored to reach the summit by the very ridge of the mountain on a short cut; I, being so much more of a weakling, was bending down *[vergebam]* toward the valley. When he called me back and showed me the straighter way *[revocantique et iter rectius designanti]*, I answered that I hoped to find an easier access on the other side and was not afraid of a longer route on which I might proceed more smoothly. With such an excuse I tried to palliate my laziness, and, when the others had already reached the higher zones *[excelsa tenentibus]*, I was still wandering through the valleys *[per valles errabam]*. . . . Thus I indeed deferred the disagreeable strain of climbing. But nature is not overcome by man's devices; a corporeal thing cannot reach the heights by descending. What shall I say? My brother laughed at me; I was indignant; this happened to me three times and more within a few hours. (p. 39)

Clearly the reader is meant to share Gherardo's laugh at Petrarch's expense. While the younger brother Gherardo calls Petrarch back, "pointing to the straighter way," Petrarch repeatedly chooses the detour, which increases his difficulties. But while Petrarch's detour and his apparent inability to learn from his mistakes may halt his progress up the mountain, they contribute to the progress of his story. The self-castigation and self-indictment that accompanies this account of erring (both in the sense of going astray and of making a mistake) draw attention to Petrarch as a sinner in need of redemption. As Petrarch later allegorizes the ascent as "the way toward the blessed life," Gherardo's higher path ascends directly to things heavenly while Petrarch's lower path "leads through the meanest earthly pleasures" *[per terrenas et infimas voluptates]* (p. 40). Being caught up in the earthly anticipates (and indeed implies) the renunciation of the earthly that will follow. In fact, Petrarch announces the strategy of his letter by antiphrasis when he says "a corporeal thing cannot reach the heights by descending." By the same logic, which we might call "the logic of error," the numerous wrong turns that Petrarch makes along the way (signaled by the verbs *vergere* and *errare*)[10] negatively anticipate the right kind of turning, the conversion (*con* + *vertere,* to turn to) at the summit.

Yet, in order to err, Petrarch needs something to deviate from, and that is Gherardo's straighter way. In "The Ascent of Mont Ventoux," younger and elder brother are differentiated as a straight line from a curve. While Gherardo ascends the mountain by the shortest, steepest path, Petrarch is "bending down" *(vergere)* toward the valley. Elsewhere in the correspondence, Petrarch opposes his own turning and bending *(versare, vergere, curvare)* to Gherardo's rectitude *(erecto, iter rectius)* and tenacity *(tenere portum)* in spiritual matters.[11] Yet the itineraries of the two brothers imply each other with the symmetry of recto and verso. Just as a curve is defined in relation to a straight line, so Petrarch, in his circuitousness, needs a straight man. And Gherardo is indeed a straight man (his laugh notwithstanding) to Petrarch's humorous self-indictment. If Gherardo's character seems flat and two-dimensional, that is because consistently righteous behavior does not possess sufficient internal conflict to create the illusion of depth. But the upright Gherardo, standing and pointing to the straight path to which he has adhered, performs an indispensable narrative function, albeit negative: to mark the crookedness that establishes Petrarch as a protagonist in a drama of salvation, to point to the path that Petrarch does *not* take. Petrarch does well to choose his younger brother as a companion for the journey because Petrarch's logic of error depends on and presupposes its opposite, which is Gherardo's stability.

When Petrarch first reaches the summit of Mont Ventoux, he continues to exhibit a spiritual blindness: "At first I stood there almost benumbed, overwhelmed by a gale such as I had never felt before and by the unusually wide and open view *[spectaculo]*. I looked back *[Respicio]*" (p. 41). This attention to the spectacle of things seen marks Petrarch's looking back as all too corporeal. But this corporeal looking does anticipate the right kind of looking, the redeemed look back upon a former corporeality that will enable him to tell his story.

Then, being led "from the contemplation of space to that of time" *(a locis . . . ad tempora)* and thus transcending his bodily location, Petrarch tries another look back, the incorporeal look of memory: "This day marks the completion of the tenth year since you gave up the studies of your boyhood and left Bologna" (p. 42). But Petrarch's retrospective look, like the Augustinian look back of *Confessions* VIII.7 that he is imitating, is only tentative, anticipatory. It takes place in the time of the "not yet": "I am not yet in port that I might think in security of the storms I have had to endure" (p. 42). The authentic recounting can only be indicated proleptically:

The time will perhaps come *[Tempus forsan veniet]* when I can review *[percurram]* all this in the order in which it happened, using as a prologue that passage of your favorite Augustine: "Let me remember *[Recordari volo]* my past mean acts and the carnal corruption of my soul, not that I love them, but that I may love Thee, my God." (p. 42)

For all Petrarch's hesitation regarding an uncertain future past, he is certain of one thing: the vantage point from which to tell his story will be *as* Augustine's. And despite his overall insecurity, he displays considerable confidence in following Augustine's example. He analyzes his instability in terms of a conflict between two rival wills in his heart—one "perverted" *(perversa)*, urging him on in his idolatrous love for Laura, the other more principled, leading him to conversion; he weeps.[12] He then reverts to an earlier mode of error (as Augustine does when he looks back at his former mistresses in *Confessions* VIII.11):

Then, dismissing my sorrows for which another place would be more appropriate, I looked back and saw what I had come to see *[respicerem et viderem que visurus adveneram]*. The time to leave was approaching, they said. The sun was already setting, and the shadow of the mountain was growing longer and longer. Like a man aroused from sleep, I turned back and looked toward the west *[verto me in tergum, ad occidentem respiciens]*. (p. 43)

He looks back once with his original "desire to see" and again with an ill-chosen turn to the west.[13] He says:

I admired every detail, now relishing earthly *[terrenum]* enjoyment, now lifting up my mind to higher spheres after the example of my body *[nunc exemplo corporis animum ad altiora subveherem]*, and I thought it fit to look into the volume of Augustine's *Confessions [visum est michi* Confessionum *Augustini librum . . . inspicere]*. (p. 44)

Petrarch makes a decisive transition: his mind, which had followed the unworthy example of his body, now follows the example of Augustine in choosing to pick up the book and read.[14] But where Augustine picks up Scripture, Petrarch picks up the *Confessions:* Petrarch's long desired vantage point, which he had identified as being *as* Augustine's, will be *in* Augustine. Moreover, since Petrarch has arrived at the summit, *respicere* has become *inspicere:* an outer-directed seeing has gained a salutary *in*wardness. In passing from *respicere* to *inspicere,* Petrarch finally turns away from physical seeing; he makes the passage from seeing to reading. The inwardness of good seeing is reading. The analogy between the two, always implicit, has become explicit. Like the illumination of the Augustinian moment of reading ("it was as though my heart was filled with a light of confidence")[15] the incorporeal light of this reading will bring Petrarch to conversion. As opposed to (and as prefigured by) the "blind," outer-directed reading of Livy, the *inspicere* of the reading of Augustine will be like a redeemed seeing.

I thought it fit to look into the volume of Augustine's *Confessions,* which I owe to your loving kindness and preserve carefully, keeping it always in my hands, in remembrance of the author as well as the donor.

It is a little book of smallest size but full of infinite sweetness. I opened it with the intention of reading whatever might occur to me first *[Aperio, lecturus quicquid occurreret]*: nothing, indeed, but pious and devout sentences could come to hand. I happened to hit upon the tenth book of the work. My brother stood beside me, intently expecting to hear something from Augustine on my mouth *[Frater expectans per os meum ab Augustino aliquid audire, intentis auribus stabat]*. I ask God to be my witness and my brother who was with me *[Deum testor ipsumque qui aderat]*: Where I first fixed my eyes *[defixi oculos]*, it was written: "And men go to admire the high mountains, the vast floods of the sea, the huge streams of the rivers, the circumference of the ocean, and the revolutions of the stars—and desert themselves" *[et relinquunt se ipsos]*. I was stunned, I confess. I bade my brother, who was avid to hear more, not to molest me *[audiendique avidum fratrem rogans ne michi molestus esset]*, and closed the book, angry with myself that I still admired earthly things. Long ago I ought to have learned, even from pagan philosophers, that "nothing is admirable besides the mind; compared to its greatness nothing is great."(p. 44)

With this reading of Augustine, Petrarch's erring comes to an end. He fixes his eyes on Augustine's text and finds stability there. He describes later his sense of election, of being personally addressed: "I was convinced that whatever I had read there was said to me and to nobody else" *(michi et non alteri dictum)* (pp. 44–45). Petrarch reads: "And men go to admire the high mountains . . . and desert themselves." Thus he understands that he has been searching outside for what was inside all along. As one critic remarks, this was prefigured when Petrarch searched among all his available friends for a companion for the ascent and found that companion at home, in his brother Gherardo.[16] The truth is at home, and Petrarch ought to have known this. The oracle says, in effect, "Know thyself!" Thus Petrarch's adventure of the self ends in the self.[17] "How greatly mortal men lack counsel," Petrarch concludes, "seeking without what could be found within" *(quod intus inveniri poterat, querentes extrinsecus)* (p. 45).

Petrarch's text thus gains from Augustine its central *in*sight: men look outside when they should be looking inside. In other words, men look physically when they should be looking spiritually. With this reading of Augustine, not only Petrarch's motivation for the ascent—the "desire to see"—but the ascent in its entirety is discredited. However, it will also be redeemed. After reading Augustine, Petrarch checks the avidity of his gaze, in effect blinding himself:

I was completely satisfied with what I had seen of the mountain [satis vidisse contentus] and turned my inner eye toward myself [in me ipsum interiores oculos reflexi]. From that hour, no one heard me speak [non fuit qui me loquentem audiret] until we arrived at the bottom. (p. 44)

This is Petrarch's Pauline renunciation of the senses (of seeing and of speaking). In a chiastic exchange between physical and spiritual, blindness and sight, Petrarch blinds himself physically and sees spiritually. This passage from blindness to sight makes possible Petrarch's specular self-understanding: he is now able to "see" that he was blind, to be both subject and object of his own gaze.

Yet, in order to blind himself, Petrarch had to read, and Petrarch's reading of Augustine has also a specular structure. When Petrarch reads the Augustinian oracle, the oracle reads him. It names his problem, just as the Livy reading had named his project "to see."[18] When Petrarch recognizes himself in Augustine's words, he appropriates being read as self-reading: he reads himself being read. Reading for conversion, whether it is called self-recognition, appropriation, or application, describes a relationship between a self and a text that is (1) specular and (2) totalizing. Petrarch's reading is so totalizing that he can read no further: "And as Anthony, having heard this, sought nothing else, and as Augustine, having read the other passage, proceeded no further, the end of all my reading [totius lectionis terminus] was the few words I have already set down" (p. 45). This reading to end all reading constitutes Petrarch as his own ideal (Godlike) reader. He is able to look back on his former reading of Livy and recognize it for what it was—partial, prefigurative, "blind." This conversionary reading of Augustine gives Petrarch the definitive vantage point from which to tell his story and constitutes him as the writer of the narrative of conversion that we read.

Petrarch's reading for conversion is also a reading of Augustine in the wider sense of following Augustine's example. For Petrarch's scene of reading appropriates, quotes, and echoes numerous Augustinian elements: (1) conversion by reading, (2) recognizing himself in a chain of anteriority that he invokes, (3) claiming personal election in the oracular address, (4) being unable to read further.[19] In following the example of Augustine's conversion, Petrarch reads Augustine in the way he wishes to be read. Augustine intends his conversion to be exemplary—a conversion that follows a saintly model (Anthony) and is itself worthy of being imitated. This pattern of exemplarity is figured in Augustine's text by his relationship to Alypius, a younger friend who accompanies Augustine through much of his life, to whom Augustine affectionately refers as "that brother of my heart" *(fratrem cordis mei)*.[20] When Augustine reads the scriptural verse that converts him, he returns to the place where Alypius waits, and tells Alypius what has happened. Alypius, following Augustine's example, receives the subsequent scriptural verse and is converted. This contagion of example has its own precedent in Augustine's prior reception of other stories of conversion, which he "burns to imitate." Augustine follows an example and becomes an example for others to follow. Alypius, who follows him, is a figure for all future readers of the *Confessions,* who, it is hoped, will fraternally share in the good news.

In having a younger brother accompany him, Petrarch would seem to be following Augustine's example. But Petrarch's behavior at the summit of Mont Ventoux is far from exemplary. Gherardo, who has accompanied Petrarch all the way up Mont Ventoux, does not get an oracle of his own.[21] When Petrarch picks up the book, Gherardo is standing by "with intent ears" *(intentis auribus)*. After Petrarch has read the oracle that applies to him, Gherardo is still standing by, hoping to hear some pious words from Augustine that might apply to him too. Petrarch recounts: "I bade my brother, who was avid to hear more, not to molest me" *(audiendique avidum fratrem rogans ne michi molestus esset)* (p. 44).

For Gherardo and by extension for Petrarch's reader, the news is anything but good. Petrarch, in denying his brother an oracle, in excluding him from conversion, brings to a halt the chain reaction his conversion could and should set off. Because of this distressing denial of fraternity and disregard of an Augustinian precedent of which he was well aware,[22] Petrarch follows an example, yet does not become an example: he follows and does not follow Augustine. He quotes Augustine (uses conversion by reading as a topic) and does not quote him (does not exemplify conversion by reading).[23]

But Petrarch's exclusion of Gherardo may indicate more than a problem in following Augustine: perhaps there is something about Gherardo that Petrarch has to exclude. Of course, one can argue that Gherardo, the straight man, the already righteous, the principle of stability, does not need a conversion. But Gherardo was not always so stable. As we learn from Petrarch in other parts of the correspondence, Gherardo himself converted from a frivolous youth to a monk in a Carthusian monastery. In *Fam.* X.3, Petrarch evokes Gherardo's youthful errors, which were so great that, as Petrarch confesses to a friend, "he [Gherardo] . . . was once my fear and anxiety" (*Fam.* XVI.9). "Suddenly," Petrarch recounts, "he was turned from a wayward and unstable young man into a firm and constant one" *(ex adolescente vago et lubrico in virum stabilem atque constantem versus)* (*Fam.* XVI.9). In these letters, Gherardo emerges as protagonist in a drama of salvation, as agent of the peripetous activity *(versus, vago)* that, in "The Ascent of Mont Ventoux," seemed to be Petrarch's sole domain. In *Fam.* X.3, Petrarch addresses Gherardo as "you who have changed from God's enemy to his friend, from his adversary to his subject" *(ex hoste familiaris ex adversario civis)* and describes Gherardo's progress from *ad*version to *con*version: "He [God] converted a noble deserter to His banners from the battle line of His enemies" *(ex agmine medio adversarum partium insignem transfugam ad sua signa convertit).* This rhetoric of Pauline conversion is apt because Gherardo's conversion was in fact a renunciation of the senses, a self-blinding to the things of this world *(terrena)* in favor of and in exchange with a spiritual sight *(celestia).* In *Fam.* X.4, Petrarch writes to Gherardo:

Of the two eyes we mortals usually use, one to gaze upon heavenly things and the other upon earthly ones, you renounced the one that beholds earthly things, being content with the better eye.

id quodam respectu proprie tibi convenire visum est, qui e duobus

oculis, quibus omnes comuniter utimur mortales, quorum altero scili-
cet celestia altero terrena respicimus, tu terrena cernentem abiecisti
oculo meliore contentus.[24]

In *Fam.* X.3, Petrarch figures yet another renunciation with
an allegorized Homeric reference, addressing Gherardo as "you
who were able to scorn the world in the flower of your youth
when it was most alluring to you and were able to cross over
[transire] with closed ears *[obstructa aure]* amidst the siren
songs." Petrarch also tells us that Gherardo maintained a near
silence—a self-imposed muteness—for seven years of his residence at the Carthusian monastery.

In short, we might summarize the threat that Gherardo
could pose to "The Ascent of Mont Ventoux" as follows: Since
Gherardo has *already* undergone the renunciation of the senses
(in the form of deafness, muteness, and especially blindness)
that Petrarch's narrative is anticipating, Gherardo's dramatic
story of conversion could usurp Petrarch's. In order to counter
this threat in "The Ascent of Mont Ventoux" (which is, after all,
Petrarch's and not Gherardo's story), Petrarch flattens out
Gherardo's story. Instead of an already (adverted and) converted Gherardo, we find an already righteous Gherardo, one
who has never strayed from the straight path—which is quite a
different story, and not much of a story at that. At the summit
of Mont Ventoux, Gherardo, who waits for his oracle "with
intent ears" (*intentis auribus,* or "all ears"), hears nothing.[25]
Petrarch renders Gherardo deaf, in effect. Gherardo's auditory
deprivation is further underscored by Petrarch's muteness for
the remainder of the outing: "No one heard me say a word until
we reached the bottom" (p. 44). But Gherardo's renunciation
of hearing is not his own, and could never become his story. It
is Petrarch's muteness (a renunciation which, like his self-blinding, is at once a physical loss and a spiritual gain) that renders
Gherardo deaf, punitively, in a loss that has no compensation in
self-knowledge. The exclusion of Gherardo at the summit of
Mont Ventoux, the refusal to pass the book on, is consistent
with the logic of Petrarch's text. Petrarch's story of blindness
and sight, of learning how to read, depends on diminishing the
threat that Gherardo's story could present.

The threat that Gherardo poses for Petrarch's spiritual autobiography is apparent even in those parts of the correspondence where the more dramatic version of Gherardo's story prevails.[26] The threat surfaces in Petrarch's preoccupation with the inequality between brothers. In *Fam.* X.3, he asks, "But why do I speak as if our states were equal *[equa]*?" and asks again, "Why is it, I ask, that although my brother and I were imprisoned by twin *[gemino]* chains . . . we have not been equally *[pariter]* liberated?" There is a biblical resonance here of the reversal of primogeniture—a passing over of the firstborn son in favor of the younger one. It seems that conversion has passed over the elder (Petrarch) in favor of the younger (Gherardo).

But Gherardo's story does not overtake Petrarch's. After a comparison of his brother's "liberty" with his own "servitude," Petrarch writes: "Pray, brother, that he [the Redeemer] may eventually restore me to liberty and that we two, born of the same womb, may find a like happy end *[pari fine]* and that I, who would normally precede you, may not be ashamed to follow *[et si preire debueram, non pudebit sequi]*" (*Fam.* X.3). With praiseworthy humility, Petrarch indicates the reversal of primogeniture: in matters of salvation his younger brother has surpassed him. But Petrarch also, rather deviously, reverses the reversal. Petrarch is the one who will follow *(sequi)* his brother's lead, chronologically as well as spiritually (if the range of meanings of the verb *sequi* is taken into account). In a metaleptic reversal, Petrarch will be, as it were, younger and Gherardo older. By granting Gherardo priority and thereby assigning him the role of elder brother to be surpassed, Petrarch establishes himself as the sole protagonist of a drama of salvation. To the same end, Petrarch, in "The Ascent of Mont Ventoux," reverts Gherardo from already converted to already righteous, does not pass the book on, does not read further.

But in "The Ascent of Mont Ventoux," Gherardo may pose a threat to Petrarch's conversion narrative in yet another and more serious sense. If Petrarch *had* read further, as Gherardo urged him to do, he might have discovered that he was misreading, misunderstanding. A look at the context of the passage in Augustine's *Confessions* indicates why this is so:

How great, my God, is this force of memory, how exceedingly great! It is a vast and boundless sanctuary. Who can plumb its depths? And yet it is a faculty of my mind. Although it is part of my nature, I cannot grasp all that I am. Therefore, the mind is too narrow to contain itself. But where is that part of it which it does not itself contain? Is it somewhere outside itself and not inside? In that case, how can it be part of it, if it is not contained in it? At this thought a great wonder *[admiratio]* comes over me. I am struck dumb with astonishment *[stupor adprehendit me]*. Yet men go to admire *[mirari]* the high mountains, the great waves of the sea, the broad streams of rivers, the vastness of the ocean, the turnings of the stars—and they forget themselves. And they see nothing marvelous in the fact that while I was mentioning all these things, I was not seeing them with my eyes *[quod haec omnia cum dicerem non ea videbam oculis]*, nor would I have been able to speak of them unless these mountains and waves and rivers and stars (which I have seen) and the ocean (which I have heard about) had been visible to me inside, in my memory, and with just the same great spatial intervals and proportions as if I saw them outside *[intus in memoria mea viderem spatiis tam ingentibus, quasi foris viderem]*. Yet when I saw them with my eyes, I did not by the act of seeing draw them into myself; it is not they but their images *[imagines eorum]* that are in me, and I know by what bodily sense each impression has come to me.[27]

Augustine is talking about memory as the condition of possibility of even speaking about mountains, seas, rivers, and oceans. He mentions them as examples of a certain capacity of memory to remember words. Mountains, seas, rivers, and oceans are not outside but inside, imprints on the mind's eye. In the line following Petrarch's oracle, Augustine makes a metadiscursive leap: he turns away from the referential value of these words (a turn marked by the figural shift *quasi*) and speaks about speaking. Petrarch, in stopping where he stops, literalizes Augustine's words precisely where Augustine turns away from their referential value. It is not *seeing* real mountains that is at stake but the possibility of *speaking* about them.

Petrarch, in taking the Augustine text to mean "seeing mountains," reenacts the very error he thinks he is correcting (looking outside instead of inside). He, in a sense, sees where he should be blinding himself, where Augustine's text has already blinded itself. His insight that men seek without what could be found within—in fact no *in*sight at all—is based on a misreading. In Augustinian terms, Petrarch's misreading could be called "carnal" because he seems to mistake a discourse

about signs for a discourse about things. Petrarch takes a sign—
the word "mountain"—for the thing signified, and (as Augustine puts it in *On Christian Doctrine* III.5) he "does not refer
the thing signified to anything else" *(neque illud quod proprio
verbo significatur, refert ad aliam significationem)*, namely, to
the possibility of speaking about mountains. He takes the word
to refer to the mountain and not, as it should be in this case, to
the word "mountain."

In *On Christian Doctrine* III.5, Augustine identifies this
practice of taking a sign for a thing not only with an understanding that is carnal *(intelligentia carni)* but also with the
related evils of (1) following the letter *(sequendo litteram)*,
which kills and (2) Jewish exegesis ("The Jews," says Augustine, "took signs of spiritual things for the things themselves").
Augustine offers an example of this carnal interpretive procedure:

If he [who takes a sign for a thing] hears of the Sabbath, he thinks only
of one day out of the seven that are repeated in a continuous cycle; and
if he hears of Sacrifice, his thoughts do not go beyond *[non excedit]* the
customary victims of the flocks and fruits of the earth *[terrenis]*. There
is a miserable servitude *[servitus]* of the spirit in this habit of taking
signs for things, so that one is not able to raise the eye of the mind
above things that are corporeal and created to drink in eternal light.[28]

To take a sign for a thing is to arrest the chain of signification,
not to go beyond the corporeal aspect of the sign to its incorporeal signified. The result of this not going beyond (according
to a certain logic of the carnal) is a *corporeal* signified, which, in
effect is the mirror of the corporeal signifier, of what Augustine
calls the "dead letter." The understanding that stops at the
corporeal signifier also mirrors the corporeal: it is carnal. And
since, for Augustine, the function of the signifier is to serve an
incorporeal signified, the carnal intelligence that stops at a corporeal signifier also *serves*.[29]

Thus Petrarch, at the summit of Mont Ventoux, reads carnally when he should be reading spiritually; he sees when he
should be blinding himself. Given this persistent carnality and
spiritual blindness, it is difficult to evaluate the self-blinding
that Petrarch does undergo when he "turns his inner eye toward

himself." Might this self-blinding be rather like the hapless Gherardo's blindness, a loss without compensation? According to an Augustinian logic of conversion, Petrarch's conversion would depend on a turn from physical to spiritual in reading and in seeing. Petrarch's self-understanding, his being able to "see" that he was blind, would depend on his specular relationship to Augustine's text. That which should be specular is in fact opaque and antiphrastic.[30]

Petrarch's reading of Augustine, seemingly inner-directed, spiritual and totalizing, turns out to be much more like his reading of Livy: outer-directed, carnal and partial. There has been no progress from the beginning of Petrarch's story; indeed there has been no story. If there is a story here, it is the story of an enslavement to things seen, an inability to go beyond the corporeal aspect of the sign. Like the "concupiscence of the eyes," it is a substitution of corporeal creation for the incorporeal creator, a substitution that would be, for Augustine, idolatrous. Petrarch, in "The Ascent of Mont Ventoux," turns out to be an "elder brother" after all: biographically or psychologically (as the one who is passed over, excluded from conversion), exegetically (he reads as a Jew, whose "literal" mode of exegesis is figured in patristic literature as the elder brother to the Christian allegorical),[31] and aesthetically (as the one whose story is "no story").

But—the question necessarily arises—what if Petrarch *wanted* to read carnally in "The Ascent of Mont Ventoux"? What if Petrarch's idolatry is strategic, part of an aesthetic strategy? The strategy would be—to follow John Freccero's reading of the *Canzoniere*—that Petrarch's portrayal of himself as idolatrous serves to vindicate his literary autonomy. Freccero bases his definition of idolatry on the Augustinian distinction between use and enjoyment: "God alone is to be enjoyed *[frui]*; all other things are to be used *[uti]*."[32] Augustine says: "To enjoy something is to cling to it with love for its own sake. To use something, however, is to employ it in obtaining that which you love."[33] In other words, enjoyment implies an end in itself; use, a means to an end. Idolatry, always a substitutive relationship, is to enjoy something *in the place of* using it, to enjoy something *in the place of* God.

A reading of Petrarch's idolatry in "The Ascent of Mont Ventoux" would want to consider the thematics of erring,[34] deferral, and perversity. For example, Petrarch's erring way up the mountain, the wrong turns (*errare, vergere, anfractus*) which suggest his distance from salvation, also suggests the turning motion of tropes.[35] This is not unusual in Augustinian terms, where a journey is always a discursive journey which is at once self-reflexive (allegorizing its own use and abuse of words) and theological (allegorizing the way toward the blessed life). What is perhaps suspicious is Petrarch's deferral of conversion ("Thus I deferred the disagreeable strain of climbing"). Petrarch claims that he defers out of spiritual weakness. But Petrarch's poetic activity (insofar as it is inseparable from the turning motion of tropes) *is* only because he errs.[36] In other words, Petrarch has to defer his conversion—prolong indefinitely his tropological activity—in order to be a poet. In Augustinian terms, Petrarch enjoys his journey and the vehicles needed on that journey (figurative language) instead of using them. He does not wish to end his journey (to be redeemed), because that would put an end to his erring.[37]

At the summit of Mont Ventoux, Petrarch laments his perverse attachment to Laura: "The third year has not yet elapsed since that perverted *[perversa]* and malicious will, which had totally seized me and reigned in the court of my heart without an opponent, began to encounter a rebel offering resistance" (pp. 42–43). Augustine's account of the robbing of the pear tree in *Confessions* II demonstrates that perversion is at least as interesting as conversion. There perversion is a turn not to God but to a nothing, a cipher. Perversion—the quintessential wrong turn, literally a turn inside out—is the negative mirror of conversion. But perversion is more than a theme, it is a negative strategy that, like conversion, constitutes a narrative. Because a narrative of conversion recounts not only the sinner's death and rebirth but also the birth of the narrator able to tell his story of death and rebirth, because the text thus recounts its own coming into being as a text, it has a claim to closure and self-reflexivity. What prevents a narrative of conversion from being merely self-reflexive is the experience of conversion (the turn to God). Because of conversion the words of a narrative of conversion are produced by and point to the Word. But when Petrarch follows the example of conversion by reading and yet does not exemplify it, he enjoys rather than uses the example of Augustine's *Confessions*. When the experience of conversion is thus drained of its theological import and aestheticized, that narrative can still claim a closure and self-reflexivity, which amounts to an absolute autonomy. The conversion narrative no longer recounts the story of how the experience of conversion made possible the story, it tells only the story of the story, a story whose only source and reference is itself. In short, Petrarch would welcome the charge of idolatry in "The Ascent of Mont Ventoux" because he wants a perversion narrative, whose principles of construction are the rigorous inversion of conversion narrative.

But such an aesthetic strategy (perversion narrative) is based on the same presuppositions as conversion narrative. The text claims to constitute itself by an aesthetic recuperation of conversion and its negation. Instead of Christ the Word redeeming words, we have words redeeming themselves. The text's unity is now aesthetic rather than theological, its specular structure no longer localized at the moment of self-understanding, but in a presumed relationship of reflection between theme and formal principle (perversion or idolatry).

Conversion by reading posits a relationship between a self and a text that is one of inside and outside. For example, when we talk about Augustine's application (literally "putting on") of the words of Scripture to himself, the words are said to have a relation to him as a garment has to a body, or a body to a soul. The scriptural text that Augustine applies to himself (puts on) is itself an admonition to put on: "Not in rioting and drunkenness, not in chambering and wantonness, not in strife and envying: but *put ye on [induite]* the Lord Jesus Christ and make not provision for the flesh in concupiscence" (Rom. 13:13–14).[38] The inside/outside relationship between language and the self that conversion by reading proposes is also said to be found within language, which is understood in terms of the oppositions outer form/inner sense, carnal/spiritual, visible/invisible, dead letter/living spirit. Thus the model of language that conversion narrative asserts, and perversion narrative necessarily shares, is based on perception: seeing and not seeing, inside versus outside. Reading for conversion is phenomenological—a bringing into the light—hence the continuity between the order of seeing and the order of reading in conversion narrative, which culminates in the light of good reading. In fact, the larger possibility of a conversion or perversion narrative depends on the same continuity between a phenomenology of the self (its death and rebirth or its desire for poetic autonomy) and a written narrative.

But if carnal in a reading did not have to do with seeing or not seeing, if carnal were no longer opposed to spiritual, if the carnal could be rewritten (not by our interpretive intervention but as something that has already taken place in Petrarch's text), then Petrarch's carnal reading, his becoming an elder brother, would not be reducible to an aesthetic strategy, because it would be neither (1) aesthetic—something phenomenally apprehended—nor (2) a strategy—part of the activity of a subject. That Petrarch's reading is indeed carnal in a sense that cannot be opposed to spiritual becomes clear if we return to his exclusion of Gherardo. For the exclusion of Gherardo puts Petrarch in a perplexing double bind.

Petrarch *had* to exclude Gherardo (suppress his story, make it into a negation and a nonstory, prevent him from reading) in order to author his own story of conversion. But because, at the summit, excluding Gherardo is also equivalent to not reading further, when Petrarch does not read further he cannot read Augustine in the right way (as referring not to seeing mountains but to an example of words), and he cannot convert.

However, even if Petrarch *had not* excluded Gherardo (i.e., read further, read spiritually), he could not have converted. Reading further, reading Augustine in the right way (in context, reading "seeing mountains" as an example of words instead of as a naming of Petrarch's experience), would not allow him to recognize himself in Augustine's text. Reading further would have given the lie to Petrarch's self-recognition because, when seeing mountains is no longer an example in a mimetic sense (a universal model to be imitated) but in a linguistic sense (a particular version that is not exemplary, i.e., worthy of imitation), then a specular reading for conversion is no longer possible. In other words, Petrarch has to exclude Gherardo (i.e., not read further; i.e., read Augustine in the wrong way, or out of context) in order to convert. And just as Petrarch has to misread Augustine in order to read him in the "right" way, so too, in order to follow Augustine's example (convert by reading), he has also not to follow it (not pass the book on).

In short, the exclusion of Gherardo is the condition of *both* possibility *and* impossibility of Petrarch's conversion. On account of the double bind the exclusion of Gherardo produces— even if Petrarch had read spiritually, he could not have converted—Petrarch's reading can no longer be called carnal in a sense that is merely opposed to spiritual. How then might the carnal be understood otherwise? What is the nature of Petrarch's misreading?

When Petrarch reads Augustine's "And men go to admire the high mountains," he takes Augustine's text as a discourse about seeing instead of as a discourse about words. Yet the way in which Petrarch misreads is not an error of vision but an error of reading. In the line following Petrarch's oracle, Augustine rereads himself, putting invisible quotation marks around his words: "And they see nothing marvelous in the fact that while I was mentioning all these things, I was not seeing them with my eyes." The passage that Petrarch quotes is already, as it were, in quotation marks. In stopping where he stops, he erases the quotation marks around Augustine's words and takes them literally, or (as Augustine would say) carnally. We say "as it were" because (1) the quotation marks are invisible and (2) quotation is one metaphor among others with which to understand Petrarch's problem in reading Augustine. The virtue of this metaphor is that it describes reading not in terms of something that is outside language (the perception of objects) but in terms that are intralinguistic. The difference here between carnal and spiritual, literal and figurative (which Augustine renders homologous with carnal and spiritual), is not based on the difference between seeing and not seeing. The quotation marks (whether invisible or visible) do not need to be seen in order to be understood; they need to be read. Here reading depends not on a phenomenological sun but on a certain nonlight, a black light. Here literal and figurative are not homologous with carnal and spiritual. "Carnal" in a reading—reading literally or, better, according to the "dead letter"—does not have to do with attaching oneself to an outer form, or to the sensuous aspect of the sign. It has to do with reading differential marks, with a materiality intrinsic to language, another kind of dead letter.

However, this possibility of reading figuratively *or* according to the dead letter is not Petrarch's possibility (the possibility of a subject who could choose between them); it is a possibility of language. An example of this may again be found in Petrarch's exclusion of Gherardo. For the exclusion of Gherardo, like the misreading of Augustine, takes place on the level of language.

Petrarch wanted to exclude Gherardo, that is, write him out of his narrative of conversion. But in order to write Gherardo out, Petrarch has to write him in *as* out. This "as" of writing is not part of the activity of a subject who can manipulate his representations (as when Petrarch represents Gherardo as two-dimensional); it is an *inscription*. At the summit, the inscription of Gherardo *as* excluded, *as* effaced, reemerges to disrupt Petrarch's conversion. Petrarch's conversion is disrupted by what is not read; but what is not read is "not" merely absent, it is a trace. In other words, Petrarch's exclusion of Gherardo is also an inclusion, but there is an asymmetrical and nondialectical relationship between the two: Petrarch's exclusion of Gherardo is psychological; the inclusion of Gherardo is linguistic.

Petrarch's difficulty in including Augustine is like his difficulty in excluding Gherardo. Just as when Petrarch excludes Gherardo he includes Gherardo *as* excluded, so too when Petrarch includes Augustine he excludes Augustine *as* included. There is more than an analogical relationship here: to exclude Gherardo (read for conversion and not pass the book on) is to exclude Augustine as included (to quote and not to quote). If Petrarch cannot quote Augustine, it is not because Petrarch has fallen away from the spiritual or historical immediacy of Augustine's Christianity nor is it because Petrarch quotes from a secondary, derivative source (the *Confessions*) instead of from a primary one (Scripture).[39] If Petrarch cannot quote Augustine, it is rather because the letter of language never quite arrives at its destination.

In short, when Petrarch excludes Gherardo in "The Ascent of Mont Ventoux" he inadvertently excludes himself. But this self-exclusion is one that Petrarch can neither master nor appropriate (as he appropriates his erring in an economy of error), because that self-exclusion is not *his* exclusion; it belongs to the erring of his text. If Petrarch's text remains a dead letter—one that is neither delivered to God (conversion narrative) nor returned to sender (self-reflexive perversion narrative)—it is because Petrarch cannot master its circulation, as he perhaps sought to do by never sending it at all.

Toward the Outside

Both Augustine and Petrarch belong to a great tradition of interiority. Augustine can be said to have initiated that tradition with his autobiographical conversion narrative; Petrarch continues it as conversion *or* perversion narrative. What the two share is first of all a mood of self-criticism or self-rebuke. The "concupiscence of the eyes" has led each one to focus on creation at the expense of the Creator, in an erring movement away from the Creator. Each laments the squandering of the gifts which were given him by God. Each recounts a prodigality—an extravagant and wasteful expenditure—followed by a peripety.

In book II of the *Confessions,* in the outpouring of remorse that follows Augustine's account of his youthful robbing of the pear tree, the narrator offers what in effect is a *theory* of prodigality and other sins. Recall here the excess and gratuitousness that characterized this theft. It was performed not out of want but out of satiety; the stolen pears were not eaten, they were thrown to the pigs, all of which landed Augustine's sinner in a *regio egestatis,* a "wasteland," "a region of lack." Such prodigality, argues the narrator, parodies and perverts the generosity that is one of God's attributes: "Prodigality *[effusio]* shows, as it were, the shadow *[umbram]* of liberality; but you [God] are the most supremely rich bestower of all good things."[1] In Augustine's analysis, prodigality "shadows" God's generosity or imitates it, insofar as prodigality, like other sins such as pride, ambition, passion, and curiosity, results from man's frenzied desire for autonomy, his attempt to be God. The profuse or

71

effuse expenditure that characterizes prodigality is, however, a poor—technically a "perverse"—imitation of the radical generosity that is God's. Of course, the appeal of the prodigal son's story—a story that determines the intelligibility of both the *Confessions* and "The Ascent of Mont Ventoux"—is its seeming radicality. The prodigal's uncalculating expenditure can be opposed to the strict accounting that his elder brother demands. The risk and adventure of the prodigal's journey "into a distant country" can be opposed to the security of the elder brother's staying at home. But, as the preceding readings of Augustine and Petrarch have tried to show, because the prodigal's itinerary is one of departure *and* return it is *his* itinerary which is ultimately economic, part of a loss and gain in a system of exchanges. The economy of personal salvation of which the prodigal's prodigality, his sin, forms part is, finally, an economy of the selfsame in which the referral to other (in the figure of the elder brother) is suppressed and in which the risk of the prodigal's adventure "in a distant country" is no risk at all.

How is this so? Surely the prodigal's journey to the outside— the "distant country" and the "region of lack"—is no comfortable experience, potentially including, as it does, the extremes of despair, self-repudiation, and self-loss. One can think, for example, of Augustine's painful sense of alienation and exile in the *Confessions:* "Your light was within," he cries to God, "and I was outside" (VII.7), or of the torturous self-division evident in his scene of self-confrontation, "You, Lord, were twisting me in between his words, turning me back toward me myself, bearing me away from behind my back where I had put myself, while I did not wish to turn toward myself; and you set me before my face, that I might see how filthy, how distorted and sordid, spotted and ulcerous I was" (VIII.7), where the image of dismemberment denotes an extreme moral discomfort. Such discomfort is the price of interiority.

Yet there is comfort in this discomfort. Or, as Emmanuel Levinas puts it, there is an ultimate "security" there.[2] For what remains constant in these experiences is the structural relation of a self to its self, that is, a fundamental identity. This identity persists through all the self's transformations, transformations which include the extremes of alienation and self-loss. (Therein, according to Levinas, lies its happiness.) For Levinas, this is the model of the self (and the selfsame) which dominates in the West. In the Christian drama of personal salvation which Augustine and Petrarch each take up, self-loss can become a type of self-gain because, if you will, the self is its own outside. In such a model of the self, what is never jeopardized is the return home, the self-reference. The prodigal's prodigality is followed by the conversionary peripety whose possibility is presupposed in advance. Such prodigality is eminently recuperable; the departure it initiates is never anything but a detour in the self's journey to itself.

Is there not, however, something other than the relation of a self to *its* self—namely, the other, the relationship *to* the other? Is there not another kind of prodigality, an extravagant movement that does *not* return to self and same? This other prodigality has already been glimpsed in the preceding chapters, where the suppressed figure of the elder brother invisibly disrupted the scenes of interiority and self-coincidence. What was suppressed in the figure of the elder brother was a referral to other—to an alterity which is in turn textual, intersubjective, and Judaic. In the second part of this study, I will seek to make this alterity explicit. The figure that will guide the readings of Kafka and Levinas that follow is not the elder brother, for the elder brother is the subordinated term in the dyadic and hierarchical opposition prodigal son/elder brother. Within conversion narratives, the elder brother receives a negative and privative interpretation as dead letter, Old Testament, Cain. In the second part of this study, according to a reinscription that has *already* taken place, the terms *dead letter, Old Testament, Cain* become *midrashic letter, Hebrew Bible, Abraham*. The figure that will guide the readings that follow is Abraham, to whom God said: "Get thee from thy kindred, from thy country, and from thy father's house" (Genesis 12:1) and also "Take thy son, thine only son, whom thou lovest, even Isaac, and get thee unto the land of Moriah" (Gen. 22:2). Abraham's itinerary is, as Levinas will remind us, a departure *without* return. His is a one-way movement, an exorbitant movement away from the familiar and the familial, another kind of prodigality.[3]

But who, Abraham? How to read Abraham? How to read

him without Kierkegaard? "Can one," as Levinas asks in *Diffi-cile liberté,* "still be Jewish without Kierkegaard?"[4] It is Kierkegaard who perhaps teaches us to read the Abraham story. It is Kierkegaard—or his pseudonymous author Johannes de Silentio—who teaches us to avoid the recuperative understand-ing of reciting the story in clichés ("'The great thing was that he loved God in such a way that he was willing to offer him the best.'. . . So we talk and in the process of talking interchange the two terms *Isaac* and *the best,* and everything goes fine.")[5] It is Kierkegaard who warns us against uncritically relying on Paul's reading of Abraham in Heb. 11:8–19, which he para-phrases ("By faith Abraham left the land of his fathers"), there-by assuming that we *know* what faith is. It is Kierkegaard who warns us against a similarly uncritical reliance on verse 1 of the biblical story ("And it came to pass after these things that God tested Abraham") lest we might think that we can get away with simply *calling* Abraham's situation a test, an ordeal, thereby assuming that we *know* what a test is. It is Kierkegaard who warns us not to rest our interpretation on the didactic verse 12 of the episode, immediately following the peripety, in which the angel of the Lord says to Abraham: "For now I know that one fearing of God are you." What do we know?

It is Kierkegaard's de Silentio who teaches us how to read the Abraham story, how not to read or understand it too quickly:

An ordeal, this word can say much and little and yet the whole thing is over as soon as it is spoken. We mount a winged horse, and in the same instant we are on Mount Moriah, in the same instant we see the ram. We forget that Abraham only rode an ass, which trudges along the road, that he had a journey of three days, that he needed some time to chop the firewood, to bind Isaac, and to sharpen the knife. (p. 52)

The slowness of the journey will require a slowness of speaking (and of reading); de Silentio says that one could speak for sev-eral Sundays just of Abraham's love for Isaac (p. 31). The task of understanding Abraham—who cannot finally be understood, who treads unintelligibility with every step—will require a slow pace: not a winged horse but an ass, and three days. It will involve an existential approach—drawing out the anguish in-herent in Abraham's situation. It will involve what seems at times the not just exegetical but compulsive gesture, "to ride along with Abraham on the three-day journey."

This impulse of existential drawing out is at once midrashic and typological. As midrash, it fills in a gap between verses three and four of the biblical story, between Abraham's early rising and "the third day." It responds to those features of Hebrew narrative that Erich Auerbach has identified: gaps, lacunae, oppressive withholding.[6] As typology, it responds to a different need. Typological interpretation, as Mark C. Taylor has usefully described it, is able "to link events as distant as an ancient Hebraic child sacrifice . . . and the suffering of a nineteenth-century Danish Christian."[7] As Taylor argues, typological interpretation thus finds "rationale" in history through the discovery of resemblances, or tropes. It also, by thus projecting the biblical past onto the present, affirms the relationship of *liber* and *speculum* discussed by Paul Ricoeur: it affirms that Scripture has an urgent application to existence.

Thus de Silentio tells the story of a man whose "sole desire was to ride along with Abraham." In *Fear and Trembling*, this journey is made innumerable times, and Kierkegaard's narrator iterates the story's paratactic details (some of them invented): Abraham "swung his leg over the ass's back" (p. 36); "he mounted the ass, he rode slowly down the road" (p. 35); "he climbed the mountain" (p. 36); "he split the firewood, he bound Isaac, he lit the fire, he drew the knife" (p. 21). The story is broken down into smaller and smaller paratactic units; it is reiterated. How many times does Abraham stretch forth his hand and take the knife to slay his son! Abraham "drew the knife" (pp. 12, 13, 14, 20, 21, 22, 23, 27); the knife "gleams" (p. 36); "Isaac's fate was placed, along with the knife, in Abraham's hand" (p. 22): "Who strengthened Abraham's arm, who braced up his right arm?" the narrator wonders, even assimilating to Abraham the story of Moses. "And Abraham stretched forth his hand and took the knife to slay his son" *(wayishlach avraham eth yado wayiqach eth hama'akhelet lishchoth eth beno) (Extendit manum et arripuit gladium ut immolaret filium suum)* (Gen. 22:10). This moment of the knife—when Abraham stretches forth his hand and takes the knife to slay his son—is on instant replay. Kierkegaard's de

Silentio is not the only one who is fixated on it. It is a key moment, an iconic moment of the story, frozen in Kierkegaard's mind and in the minds of other Christian typological interpreters, who perhaps marvel at the knife—that killing letter—which, read typologically, becomes a life-giving spirit.

Yet this is a knife that cuts both ways. The midrashic commentators handle the killing letter otherwise. (And if the "man" of whom Kierkegaard speaks, who is obsessed with the Abraham story, "had known Hebrew" [p. 9], would he have known this?) In *Genesis Rabbah,* section *Vayera,* we find a rabbinic comment on the scriptural verse that revokes the command, the peripety of the episode, verse 12, when the angel of the Lord says, "*Lay not thine hand upon the lad* [or *Do not stretch forth your hand upon the lad*]. Where was the knife? Tears had fallen from the angels upon it and dissolved it."[8] The comment continues a recurrent image in this midrashic unit, that as Abraham, in the words of verse 10, "stretches forth his hand and takes the knife to slay his son," the angels are weeping. But here the rabbis are especially concerned with a gap in the text, and they tell us what their question is. Since verse 10 reads "And Abraham stretched forth his hand *and* took the knife to slay his son," in revoking the command, why doesn't Scripture repeat the phrase—the double verbal construction—in its entirety? Why is the knife not mentioned? Because when the angels wept, their tears, which evidently consist of a special solvent, fell on the knife and dissolved it.

Thematically, this exegesis suggests the sorrow the angels expressed previously (because, as it appears in context, God is breaking the convenant) and also relief. For despite the tears' magical powers, as an intervention they are too late. The command "Take thy son" has already been revoked (how *can* one revoke a command, a performative?). On the level of interpretive procedure, this exegesis also requires comment. A gap in the text—the missing knife—is imaginatively filled in with the story of the angels weeping. Yet the gap in question, or the scriptural problem, is as fanciful as the solution (and the tears are the solution—quite "literally"—to the problem of both the missing knife and the presence of the knife in the first place).

The killing letter that Abraham takes up is dissolved but not in the way of the letter becoming spirit. The literal is "literally" dissolved. What does "literal" mean, in its opposition to figurative, in a case like this?

Suffice it to say that there is also much to learn from the midrashic commentators about reading Abraham, indeed about reading. Their painstaking attention to the scriptural text is apparent, proceeding metonymically from hand to knife, interpreting what is there and what is not there. The pace of midrashic exegesis is also exemplary; it is slow going and excruciatingly careful. The name for such a critical attitude or approach is patience. This is a discourse of patience. It is a discourse to which I will often have recourse in the pages that follow when it comes to the reading of Abraham.

But who, Abraham? Kafka's Abraham (who is also to a certain extent, in my reading, Blanchot's Abraham) is a nomad. He errs. But his exile is distinctive. For unlike Augustine's place of exile—the *regio egestatis,* the "region of lack"—and unlike the prodigal son's *regio longinqua*—the "distant country" which he inhabits before he "returns in himself"—Abraham's exile is not a region or place at all. *This* Abraham, Kafka's Abraham (who is also, in my reading, Kafka "himself"), is in exile. But this exile is not a place he inhabits; it is not an exile where he could *find himself* exiled. His is a radical exile; he is exiled even *from* this exile, as Blanchot argues.[9] Thus excluded from himself, his is a peripety *without* anagnorisis, as I will show.

For Levinas, it is as if the very question "Who, Abraham?" is too much a question of essence. Abraham's peripety must be, for Levinas, a peripety *of* essence and ontology, that is, an inversion or reversing of the dominant tendencies of thought in the West. In other words, the question of Abraham is very much linked to Levinas's particular philosophical project. Levinas poses Abraham paradigmatically for an ethics that is specifically Hebraic. "To the myth of Odysseus returning to Ithaca, we would like to oppose the story of Abraham leaving forever his homeland for a land yet unknown and forbidding his servant to bring even his son to this point of departure."[10]

In Levinas's reading, Abraham's departure *without* return figures the very departure from self and from self-reference that is the movement of ethics and responsibility. For ethics, the imperative to be responsible to the other, requires such a departure from self-reference. Responsibility to the other is not something that is first filtered through the self; it is not an imperative that I deliver to myself. Rather, it is a being delivered over to the other. As Levinas describes it, responsibility cannot be the result of the kind of self-criticism in which we see Augustine and Petrarch engaging; it is a radical departure from self toward the other. "And God said to Abraham, 'Abraham.' And he said, 'Here I am' *[hineni]*" (Gen. 22:1).

Many commentators have found Abraham's response to God's call extraordinary, Kierkegaard among them: "Cheerfully, freely, confidently, loudly he answered: Here I am" (p. 21). In the biblical context, "Here I am" *(hineni)* indicates readiness, usually in response to God's call. It is used in this way by Jacob, Moses, Samuel, and Isaiah. The rabbinic interpretation found in *Genesis Rabbah* stresses the legal and performative aspect of the phrase. Rabbi Joshua says: "Now Abraham said, *Here I am*—ready for priesthood, ready for kingship."[11] Rabbi Joshua takes the word *hineni* according to its other predominant biblical usage, where it introduces a solemn and important declaration and has the legal force of "hereby." Thus Abraham's *hineni* indicates not just readiness but a legal commitment to serve (as priest, as king): it signals a performative utterance in which someone commits himself to something. Yet even if Abraham's *hineni* is not a legal usage, it is performative in another sense. In nonlegal as well as legal contexts, *hineni* is glossed by the rabbis as "joyfully." Joy here is not a description of an inward state but denotes readiness, absence of duress.[12] When Abraham responds to God's call with *hineni,* he is joyful to sacrifice Isaac, not because he is a murderer but because he is ready. He is entering into a commitment to fulfill God's word.

In his later work, Levinas makes *hineni* the paradigm for responsible subjectivity. "The word 'I' signifies 'here I am,' responding to everything and to everyone."[13] He refers us to the call of Isaiah: "And I heard the voice of the Lord saying, 'Whom shall I send, and who will go for us?' Then I said, 'Here I am, send me'" (Isa. 6:8). Levinas writes: "'Here I am' means 'send me'" (OB, 199). In glossing Isaiah's *hineni* as a being sent, as service, Levinas draws implicitly on the rabbinic interpretation of the phrase and thus emphasizes its performative force. For Levinas, the first response to the other is always "here I am."

The temporality of this response is unusual. In Levinas's account, "here I am" is not, strictly speaking, a response *to* a call. The response *precedes* the call, anachronistically. It precedes the call, as in a passage from Isaiah that Levinas quotes concerning God's promise for the messianic days: "Before they call, I will answer" (OB, 150). Here there is response before (or even in the absence of) there being anyone to respond to. In this asymmetrical call and response, there is neither reciprocity nor meeting nor even necessarily understanding. "Here I am" is the response of responsibility. It is prior to the call, but its priority cannot be understood in terms of ordinary time intervals. It will have to be understood otherwise.

3/

Kafka's Parables

In Franz Kafka's unfinished novel *The Castle*, K. visits the Mayor to find out about the terms of his employment as Land Surveyor. The Mayor explains to him at length that no Land Surveyor is needed, and that K.'s being summoned was an error.

"Allow me, Mr. Mayor, to interrupt you with a question," said K. "Did you not mention once before a Control Authority? From your account of the way things are run here, the very idea that the Control could be lacking makes one feel unwell."

"You are very rigorous," said the Mayor, "but multiply your rigor a thousand times and it would still be nothing compared with the rigor that the Authority imposes on itself. Only a total stranger could ask a question like yours. Is there a Control Authority? There are only Control Authorities. Of course, it isn't their function to hunt out errors in the vulgar sense of the word, for errors don't happen, and even if once in a while an error does happen, as in your case, who can say finally that it's an error?"

"This is something entirely new!" cried K.

"To me it is something very old," said the Mayor.

"Erlauben Sie, Herr Vorsteher, daß ich Sie mit einer Frage unterbreche," sagte K., "erwähnten Sie nicht früher einmal eine Kontrollbehörde? Die Wirtschaft ist ja nach Ihrer Darstellung eine derartige, daß einem bei der Vorstellung, die Kontrolle könnte ausbleiben, übel wird."

"Sie sind sehr streng," sagte der Vorsteher. "Aber vertausendfachen Sie Ihre Strenge, und sie wird noch immer nichts sein, verglichen mit der Strenge, welche die Behörde gegen sich selbst anwendet. Nur ein

völlig Fremder kann Ihre Frage stellen. Ob es Kontrollbehörden gibt? Es gibt nur Kontrollbehörden. Freilich, sie sind nicht dazu bestimmt, Fehler im groben Wortsinn herauszufinden, denn Fehler kommen ja nicht vor, und selbst, wenn einmal ein Fehler vorkommt, wie in Ihrem Fall, wer darf denn endgültig sagen, daß es ein Fehler ist."
"Das wäre etwas völlig Neues!" rief K.
"Mir ist es etwas sehr Altes," sagte der Vorsteher.[1]

The Mayor's logic is characteristic of Kafka's witing—a double or triple movement of interpretation that cancels itself out: (1) errors don't happen; (2) K.'s being summoned is an error; (3) who can say, finally, that it's an error? Here the movement is further complicated by a question that runs throughout the novel: was K. in fact summoned by the Castle at all? (The first words K. utters upon his arrival are: "What village is this that I have wandered into? *[In welches Dorf habe ich mich verirrt?]* Is there a Castle here?")[2] The Mayor himself is not sure if K. was indeed summoned. Shortly after this exchange, the Mayor says: "I don't know whether in your case a decision of this kind happened—some people say yes, others no—but if it had happened, then the summons would have been sent to you."[3]

But the authority of the Mayor—the one who names K.'s being summoned an error and not—is in turn discredited by the Landlady ("The Mayor is a person of no importance," she informs K.)[4] Perhaps the statement about the possibility of error, a statement made by one who has no authority, is itself in the mode of error. This suspicion is reinforced by K.'s progressive insight throughout the novel that all his perceptions—all his figurations of the Castle bureaucracy, the Mayor, and the Landlady—may be illusory, that is, in the mode of error. But what if, in a kind of infinite regress, this insight that everything is illusory is itself illusory; what if the statement that everything is an error is also an error? The kinds of conclusions that a reader of Kafka might draw from the larger context of the Mayor's statement about error are hardly encouraging. If the putting into question of the Mayor's authority is not authoritative, if the metadiscursive comment on the status of the Mayor's discourse about error is not free of the error it identifies and denounces, then the possibility of an interpretive metadiscourse on Kafka's writing seems to be discredited in advance.

Interpreters of Kafka will at one time or another come up against the two problems we have tried to identify here. The first, which is exemplified by the Mayor's logic, we might call "Kafka's law." We do this to avoid calling this movement of self-cancellation "paradox," as some commentators have done, thereby reducing it to a concept at the expense of its distinctive rhetorical features.[5] Indeed, a more felicitous model for the kind of "logic" that is at work here is summoned up by Freud when he recounts the joke about the borrowed kettle:

A. borrowed a copper kettle from B. and after he had returned it was sued by B. because the kettle now had a big hole in it which made it unusable. His defence was: "First, I never borrowed a kettle from B. at all; secondly, the kettle had a hole in it already when I got it from him; and thirdly, I gave him back the kettle undamaged.

Freud notes that "Each one of these defences is valid in itself, but taken together they exclude one another. A. was treating in isolation what had to be regarded as a connected whole." *(Jede einzelne Einrede ist für sich gut, zusammengenommen aber schließen sie einander aus. A. behandelt isoliert, was im Zusammenhange betrachtet werden muß.)*[6] In such a treatment, says Freud, "there is no such thing as an either-or, only a simultaneous juxtaposition" *(kein Entweder-Oder, nur ein gleichzeitiges Nebeneinander).*[7] The discourse of the Mayor, like that of A., the borrower of the kettle, involves a *paratactic* juxtaposition of mutually exclusive claims. Parataxis (from the Greek word meaning "placing side by side") refers to "clauses or phrases arranged independently, a coordinate rather than subordinate construction," "sometimes . . . without the customary connectives."[8] The Mayor and A. place contradictory statements side by side. The connectives that are missing between these statements are logical ones—a gap in thought in violation of the principle of noncontradiction, for example. But a closer look at the Mayor's discourse reveals that its juxtaposition is paratactic on the level of logic only. For the Mayor's discourse does employ subordinate construction and connectives: "Of course, it is not their function to hunt out errors in the vulgar sense of the word, *for* errors don't happen, *and even if* an error does happen, *as* in your case, who can say finally that it's an error?" On what one could call the level of rhetoric, the Mayor's discourse is, if anything, hypotactic.[9] The simultaneous absence of logical connectives and presence of "rhetorical" connectives in the Mayor's discourse signal what could be a potential tension or mutual interference between logic and rhetoric in Kafka's writing. Perhaps the burden of Kafka interpretation—if it is not to reduce Kafka's writing to mere self-contradiction or self-cancellation—is precisely to read the connectives.

The importance of these connectives, these particles of speech, has been noted by at least two of Kafka's commentators. Horst Steinmetz, for example, has pointed to "the high frequency of conjunctions, adverbial modifiers and prepositions. The texts are shot through with *aber, freilich, allerdings, vielmehr, trotzdem, übrigens, vielleicht*" (but, of course, certainly, rather, in spite of, moreover, perhaps). Steinmetz draws on the work of Herman Uyttersprot, who links the use of these particles to "the interplay between hypothesis and fact that can be seen in almost all the argumentative procedures in Kafka. Given facts are reflected on, hypotheses are won out of them, hypotheses are in turn explained into facts, out of which again hypotheses are derived." Says Uyttersprot, "Every known fact . . . often appears in a bright veil of doubt, every hypothesis, on the other hand, contains something of the rigor of certainty." Uyttersprot, whose study of Kafka's use of particles centers on the occurrence of the word *aber* (but), claims statistical support for his observation that "of all German authors, Kafka uses the adversative conjunction 'aber' by far the most. Indeed, he uses it on the average two and three times more often than all other authors. . . . The cause of this lies in the remarkable complexity of a soul which cannot simply see and feel in a straight line, a soul which didn't doubt and hesitate out of cowardice and caution, but rather out of clear-sightedness. A soul which at every thought, every perception, every assertion, instantly heard a little devil *[ein Teufelchen]* whispering to him: *aber.* . . . And then this soul had to write down this devilish 'aber' to our greater 'confusion inside of clarity.'"[10]

These particles certainly play a role in the confused clarity of the Mayor's discourse. He moves from fact, "of course *[freilich]*, errors don't happen," to hypothesis, "and even if *[und selbst wenn]* an error does happen," to fact, "as *[wie]* in your case," to a question, "who can say finally that it's an error?"

A second problem in the passage with which we began is the status of interpretation in and of Kafka's writing. Interpretation is thematized in this passage not only in the kind of unstable reasoning we find on the part of the Mayor but, as we recall, in the unreliable discovery that the Mayor's discourse is not reliable, in the nonauthoritative putting into question of the Mayor's authority. If the metadiscursive comment on the Mayor's discourse about error is not free of the error it identifies and denounces, if the metadiscourse is subject to the same error that conditions the discourse that it talks about, then the metadiscourse is no *meta*discourse, and there is a certain return to the Mayor's question, "Who can say finally that it's an error?"

Many other examples of this thematization of interpretation in Kafka's writing could be cited: the messages that don't get there in "An Imperial Message"; the exhortation to "Go over" *(Gehe hinüber)* in "On Parables," which is followed by a demonstration of the impossibility of going over;[11] the commentary that follows the parable "Before the Law," in which each interpretation that is put forth is in turn discredited. In "Before the Law," we also find the priest's (nonauthoritative) reflection on the status of all particular interpretations: "The scriptures are unalterable and the comments often enough are merely an expression of the commentators' despair" *(Die Scrift ist unveränderlich, und die Meinungen sind oft nur ein Ausdruck der Verzweiflung darüber).*[12]

It is not surprising then that the bewildering multiplicity of incompatible interpretations has become a *topos* of Kafka criticism, as well as the suggestion that Kafka's work defies interpretation and thematizes its impossibility. Heinz Politzer is exemplary in this regard when he outlines his method of Kafka interpretation with a motto borrowed from Kafka: "Give it up!" *(Gib's auf!).*[13] Similarly Stanley Corngold entitles his critical bibliography on Kafka's "The Metamorphosis" *The Commentators' Despair.*[14] This despair certainly demonstrates an attentive reading of Kafka, but it risks falling into the smug assurance of a negative knowledge. For example, Politzer argues that Kafka developed the form of the paradoxical parable to demonstrate, in Kafka's words, "that the incomprehensible is incomprehensible, and we knew that already."[15] Corngold, reading the same phrase, writes: "At this point, it is clear, the literary enterprise is seen in its radically problematical character."[16] But a reading of Kafka's "On Parables" would "show" that this kind of *negative* knowledge is precisely not available, especially in the form of a generality. The commentator can make the mistake of believing that something like a negative knowledge can be gained from Kafka's writing, only as long as the nonunderstanding that Kafka's work relentlessly explores is conceived within a hermeneutic model—namely, as the opposite of understanding, as its negative. Returning to the priest's remark about the status of particular interpretations and the interpretation of interpretation—"the comments often enough are merely an expression of the commentators' despair"—we might ask: is this despair of hermeneutics a despair that is proper to hermeneutics, that is, something that the interpreter can appropriate? Or, to return to the Mayor's question—"who can say finally that it's an error?"—is there anything like an "I" who can say this?

At stake here is the problem of how one can speak about problems in Kafka criticism. Frank Kermode remarks in *The Genesis of Secrecy* that much commentary takes place according to a revelatory model based on the New Testament's relationship to the Old. Former interpreters are seen, Kermode says, "like the Israelites, men in shadow, possessing a text that only *seemed* to be intelligible,"[17] while the present interpreter reveals the text in all its intelligibility and sees the blindness of the former interpreters with a new, spiritual sight. This pervasive revelatory model, which, one may note, has the structure of a conversion experience, is, simply, hermeneutics. We are certainly working within this model when we discuss the limits of former interpretations of Kafka. But can Kafka's discourse— marked by the oscillation between fact and hypothesis, misunderstanding and understanding—be accounted for by such a revelatory model?

In order to pursue the question of models for interpretation, we turn to the reading of Kafka in *The Genesis of Secrecy.* "Leopards break into the temple and drink to the dregs what is in the sacrificial pitchers; this is repeated over and over again; finally it can be calculated in advance, and it becomes a part of the ceremony" *(Leoparden brechen in den Tempel ein und saufen die Opferkrüge leer; das wiederholt sich immer wieder; schließlich kann man es vorausberechnen, und es wird ein Teil der Zeremonie).*[18] Here we will bypass Kermode's discussion of the parable in terms of the assimilation of an intrusion by a cultus and the intrusion's becoming liturgical, as well as other strong interpretations the parable has received,[19] in order to focus on an interpretation of the parable that thematizes its interpretation. This interpretation is not by Frank Kermode. Following his discussion of the parable, he writes:

> Here I will interpolate a reading of the parable by another hand, my wife's. "The letter of the parable," she writes, "masters our freedom to interpret it. The words, we know, must mean more and other than they say; we would appropriate their other sense. But the parable serenely incorporates our spiritual designs upon it. The interpreter may be compared to the greedy leopards. As their carnal intrusion is made spiritual, confirming the original design of the ceremony, so is this figurative reading pre-figured; only complying with the sense, it adds nothing of its own and takes nothing away. In comparing himself to the leopards, the reader finds himself, unlike the leopards, free—but free only to stay outside. Thus dispossessed by his own metaphor, excluded by his very desire for access, he repeatedly reads and fails to read the words that continue to say exactly what they mean."[20]

Kermode's wife (not named in any other fashion) offers a reading of the way in which the parable refers to itself which enjoys, much like her denomination, something like a secondary status in the economy of Kermode's book. Kermode (whose book, incidentally, focuses on interpretive exclusions and which is dedicated, in the words of Mark, "to those outside") inscribes his wife's discourse—the discourse of one outside a proper name, a discourse about the discourse of the outside—in his book *as* outside. Into his own discourse he interpolates her reading—a reading of the parable that thematizes the reader as "outside," as "excluded by his very desire for access"—and excludes it. Appropriately enough, the reading that Kermode's wife offers—let us, for convenience's sake, refer to her as "Mrs. K."—dramatizes most sharply the problem of how one can speak about the interpretive exclusions that Kafka's writing thematizes.

Mrs. K. opposes the letter of the parable (the words that "say exactly what they mean") to its other, figurative sense (the words that "mean more and other than they say"). "The interpreter may be compared to the greedy leopards. As their carnal intrusion is made spiritual . . . so is this figurative reading pre-figured." The leopards' going from carnal to spiritual is a figure for what the reader does, which is making the "literal" figurative. Thus, to interpret the parable is to do exactly what the parable says the leopards do—to make the passage from carnal to spiritual, literal to figurative. In this way, the parable figures (and prefigures) its own interpretation. Mrs K. then reflects on the status of that insight, of the self-referential reading. "In comparing himself to the leopards, the reader finds himself, unlike the leopards, free—but free only to stay outside." The interpreter, like the leopards, comes from outside the text. But unlike the leopards, who make it inside the text, the interpreter remains outside the text, which has again become a letter. In other words, the only recognition that the interpreter gains from this self-referential reading is that he was an intruder, an outsider who remained outside, that his interpretation is superfluous (he is "dispossessed by his own metaphor"); he recognizes himself as excluded.

But is Mrs. K's reading of the parable as closed and as self-referential as she seems to imply? Is there not an asymmetry within her analogy between the interpreter and the greedy leopards? "As their carnal intrusion is made spiritual . . . so is this figurative reading *pre-figured*." The relationship between carnal and spiritual is a *figure* for what the reader does, which is to pass from literal to figurative. The relationship between carnal and spiritual is itself a *figure* for the relationship between literal and figurative. The asymmetry is that the analogy between carnal/spiritual and literal/figurative is itself based on a *figural* relation, that is, the relationship between literal and figurative. Mrs. K's reading knows more about this asymmetry than she does. After saying why the interpreters are *like* the greedy leopards, she says: "the reader finds himself, *unlike* the leopards, free—but free only to stay outside."

The leopards are included in the text by being spiritualized.

The reader is included in (and excluded by) the text by being *prefigured*. The leopards get into the text because they pass from carnal to spiritual. The reader stays outside the text because he passes from literal to figurative. Insofar as the reader's activity is *not* like what the leopards do—drinking up what is in the sacrificial pitchers—insofar as the reader is in a relationship of literal and figurative to a text, (the *in*scription of) his *ex*clusion from the text is far more radical than Mrs. K. lets on. How is this exclusion to be understood?

Frank Kermode argues that the paradigm for the interpreter's exclusion, including the one we find in Kafka, is authorized by a certain reading of Mark 4: "To you has been given the secret of the kingdom of God but for those outside everything is in parables; so that seeing they may indeed see but not perceive, and they may indeed hear but not understand; lest they should turn again, and be forgiven" (vv. 11–12). The scholarly literature and controversy surrounding this statement ranges from discussions of Mark's theology of secrecy to claims of scribal and redactional errors.[21] Kermode summarizes the two predominant readings this passage has been given as (1) "the stories are obscure on purpose to damn the outsiders" and (2) a modified version of what Kermode calls Jesus' "gloomy ferocity," the stories "are not necessarily impenetrable, but . . . the outsiders, being what they are, will misunderstand them anyway."[22]

The interpretive exclusion in and from Kafka's writing can indeed be linked to Mark's theory of parable. But Kafka's work is an outsider's rewriting of New Testament parable, that is, from the point of view of the unredeemed. In other words, the nonredemption in Kafka's work is not simply that of the Jew in the Gospel who refuses to accept Christ but a certain return to an older model of interpretation. That the answer to the question of unredemption, exile, and erring may be formulated in terms of old and new is hinted in *The Castle*, in the Mayor's final exchange with K.:

". . . errors don't happen, and even if once in a while an error does happen, as in your case, who can say finally that it's an error?"

"This is something entirely new!" cried K.

"To me it is something very old," said the Mayor.

A number of critics, among them Walter Benjamin, Maurice Blanchot, Martin Buber, and Heinz Politzer, have suggested in different ways that Kafka be returned to the Jewish tradition. Benjamin draws an analogy between Hasidic parable and Kafka's writing. Buber talks about Kafka's "Paulinism of the unredeemed." Politzer has suggested that Kafka's style resembles that of the Elohist, as analyzed by Erich Auerbach; it is "fraught with background." Blanchot, who uses metaphors from the Jewish tradition to talk about Kafka's work, suggests that Kafka be read not from the perspective of Christianity but "from the perspective of Abraham."[23]

Kafka's fragmentary writings on Abraham are, then, of no small interest. But it is perhaps significant that all the writings by Kafka on Abraham that we possess are glosses on Søren Kierkegaard's Abraham. It is as though Kafka, in order to read the Hebrew Bible, had to read the New Testament first. But before we draw any conclusions from this, a little background for Kafka's readings of Kierkegaard is in order.

Kafka first read Kierkegaard in 1913. He notes in a diary entry: "As I suspected, his case, in spite of essential differences *(trotz wesentlicher Unterschiede)*, is very similar to mine. . . . He confirms me like a friend."[24] The similarity that Kafka speaks of here (and elsewhere) is the history of the broken engagement.[25] Kafka, who had proposed to Felice Bauer just two months before, was already regretting his proposal. This twice-broken engagement is documented in Kafka's *Letters to Felice,* which are in length equivalent to nearly his entire novelistic output. Kierkegaard also broke his engagement to Regina Olsen and generated an excess of texts concerning that rupture. But this similarity "in spite of" *(trotz)*—a characteristic Kafkan preposition—sums up the history of Kafka's reading of Kierkegaard as a history of ambivalences. Four years later Kafka, who has read more Kierkegaard, says of his friend's *Either/Or* that the book's "hatefulness grows under my hands."[26] A problem of proximity and distance is evident in all of Kafka's writings on Kierkegaard.[27] Kafka's earlier fragments about Abraham all take up Kierkegaard's terminology despite essential differences. Commenting on these obscure and difficult fragments, Jean Wahl writes: "Kafka directs our attention to two traits of Abraham (but is Abraham not Kierkegaard himself? one might ask). . . .

Here Kafka draws a portrait of Kierkegaard. . . . But Kafka does not say: Kierkegaard. He repeatedly speaks of Abraham."[28] Against Wahl's weak explanation for this valuable insight (namely, that Kafka saw Kierkegaard in the image of Abraham because the first book he read by Kierkegaard was *Fear and Trembling*), against an idea that Kafka was simply "inspired" by *Fear and Trembling,* one could say that this substitution of proper names poses the question: what kind of return to the Jewish tradition is possible for Kafka? This return is neither unmediated nor nostalgic: when Kafka reads Abraham, he can't not read Kierkegaard's Abraham.

But who is Kierkegaard's Abraham? In *Fear and Trembling,* Kierkegaard (or rather the pseudonymous author Johannes de Silentio) speaks of a man whose sole wish was "to go along on the three-day journey when Abraham rode with sorrow before him and Isaac beside him."[29] The Bible says:

And He [God] said, "Take now thy son, thine only son, whom thou lovest, even Isaac, and get thee into the land of Moriah; and offer him up there for a burnt offering upon one of the mountains which I will tell thee of." And Abraham rose up early in the morning, and saddled his ass, and took two of his young men with him, and Isaac his son; and he cleaved the wood for the burnt offering, and rose up, and went unto the place of which God had told him. On the third day Abraham lifted up his eyes and saw the place afar off. (Gen. 22:2–4)[30]

Kierkegaard's version*s* of Abraham are an attempt to fill in the gaps between verses 3 and 4 of the biblical story, between Abraham's early rising and "the third day." They are also an-swer*s* to a question that Kierkegaard poses of the biblical text: did Abraham communicate the purpose of the journey to Isaac?[31] The final answer that Kierkegaard gives to this question is that Abraham cannot speak, because he cannot make himself intelligible. "The ethical expression for what Abraham did is that he meant to murder Isaac; the religious expression is that he meant to sacrifice Isaac."[32] Abraham's willingness to obey God's command involves renouncing the ethical, which is the general, and with it all possibilities of making himself intelligi-ble. That is why Abraham's answer to Isaac's question—"Where is the lamb for the burnt offering?" "God will provide the lamb for the burnt offering my son."—is in the mode of irony, "for it is always irony when I say something and still do not say anything."[33] When Abraham sacrifices the ethical, he also sacrifices the finite, the temporal; he makes the movement of infinite renunciation. But he does not lose his faith; he still has faith in God's promise that "in Isaac thy seed shall be called to thee" (Gen. 21:12). He is a "knight of faith" who makes the movement of faith by virtue of the absurd in such a way that, says Kierkegaard, he "does not lose the finite but gains it whole and intact," in such a way that he "who draws the knife gets Isaac" again. Faith, says Kierkegaard, is this "prodigious paradox" "that makes murder into a holy and God-pleasing act, a paradox that gives Isaac back to Abraham again."[34]

In a letter to Max Brod, Kafka remarks of Kierkegaard's *Fear and Trembling:* "He doesn't see the ordinary man . . . and paints this monstrous Abraham in the clouds" *(und malt den ungeheuren Abraham in die Wolken).*[35] Kierkegaard's Abraham is perhaps monstrous because Kierkegaard's Abraham is a murderer and, by antiphrasis, a Cain:

In the moment he is about to sacrifice Isaac, the ethical expression for what he is doing is: he hates Isaac. But if he actually hates Isaac, he can rest assured that God does not demand this of him, for Cain and Abraham are not identical. He must love Isaac with his whole soul. . . . Only in the moment when his act is in absolute contradiction to his feelings, only then does he sacrifice Isaac, but the reality of his act is that by which he belongs to the universal, and there he is and remains a murderer.[36]

This disclaimer, and the use of the word "murderer" makes one pause. But Kierkegaard does not say: Cain. He speaks instead of Abraham.[37]

Kafka's most sustained reflection on Abraham is part of a letter he wrote to Robert Klopstock in 1921:

I could think of another Abraham for myself—who certainly would not make it to a patriarch, not even to an old clothes dealer—who would be ready to fulfill the demand of the sacrifice immediately, with the promptness of a waiter, but who could not bring off the sacrifice, because he can't get away from the house, he is indispensable, the household needs him, there is always something more to put in order, the house is not ready.

Ich könnte mir einen andern Abraham denken, der—freilich würde er es nicht bis zum Erzvater bringen, nicht einmal bis zum Altkleiderhändler—der die Forderung des Opfers sofort, bereitwillig wie ein

Kellner zu erfüllen bereit wäre, der das Opfer aber doch nicht zustandebrächte, weil er von zuhause nicht fort kann, er ist unentbehrlich, die Wirtschaft benötigt ihn, immerfort ist noch etwas anzuordnen, das Haus ist nicht fertig.[38]

Like Kierkegaard, Kafka is involved in the project of *thinking* Abraham (or Abraham*s*). Kafka thinks *another* Abraham, who is so capable, so much in the finite, that he is incapable of leaving the house. And, as Kafka reasons, Abraham did have a house: "If he hadn't had a house, where else would he have raised his son—in which rafter would the sacrificial knife have been stuck?" *(Wenn er nicht das Haus gehabt hätte, wo hätte er denn sonst den Sohn aufgezogen, in welchem Balken das Opfermesser stecken gehabt?)* This is *another* Abraham, other than the biblical Abraham, other than Kierkegaard's Abraham—or is it? This is not "the monstrous Abraham in the clouds"; it is an Abraham whose ordinariness is stressed. But it is also to some degree an extension of Kierkegaard's description of the knight of faith. The knight of faith has, externally, "a striking resemblance to bourgeois philistinism"; he expresses "the sublime in the pedestrian"; "his gait is as steady as a postman's."[39] But, as Kafka will continue his reasoning: Yes, Abraham had a house, but did he have a son? He says: "It was different for the above-cited Abrahams, who stood in the houses they were building and suddenly were supposed to go up Mount Moriah; possibly they don't even yet have a son, and are supposed to sacrifice him already" *(Anders die oberen Abrahame, die stehn auf ihrem Bauplatz und sollen nun plötzlich auf den Berg Morija; womöglich haben sie noch nicht einmal einen Sohn und sollen ihn schon opfern).* Kafka's hypothesis *(womöglich)* is a devastating one because, for Kierkegaard, it was a fact. Kafka has put his finger on a central embarrassment of Kierkegaard's *Fear and Trembling,* which lies in the autobiographical allegory of Kierkegaard's broken engagement.[40] This autobiographical allegory is based on the analogy: As Abraham sacrificed Isaac, so Kierkegaard sacrificed Regina.[41] The embarrassment here is that Kierkegaard never had any finite to sacrifice. Kafka says, "possibly he didn't even yet *[noch nicht]* have a son and is supposed to sacrifice him already *[schon]*." We could read this "not yet" and "already" as an "always not yet" and an "always already," that is, as an unreachable futurity and an unreachable anteriority. He had no present, no temporal, no finite, to sacrifice. Neither, for that matter, did Kafka.

Jean Wahl said that Kafka substitutes the proper name of Abraham for Kierkegaard. Could we not also say that Kafka at times substitutes the proper name of Abraham for Kafka? Perhaps Kafka's autobiography—the one he never wrote—is also in the Abraham story. In a letter to Felice, Kafka writes that he is held back from their marriage, their union, "by what is almost a command from heaven" *(Aber was mich hält, ist förmlich ein Befehl des Himmels)*.[42] Yet is this "command from heaven" not also ridiculous, something of a joke? Possibly they haven't even yet a son and are supposed to sacrifice him already. Kafka continues: "These are impossibilities and Sarah is right, when she laughs" *(Das sind Unmöglichkeiten und Sarah hat Recht, wenn sie lacht)*. Who is Kafka's Abraham?

The last part of Kafka's letter to Klopstock introduces yet another "other" Abraham. If the first version of Kafka's Abraham is he who does not yet have a son and already has to sacrifice him, Kafka's second version of Abraham is he who comes unsummoned. The first version questions the Abraham of Kierkegaard. The second version asks a question of the biblical Abraham and of the biblical text. The ridicule attached to the Abraham who had no son to sacrifice still clings to this other Abraham, and it gets worse. Kafka writes:

But another Abraham. One who wants to sacrifice altogether in the right way, and who has the right mood in general for the whole thing, but who cannot believe that he is the one meant, he, the repulsive old man and his child, the dirty boy. The true faith is not lacking to him, he has this faith, he would sacrifice in the right frame of mind if he could only believe that he is the one meant. He fears, he will ride out as Abraham with his son, but on the way he will metamorphose into Don Quixote. The world would have been horrified at Abraham if it could have seen him, he however fears that the world will laugh itself to death at the sight of him. But, it is not ridiculousness as such that he fears—of course, he fears that too, and above all his laughing along with them— but mainly he fears that this ridiculousness will make him even older and uglier, his son even dirtier, more unworthy really to be summoned. An Abraham who comes unsummoned!

Aber ein anderer Abraham. Einer, der durchaus richtig opfern will und überhaupt die richtige Witterung für die ganze Sache hat, aber nicht glauben kann, daß er gemeint ist, er, der widerliche alte Mann und sein Kind, der schmutzige Junge. Ihm fehlt nicht der wahre Glaube, diesen Glauben hat er, er würde in der richtigen Verfassung opfern, wenn er nur glauben könnte, daß er gemeint ist. Er fürchtet, er werde zwar als Abraham mit dem Sohne ausreiten, aber auf dem Weg sich in Don Quixote verwandeln. Über Abraham wäre die Welt damals entsetzt gewesen, wenn sie zugesehen hätte, dieser aber fürchtet, die Welt werde sich bei dem Anblick totlachen. Es ist aber nicht die Lächerlichkeit an sich, die er fürchtet—allerdings fürchtet er auch sie, vor allem sein Mitlachen—hauptsächlich aber fürchtet er, daß diese Lächerlichkeit ihn noch älter und widerlicher, seinen Sohn noch schmutziger machen wird, noch unwürdiger, wirklich gerufen zu werden. Ein Abraham, der ungerufen kommt![43]

This chain of reasoning recalls Uyttersprot's remark: "Every known fact appears in a bright veil of doubt; every hypothesis, on the other hand, contains something of the rigor of certainty." Kafka begins with a fact that the Abraham story presupposes: Abraham was summoned to sacrifice his son. In contrast to Kafka's earlier version of him, this Abraham is perfectly capable of fulfilling the sacrifice, but *(aber)* he cannot believe that he is the one meant. In other words, the fact is doubted and becomes a hypothesis. The hypothesis, perhaps he is not the one meant, in turn becomes a fact: "An Abraham who comes unsummoned!" Kafka continues:

It is as if at the end of the year, the best student is ceremoniously supposed to receive a prize, and in the expectant stillness the worst student, as a result of an error of hearing, comes forward from his dirty last desk and the whole class explodes. And it is perhaps no error of hearing, his name was really called, the rewarding of the best is supposed to be, according to the intention of the teacher, at the same time the punishment of the worst.

Es ist so wie wenn der beste Schüler feierlich am Schluß des Jahres eine Prämie bekommen soll und in der erwartungsvollen Stille der schlechteste Schüler infolge eines Hörfehlers aus seiner schmutzigen letzten Bank hervorkommt und die ganze Klasse losplatzt. Und es ist vielleicht gar kein Hörfehler, sein Name wurde wirklich genannt, die Belohnung des Besten soll nach der Absicht des Lehrers gleichzeitig eine Bestrafung des Schlechtesten sein.[44]

The analogy turns on a humiliating pedagogical scene. The worst student (out of nervousness? overanxiousness? because he is error-prone?) mishears his name being called. He who always sits in the last row (because he is the worst) tries to come up to the first row (because he would like to be better, he makes himself even worse?); he becomes an object of ridicule.

But is it an error of hearing? The whole analogy is in the form of a hypothesis: it is as if *(es ist so wie wenn)*. The error of hearing is stated as a fact: *(infolge)* "due to, as a result of, in consequence of" an error of hearing, which is in turn doubted. The doubt becomes a hypothesis: perhaps *(vielleicht)* it is no error, which becomes a fact: his name was really *(wirklich)* called. However, it is not a question of an error of hearing after all, the teacher merely wanted to teach the worst student a lesson.

Let us draw out the analogy this distressing pedagogical scene summons up. Abraham's obedience to God's command is like the worst student's mishearing. (The dirt that attaches to Abraham's son is now attached to the worst student's desk—because he is always making errors and erasing them, and never gets the answer right?) If Kafka's Abraham is the Abraham of Kafka here—the autobiographical allegory—then Kafka's "command from heaven" is like the worst student's mishearing. The difficulty of deciding whether or not it is an error of hearing is like the difficulty of not yet having a son and already having to sacrifice him.

But why not the Abraham of the Bible here? The question Kafka poses of the biblical text—did Abraham come unsummoned?—is not without precedent. A midrashic commentator on the binding of Isaac has asked the same question of the biblical text, although there the question is more bound to and bound up with the text. The occasion for the midrashic remark is verse 12 of Genesis 22, which begins, "Lay not thine hand upon the lad." This verse marks the peripety of the episode:

And Abraham stretched forth his hand and he took the knife to slaughter his son. And an angel of the Lord called unto him from the heavens, and said, "Abraham, Abraham." And he said, "Here I am." And he said, "Lay not thine hand upon the lad, neither do thou anything unto him, for now I know that thou art one fearing of God, because thou hast not withheld thy son, thine only son, from me."

Rabbi Aba said: Abraham said to God: "I will lay my complaint before you. Yesterday (on an earlier occasion) you told me 'In Isaac shall thy seed be called to thee' (Gen. 21:12), and then again you said, 'Take now thy son' (Gen. 22:2), and now you tell me 'Lay not thine hand upon the lad!'" The Holy One, blessed be He, said to him, in the words of Ps. 89:35, "'My covenant will I not profane, nor alter that which is gone out of my lips.' When I told you 'Take thy son,' I was not altering that which went out from my lips, namely, my promise that you would have descendants through Isaac. I did not tell you 'kill him,' but 'bring him up' to the mountain. You have brought him up—now take him down again."[45]

In this midrashic unit, Abraham is portrayed as wondering about the contradiction, on the one hand, between God's earlier promise to him, "In Isaac shall thy seed be called to thee," and the command to sacrifice Isaac (the contradiction Kierkegaard wondered about) and, on the other hand and more at issue here, the contradiction between God's first command to sacrifice Isaac, "Take thy son," and God's second command, "Lay not thine hand upon the lad." Abraham is saying to God, you're contradicting yourself here and you've done it before (or, why do you keep contradicting yourself?). God replies that he is not contradicting himself and that Abraham has, in effect, misunderstood the command.

When, in verse 2, God says to Abraham, "Take thy son, thine only son, whom thou lovest, even Isaac, and offer him up there for a burnt offering," the verb used is *alah* ("to go up, ascend, climb"), which appears here in a form where it has a causative force: "Cause him to go up, cause him to be brought up there." In its entirety, the phrase has the idiomatic meaning "to offer sacrifice," but a more literal (if less obvious) translation would be "bring him up there for a burnt offering." In other words, perhaps Abraham misunderstood the phrase. God says, "I did not tell you 'kill him,' but 'bring him up' to the mountain. You have brought him up—now take him down again." In this midrashic unit, the episode has the structure of a misunderstanding, indeed the structure of a joke (although perhaps not a very funny one). (In a much later document, one midrashist— Woody Allen—has Abraham pose the question to God thus: "How am I supposed to know when you're kidding?")

In short, Kafka's question—did Abraham come unsummoned—is not far from a question that Rabbi Aba, for different reasons, asks of the biblical text. The midrashic reading—the question and its resolution—is bound to the biblical text in a way that Kafka's is not. And of course Kafka, in reflecting on a ridiculed Abraham, departs substantially from the dominant rabbinic view that Abraham was exalted by this episode.[46] Perhaps Kafka is again closer to Kierkegaard, who, comparing the distress of Abraham's situation to that of the Virgin Mary ("the one who God blesses he curses in the same breath"), asks in effect: is this what it means to be God's chosen one? But the ugliness of Kafka's Abraham is not quite the same ugliness of Kierkegaard's Abraham. And there are perhaps, in Kafka's analogy, this story and another story to be read.

When the worst student gets up from his grimy last desk, the opposition best/worst, first desk/last desk, and the reversal of rank that results from the error of hearing recall the New Testament reversal: "The last will be first and the first, last." One place in which this phrase may be found is at the close of the parable of the laborers in the vineyard. As the story goes, the owner of a vineyard pays the same wage to the laborers who worked all day and to the laborers who were hired at the eleventh hour. When the ones hired first see this, they grumble at the owner, saying, "These last worked only one hour, and you have made them equal to us who have borne the burden of the day and the scorching heat." The owner dismisses the complaining workers from his presence, saying, "Take what belongs to you, and go. . . . Do you begrudge my generosity?" Jesus concludes, "So the last will be first and the first, last" (Matt. 20:1–16).

The parable is generally understood as an illustration of God's generosity and as a vindication of the Gospel against its critics. As one critic puts it, Jesus' purpose was to "defend his association with the sinners and to attack any legalistic merit doctrine." For, indeed, the grumbling workers insist on just such an application of merit, in which "reward should be exactly proportionate to achievement." Their "flawed self-understanding" is "challenged" by "the surprising payment" to the eleventh-hour workers, by "the graciousness" (or grace) of the owner. Because of this legalist understanding, however, they "exclude themselves from the source of grace,"[47] and, as another critic says, "they reject God's gift" and "cut themselves off from salvation."[48] Joachim Jeremias remarks that "the parable is clearly addressed to those who resembled the murmurers, those who criticized and opposed the Good News, Pharisees for example."[49] The Jerusalem Bible glosses the parable: "Into his kingdom God brings latecomers, sinners and pagans. Those who were called first (the Jewish people who, from Abraham's time, had been privileged with the covenant) have no right to be offended." Another source invokes Irenaeus, who "proposed that the men who worked longer hours represent the patriarchs and the prophets of the Old Testament, while the eleventh-hour servants represent the disciples of Christ."[50]

In Kafka's analogy, there is a reversal of rank: best/worst, first/last. But the reversal of rank (the worst student's coming forward) is the result of an error of hearing. In other words, there is no reversal of rank. Kafka in effect rereads the New Testament reversal and reverses it, unreads it, calls it an error. But perhaps it is no error of hearing, the name of the worst student really was called, and the teacher's intention was at once to reward the best and punish the worst. It is as though Kafka had to unread the New Testament back to the Old—to unread grace back to a legalistic, punishing God who says that the first will be first and the last will be last. But this reversion (turn back) to the "Old Testament"—a scripture defined by its relationship to the Gospel—is followed by another turn: a turn away from the question of an error of hearing ("who can say finally that it's an error?") and a turn to somebody else's—the teacher's—intention (nach der Absicht des Lehrers). That intention is not like the intention of a subject but the kind of intention that is a law of Kafka's writing: the road to the Castle "did not lead up the Castle hill; it only led near it, but then, as if intentionally, it turned aside, and if it did not lead away from the Castle, it did not lead nearer to it either." (Die Straße nämlich, die Hauptstraße des Dorfes, führte nicht zum Schloßberg, sie führte nur nahe heran, dann aber, wie absichtlich, bog sich ab, und wenn sie sich auch vom Schloß nicht entfernte, so kam sie ihm doch auch nicht näher).[51]

In short, it is as if, in order to read Abraham, Kafka has to read him back through the New Testament (typology,

Kierkegaard) and back through the "Old Testament" (an "old" law which opposes merit to grace or justice to mercy) in order to return him to an other law, which is not yet and always already the "law" of the Hebrew Bible, which is the law as other, in other words, an other Abraham.

4/

Alterity and the Judaic: Reading Levinas

For an inquiry into the place of the Judaic in literary criticism, the work of the philosopher Emmanuel Levinas provides an exemplary way of access. In contemporary French philosophy, Levinas is best known for having renewed the question of the ethical, the discourse inclined toward the infinitely other. He describes ethics as the upsurge of responsibility that is born(e) in the encounter with the "face of the other" *(le visage d'Autrui)*. He also marks out with admirable caution and rigor the conjunction between the alterity of the other and the alterity of the Judaic. He does so from within a tradition of French phenomenology in which he is a leading figure. Levinas studied with Husserl and Heidegger in Freiburg in 1928–29 and virtually introduced Husserl to the French-speaking world with his cotranslation of the *Cartesian Meditations* in 1930. Although he published important short works and essays in the 1930s and '40s, Levinas's major philosophical impact has come from the publication of *Totality and Infinity* (1961) and *Otherwise than Being or Beyond Essence* (1974).[1]

The way of access that Levinas's work provides for an inquiry into the place of the Judaic in literary criticism is already and necessarily a detour. The detour is not merely extrinsic, the result of an obstacle created, say, by the genuine remove of Levinas's project from literary critical concerns. Such an obstacle could in any case be circumvented in part by situating Levinas in the intellectual context of Blanchot, Bataille and Derrida, with whom he has numerous affinities. A related way

100

of linking Levinas's work with literary critical concerns would be to cite his ongoing preoccupation with Heidegger, whose importance for literary criticism is widely recognized if not always well assimilated. However, the detour in question is not merely due to having to go by way of philosophy to pursue the conjunction between the alterity of the other and the alterity of the Judaic in Levinas's work. It is, as we will see, a detour intrinsic to Levinas's saying of this conjunction (indeed, does he ever say it?). It is a problem of how to speak of Judaism and alterity or, better, to recontextualize Derrida's formulation about negative theology, "how not to speak?" *(comment ne pas parler?)*. How not to speak of Judaism and alterity, namely: (1) how is it possible to avoid speaking of it? how not to speak of it? (2) how must one avoid speaking of it? how *not* to speak of it? how to avoid speaking of it badly, glibly, etc.?[2]

We can point to some of the difficulties that beset Levinas's saying of Judaism and alterity. They begin with the saying of alterity, the transcendence of the infinitely other, namely, the ethical. Levinas does not merely renew the question of the ethical in contemporary philosophy in the sense of breathing new life into a question that had died. He *reinscribes* the question of the ethical because in order to pose it he must (re)read and repeat a philosophical tradition that suppresses this question. In order to restore priority and fundamental sense to the question of the ethical, he must detach the question from the conventional senses with which the philosophical tradition covers up the question. Thus, in order to pose the question of the ethical anew, to re-pose the question, he must bring the question out of *its* repose or dormancy.

The manner of Levinas's question owes much to Heidegger; yet for Levinas, Heidegger is the culmination of a tradition in the West in which the question of the ethical is in repose. (In Heidegger, one could say, the question of the ethical re-poses.) Heidegger is the culmination of a history of philosophy (a history viewed solely from the perspective of its suppression of the question of the ethical) that suppresses consideration for the other, that fails to "do justice" to the other. Levinas characterizes it as an "allergy": "Since its infancy, philosophy has been filled with a horror of the other that remains other, with an insurmountable allergy" (T, 346). From Socratic maieutics (where you can only learn what you already know) to Husserlian phenomenology (where the totalizing, synoptic power of the gaze would convert all alterity to my transcendentally reduced *Sinngebung*) to Heideggerian ontology (where the description of *Dasein*—man insofar as he is the *being* who asks the question of the meaning of being—determines and secondarizes the relationship with the other as a symmetrical and indifferent *Mitsein* [being-with]), Western philosophy has been a philosophy of the Same. (The Same is a term which for Levinas denotes the concrete way in which the "I" "recovers its identity through all that happens to it" [TI, 36].) Over and against this suppression of the other in the tradition, Levinas seeks a "non-allergic relation with alterity," a "heteronomous experience." This heteronomous experience, this subjection to an other law *(heteron,* other + *nomos,* law), is a relationship to the other in which generosity, responsibility, and language are primordial structures. These structures are *prior* to the violent suppression of the other in a relationship of knowing, phenomenology, or ontology. As Levinas emphasizes throughout his work, they respond to the infinite alterity of the other's face.

Levinas identifies two precedents in the history of philosophy for his "non-allergic relation with alterity," two exceptional moments that do not (as Derrida says in "Violence and Metaphysics") "repress ethical transcendence" (VM, 91), that escape from the domination of the Same. These are the Platonic good beyond being (the *epekeina tes ousias* of *Republic* 509) and the Cartesian idea of infinity, as a thought which overflows my thinking of it. Not evoked as such in Levinas's work yet nonetheless clearly marked is, in fact, a third precedent for this unheard-of escape from the domination of the Same: the talmudic tradition and/or biblical "ethics." How is this third precedent marked? In short, how does Levinas say "Judaism?"

The talmudic tradition is evoked explicitly only in Levinas's nonphilosophical works, namely, in the three collections of talmudic readings, *Quatre lectures talmudiques* (1968), *Du sacré au saint* (1977), and *L'au-delà du verset* (1982), and in *Difficile liberté: Essais sur le judaïsme* (1963, 1976). In the philosophical works, the evocation is implicit, in the form of biblical

allusions and biblical citations.[3] (In neither the philosophical
nor ultimately in the nonphilosophical works is this tradition
evoked *as such,* as we will see.) Levinas himself insists on this
distinction between his two types of writing for good philosophical reasons.[4] For the same good reasons, this third precedent, the talmudic tradition, does not really belong in Levinas's
account of the history of philosophy. Talmudic interpretation
would belong instead to religion. Insofar as its starting point
and the object of its discourse are God, it is philosophy's nonphilosophical other. But the Talmud, as Levinas describes it in
Quatre lectures talmudiques, is not a fideistic, dogmatic, or
theological document.[5] Beneath its apparent preoccupation
with minutiae of ritual observance, it conceals a philosophical
discourse: "The rules [concerning ritual, social, and economic
life] have in fact a philosophical prolongation often dissimulated beneath problems concerning 'positive commandments'
or 'negative commandments'" (QLT, 12). It gives us access to
a thinking "older" than the conceptual oppositions in the West
(QLT, 79).

Levinas's interpretive procedure with respect to the Talmud
is exemplified in the reading he gives of *Shabbath* 88a–88b in
Quatre lectures talmudiques. This talmudic text concerns the
acceptance of revelation. It begins with the scriptural verse immediately prior to the giving of the law: "And the people stood
at the foot of [literally "under"] the mountain" *(betachtith
hahar)* (Exod. 19:17). Rabbi Abdimi bar Chama bar Chasa
comments: "This teaches that the Holy One, blessed be He,
held the mountain above them like an inverted cask and said to
them: 'If you accept the Torah, it is well. If not, there will be
your tomb.'" At the foot of Mount Sinai, then (or "under it,"
if one takes the prepositional phrase literally), the people were
faced with the alternative between the Torah and death. Levinas
argues that the Torah, which renders free choice possible, cannot have been the result of free choice. It is a violent imposition
of freedom that is prior to the alternative freedom/violence.
"That which must be received to render free choice possible
cannot have been chosen, unless it is after the fact *[après coup].*
In the beginning was violence" (QLT, 82).

In fact, as Levinas argues, there is an originary adhesion to the law that precedes not only free examination and rational assent but any apprehension of it. Levinas's reading relies here on another scriptural verse which, as a cross-reference, engages the rabbinic commentators considerably. The verse, from Exodus 24:7, relates the people's words following the donation of the law, affirming their acceptance of it: "And the people said: All that the Lord has spoken we will do and we will obey [literally "hear, hearken"]" *(na'aseh venishmah)*. As the rabbinic commentators read these words, the syntactical order signifies a temporal order, namely, the people did the law first, then heard it. Or, as Levinas extends the sense of "hear, hearken" in a way that the Hebrew *(shema)* as well as its French translation *(entendre)* allows, they did the law first, then they understood it.

Doing before understanding is certainly not the logical order. But this error of logic has "hidden resources" that Levinas will draw out in the course of his reading. That is why he resists interpretive efforts that would make this verse conform too much to logic, to ordinary ways of thinking. For example, "we will do and we will understand" might express the people's confidence: "Because of this confidence in him who speaks we promise to obey and now we will hear what he has to say to us" (QLT, 92). But let us not cease to wonder, says Levinas, at this confidence that precedes examination. Let us not assume that we know what it is. Even if we take the verse as "we will do *in order to* understand," we risk transforming the "we will do" into a mode of understanding (QLT, 93). Let us not cease to wonder at this doing before understanding. The rabbinic commentators maintain its extraordinary nature, calling it a secret of the angels. They delight in the inversion of the normal order that doing before understanding implies.

In Levinas's argument, doing before understanding simply goes against the grain of the entire conceptuality of the West. Ultimately this is not just a matter of logic; it is in accordance with the philosophical priority of the knowledge we have *of* an act over that act itself (QLT, 76). Generally we want to understand what we do and certainly to understand before we do. The spontaneous engagement that characterizes doing before understanding can only be conceived as a blind practice, an ignorance, a naive and infantile innocence (QLT, 77–78)—unless, concludes Levinas, the unconditional and unreflective acceptance of the law suggests a notion of the act which is *prior* to the opposition between theory and practice and which in fact *conditions* this opposition (QLT, 78–79). The apparent inversion of normal chronology—doing before understanding—is in fact fundamental. Doing before understanding reveals the way in which the world is not a space of possibilities but is responsibility to the other. It suggests a way of actualizing that does not begin with the possible (QLT, 95).

For Levinas, as these kinds of conclusions suggest, talmudic discourse is a rigorous delineation of the very ethical situations that he himself is trying to describe.[6] Everything has perhaps already been thought there! (DL, 11). Thus, in Levinas's nonphilosophical writing, the Talmud plays a privileged role, perhaps analogous to the interpretation of the pre-Socratics in Heidegger. The question of the ethical is posed (and dissimulated) there before it becomes congealed in the tradition, before it reposes in its derivative form.

Levinas's readings of the Talmud effect a remarkable "translation" of talmudic thought into philosophical terms that demonstrates both the rigor of talmudic thought and its pertinence to "philosophical ethics." In this sense, Levinas can be said to form part of a tradition of Jewish philosophizing that performs a "translation" or encounter between philosophy and Judaism, a tradition that would include names as diverse as Philo, Maimonides, Spinoza, Moses Mendelssohn, Hermann Cohen, Solomon Maimon, and especially Franz Rosenzweig. Levinas refers to his readings as a "translation" of the Talmud into "the modern" (QLT, 15), or a "translation of the wisdom of the Talmud into Greek" (QLT, 24), "which is our university language" (TrI, 43), the language of philosophy. He stresses the importance of further translation of the Talmud into "Greek": "The Septuagint is not yet complete; the translation of biblical wisdom into Greek language remains unfinished."[7] His reading model for the philosophical translation/appropriation of the Talmud is a Septuagint in the making.

When we turn to Levinas's saying of Judaism in the philosophical works, we find little trace of this voluble and inspired translation project (which, as we will see, is by no means as absolutely hermeneutical as it first sounds). We find instead a reticence, a discretion, allusions that are iterated but almost invisible, scattered through his texts, never pursued in sustained form. We find a type of negative indication. In the philosophical works, we gain access to "biblical ethics" by allusions to a certain Abraham. The following citation is from the important 1963 essay "The Trace of the Other," a transitional essay between his two major works which marked a certain departure from an ontological language. We quote from this essay at some length to show how the allusion to Abraham is embedded in a conventional(!) philosophical context.

The heteronomous experience that we are seeking would be an attitude that cannot be converted into a category and whose movement toward the other is not recuperated in identification, does not return to its point of departure. Is not this experience furnished by what one all too flatly calls goodness and the work? . . . But then we must not conceive of the Work as an apparent agitation of a ground which afterwards remains identical with itself, like an energy which, in all its transformations, remains equal to itself. . . . The Work thought radically is in effect a movement of the Same toward the Other which does not ever return to the Same. To the myth of Odysseus returning to Ithaca, we wish to oppose the story [l'histoire] of Abraham, leaving his fatherland forever for a land yet unknown and forbidding his servant to bring even his son to the point of departure. (T, 348)

The certain heterogeneity between the philosophical discourse and the literary and religious discourse to which it alludes is mastered, unified, in a style that might be called seamless. The characteristic discursive strategy of the passage as a whole resembles a *via negativa*. The passage begins by describing what the heteronomous experience is not: "an attitude that *cannot* be converted . . . whose movement is *not* recuperated." It then says what the heteronomous experience is, identifying it positively as goodness and work—but indicating that these commonplace terms need to be reinscribed. Then follows a *non*-heteronomous conception of the work—"But then we must *not* conceive of the work as an apparent agitation of a ground" (i.e., as self-identical)—to which is contrasted a heteronomous (or a

non-nonheteronomous?) conception of the work as "a movement which does *not* ever return to the Same," followed by an
oppositional allusion: Odysseus (departing and) returning, the
*non*heteronomous experience, and Abraham departing *without*
returning, the non-nonheteronomous experience, or, if you
will, what the heteronomous experience is [not]. Abraham is
introduced within an oppositional economy, not only of
"Greek" and "Hebrew," "myth" and "story" (or "history"),
but of two kinds of itineraries, as if the significance of his itinerary can only be indicated by contrasting it with what it is not.

The allusion is also appositional. It functions in apposition
to the two kinds of experience and two conceptions of the work
expressed. The apposition is metaphorical because it turns on
an analogy between four *movements,* based on their resemblance—a resemblance between, on the one hand, a non-
heteronomous movement which returns to the Same and the
movement of Odysseus' return and, on the other hand, a heteronomous movement which does not return to the Same and
Abraham's movement of departure without return. In this way,
the opposed itineraries of Odysseus and Abraham can evoke,
respectively, the circular identification of egological life versus a
radical going out toward the other, a negative that is recuperable versus a negative that is not recuperable, the return to a *site*
of the Same versus a departure from the site of the Same, indeed
a departure from all sites.[8]

Could one not say that in order to make this metaphorical
apposition based on a perceived resemblance between itineraries and then to oppose them, Levinas has to reduce both his
literary and religious source texts to the level of plot, to the
arrangement of incidents? (The Abrahamic plot, as recounted
by Levinas, is already more exegetical to the extent that it is a
conflation of Genesis 12, the leavetaking, and Genesis 22, the
Akedah [the binding of Isaac], in which Abraham bids his servants [presumably father and son] not to accompany him to the
sacrifice [Gen. 22:5]. It thus reads together two instances of
radical departure.)[9] What is the necessity in which the Greek
text that covers up the Hebrew must itself be covered up in
order to recover the Hebrew? Matthew Arnold describes it as

follows: "When the two [Hellenism and Hebraism] are con-
fronted . . . the speaker's whole design is to exalt and enthrone
one of the two, and he uses the other only as a foil and to enable
him the better to give effect to his purpose."[10] Is this necessity
then "rhetorical" in the broadest sense of the term? Of course
it could be argued that the Odyssean itinerary is also not a plot
in the derived sense: it is the fundamental plot of Western philosophy, the plot in which one will never encounter the other.
For nothing other can befall Odysseus, "all of whose adventures
are but the accident of a return" (TrH, 92). Elsewhere in the
philosophical work, Levinas alludes to the Odyssean itinerary to
evoke this would-be adventure that is in fact a spurious alterity,
a false outside, the insistence on adequation, the refusal of exteriority that is the very figure of philosophical thought.[11] And
in each case, one could note a certain heterogeneity between
the allusion and its philosophical context, a heterogeneity that
is both presupposed and mastered by the use of allusion itself.
Disruptive in its very unobtrusiveness, is not this other rhetorical necessity, namely, the "use" of allusion, even more trou-
bling than the reduction of the *Odyssey* to plot?

The reference to Abraham and Odysseus is an allusion, that
is, a tacit reference to a literary and to a religious text which
presupposes the reader's familiarity with those texts. It thus
presupposes a shared tradition, a community, a fusion between
author and reader. Of course the reader can not "get" the allusion; but within the prevailing concept of allusion, whose model
for text understanding is overwhelmingly hermeneutic, the
reader's competence or lack thereof is necessarily going to be
understood as a fusion or incomplete fusion of horizons.[12] Our
question is then: does not what Levinas is doing with allusive
apposition contradict what he is saying (and "reinforcing") by
allusive apposition, at this very moment, about the Work? "The
work thought radically is in effect a movement of the Same
toward the Other which never returns to the Same. To the myth
of Odysseus returning to Ithaca, we wish to oppose the story of
Abraham." Does not Levinas's "use" of allusion, with the
shared tradition, the hermeneutical fusion and exchange between work and reader that it presupposes, contradict what he

is saying here about the non-self-identity of the work, about the asymmetrical, nonreciprocal relationship between work and reader? In the two sentences immediately following, Levinas writes: "The work thought to the limit demands a radical generosity of the Same, which in the Work goes toward the Other. It therefore demands an *ingratitude* of the Other. Gratitude would be precisely the *return* of the movement to its origin" (T, 191). In this thinking of the gift, Levinas argues against a balanced economy of exchange, a circle of debt and restitution that would symmetricalize the work-reader relationship. He argues elsewhere against a symmetrical and sentimental communion between interlocuters, between addresser and addressee.[13] The radical asymmetry between Same and Other which he describes in the work, in the face-to-face encounter, in the saying *(le dire)* could never become a reciprocal contract, a fusion of horizons, a dialogue. This is part of his implicit critique of the dialogical model for text interpretation proposed by Heidegger's successors in philosophical hermeneutics.

The discrepancy between doing and saying that emerges with Levinas's "use" of allusion does not indicate an authorial naiveté or the author's betrayal of his own intentions. It is not as if any text, philosophical or otherwise, could "do without" allusion (that would be like trying to do without a structure of reference in general). It is also not simply Levinas who, in the manner of an authorial subject, "uses" allusion; it uses (up) his text. Rather the discrepancy between what his text does with allusion (namely, symmetricalizes and returns to Same the work-reader relationship) and what his text says by allusion (namely, that the work-reader relationship should be asymmetrical, should go from Same to Other) indicates a larger tension in Levinas's work between, in short, its performative and constative dimension.

This tension has been explored by Jean-François Lyotard and Jacques Derrida as a particular kind of double bind. Let us summarize the double bind in general terms. Levinas says that the work ought to be non-self-identical. But if Levinas's work is non-self-identical in the way that his work says that the work ought to be non-self-identical, then it is self-identical. In fact, if Levinas's work doesn't do what it says about the work (as seems to be the case with his allusion to Abraham: when he "says" Abraham, he "does" Odysseus), if his work is non-self-identical, then it does what it says about the work, and it is self-identical.

This double bind in which Levinas's work is caught also encircles his *reader*. For example, Lyotard asks how Levinas's reader is to read the talmudic wisdom of "doing before understanding": "Is this not what the commentator is bound to do with this work, if he understands it?"[14] But if the reader understands, he has to do before understanding; he has not to understand. For Lyotard, the performative dimension of the talmudic "do before understanding" always risks falling into a constative which neutralizes the executive force of the order and to which it is incommensurable. In fact, all of Levinas's ethical discourse runs this risk of falling into a discourse *on* the ethical. The ethical utterance falls into a denotative metacommentary; a speaking to the other becomes a speaking about the other. How to read/receive the Levinasian ethical discourse, the performative description? In his second essay on Levinas, "En ce moment même dans cet ouvrage me voici," Derrida speculates about the case of the archperformative, the gift:

Suppose that I wish to *give* to him, to Emmanuel Levinas. Not to return something to him, an homage for example . . . but to give him something that escapes from the circle of restitution, of the meeting *[rendez-vous]*. . . . It would thus be necessary that, beyond all possible restitution, my gesture operates beyond debt, in absolute ingratitude. . . . It would however be necessary to do that in conformity to what his Work says of the work. I would still be caught in the circle of debt and restitution. . . . If I restitute, if I restitute without fault, I am at fault. And if I don't restitute, by *giving* beyond recognition, I risk being at fault.[15]

To escape from the circle of the meeting (from the *rendez-vous*, the "render you"), from the contract, and from symmetry necessitates a radical ingratitude. But to be ungrateful is to conform to Levinas's thinking of the structure of the gift; it is to be grateful. The fault in either case is constitutive. Derrida continues:

If someone says to you: do not render/return to me what I give you—
you are at fault even before he has finished speaking. It suffices that you
hear/understand [entendre] him, that you begin to understand and to
recognize. You have begun to receive his injunction, to render to yourself what he has said, and the more that you will obey him by restituting
nothing, the better you will disobey him and will render yourself deaf
to what he addresses to you.[16]

To receive the Levinasian gift of the gift (to preserve it *as* a
gift, but the gift is not, *as* a gift, and the gift *is* not), the reader
must do before understanding, must be deaf to Levinas's injunction. The asymmetrical structure of the gift necessitates an
ingratitude so radical that it approaches ambivalence and persecution. For, as Lyotard explains, the guiding principle of
Levinas's work is "that thou shall never be 'I.'" But, as Lyotard
pursues the logic of this principle, if the reader does not want
"to flatten the alterity of his work" (in accordance with "the
hermeneutic, discourse of good faith"), he *has* to flatten the
alterity of his work ("discourse of ambivalence"): "Since you
ask for it, I will not treat you as my similar, but as my dissimilar.
I can do you justice only by mistreating you. Indeed, if in your
view to be just is to court alterity, the only way to be just
towards your discourse of justice is to be unjust about it" ("discourse of persecution").[17] At the limit the discourse of the ethical is *almost* indistinguishable from the discourse of persecution. This is the logical form to which Levinas's ethical
discourse is absolutely vulnerable.

But while these double binds look like paradoxes, they in fact
indicate a structure that is *prior* to formal logic. Derrida calls it
"an incredible logic, formal and non formal."[18] In other words,
they are not reducible to logical deficiencies or traps in
Levinas's discourse (and our use of the words "contradiction"
and "discrepancy" to talk about Levinas's "use" of allusion
should also not be reduced thus). Although these double binds
are anterior to logic, they are, if you will, the logical form in
which Levinas's discourse necessarily dissimulates itself. Dissimulated thus, all of Levinas's saying, and not just the saying of
Judaism and alterity, is beset by a certain incapacity. Is Levinas's
other saying a saying otherwise? Would it demand in turn to be
read otherwise?

With these problems and questions in mind, let us come back to this particular and problematic saying: "To the myth of Odysseus returning to Ithaca, we wish to oppose the story of Abraham, leaving his fatherland forever for a land yet unknown, and forbidding his servant to bring even his son to the point of departure." The risks of this saying thus multiply. In addition to the necessary possibility that the Levinasian performative fall into the constative, there is the necessary risk, even the necessity, that this saying be misunderstood, be received in absolute ingratitude. But in order to grasp the stakes of this misunderstanding and this ingratitude, we have to be grateful, we have to understand what is to be misunderstood, lest we "flatten the alterity" of this saying and obscure its considerable merits. To Odysseus, Levinas still opposes Abraham.

Odysseus' journey is the Greek and philosophical journey par excellence. Levinas writes: "Action recuperated in advance by the light that was supposed to guide it, this is perhaps the very definition of philosophy" (T, 347). Because of the structure of the return home, there is an essential intelligibility which governs this journey, even its unforeseeable adventures. In his reading of the talmudic tractate *Shabbath* 88a–88b (discussed above), Levinas describes the structures of Christian experience as having the same kind of intelligibility. Addressing an audience of the Colloque des intellectuels juifs de langue française, to whom this reading was originally delivered, Levinas says that while Jews are "particularly insensible to Jesus, the figure that Christians find most moving," they are also "particularly interested," indeed "tempted," by "the dramatic life" and "the life of temptations" that Christianity announces. The temptation for Jews that Levinas identifies here is precisely the temptation *of* temptation:

Christianity tempts us by the temptations —be they surmounted —that fill the days and nights of its very saints. We are often repelled by the "flat calm" that reigns in a Judaism regulated by law and ritual. . . . The tempted self . . . can listen to the siren's song without compromising the return to its island. It can brush past, it can know evil without succumbing to it, experience it without experiencing it, try it without living it, venture forth *in security.* . . . The temptation of temptation is the temptation of knowledge. The temptation of temptation is not the attraction exerted by this or that pleasure over to which the one tempted risks to surrender himself, body and soul. What is tempting here is not the pleasure but the ambiguity of a situation in which pleasure is still possible, but in which the self conserves its freedom, in which it has not renounced its security, its self-reference. What is tempting here is the situation in which the self remains independent, but in which this independence does not exclude the self from that which must absorb it—to exalt it or to lose it—in which the self is at once outside of everything and a participant in everything. . . . The temptation of temptation is philosophy, . . . it takes off from a self which, in engagement, is assured of a permanent disengagement. The self is perhaps nothing other than this. (QLT, 73–75)

Levinas does not hesitate here to assimilate the structures of Christian experience to the structure of philosophical knowledge. Both are Odyssean in that they constitute the interiority of the self by the recuperation of an outside. (Is philosophy's insurmountable allergy to the Other also an insurmountable allegory? The Christian adventure, with its emphasis on personal salvation, misses the other.) This self that "tries things without trying them" is precisely a self for whom the adhesion to the law (doing it) would proceed from a rational choice (understanding it). The self, in this Greco-Christian economy, stands precisely opposed to doing before understanding. But the Judaic economy, after all, offers no interiority of the self, none of the peripeties or the retrospective illumination of a drama of personal salvation. Small wonder that Levinas speaks of the aversion we often feel toward "the 'flat calm' that reigns in a Judaism regulated by law and ritual" (QLT, 73). For while Odysseus' journey takes place in the light, Abraham's journey (or, if you will, the doing that precedes understanding), takes place in darkness and unintelligibility, is characterized by non-return and absence. Levinas writes that if doing the law before understanding is conceived as pure praxis as opposed to contemplation, it is "a movement in the night" (QLT, 78). But Levinas, attentive to the hierarchical oppositions—inside and outside, presence and absence, seeing and blindness—that organize the opposition Greek/Hebrew (and Christian/Hebrew as well), does not merely reverse the dyadic hierarchy (i.e., privilege the outside, nonseeing, absence). He reinscribes it so that the subordinated term is no longer the (dialectical) opposite of the first. Perhaps the adhesion to the law that precedes understanding is not merely external (i.e., a blind or infantile naiveté) but an adhesion which is anterior to the internal adhesion that operates in the light of evidence (QLT, 82). Perhaps the "without" of Abraham's departure *without* return should "not" be understood in a privative sense but as a radical departure, a movement toward the Other, a heteronomous experience. The experience of absence that dominates Abraham's itinerary can be reread: the absence in which Levinas's other is manifested is, as Derrida explains, "not pure and simple absence, for there logic could make its claim, but a *certain* absence" (VM, 91). Thus, one can understand the inscription of the Judaic in Levinas's work as its reinscription in a differential structure analogous to the logic of the Derridean "deconstruction" of the metaphysics of presence.[19]

This reinscription has considerable exegetical force. It opens up possibilities of rereading the Judaic in its opposition to the Greek or Christian and suggests a way of access for this rereading. For example, Derrida writes about the encounter with the other in Levinas's work as "a community of non-presence and therefore of non-phenomenality. Not a community without light, not a blindfolded synagogue, but a community anterior to Platonic light" (VM, 91). Here Derrida, following Levinas (who follows Rosenzweig), not only rereads but unreads an entire medieval iconography of the synagogue with its broken staff and its blindfold.[20] That iconography is exegetical; it is based on the typological relationship between the two testaments. Judaism prefigures and announces Christ. But since Judaism does not accept Christ, it is blind to the light it gives off. It is, as Bernhard Blumenkranz writes, "like a blind man with a lantern who shows the way to others but doesn't see it himself."[21]

According to the antisemitic Christian (typo)logic we traced out in our discussion of Augustine in earlier chapters, blind(folded) Judaism is necessarily blind *to* its blindness, that is, has a radical self-opacity. However, what if this blindness, or this self-opacity, were not a lack of (sensible or intelligible) seeing but a *prior* turning away from the light? What Derrida calls an entire "heliopolitics" is no doubt at stake here. Could the certain nonlight of Abraham's itinerary be *prior* to a helio-tropics as well? These are questions which must be posed with great caution. But Levinas enables these questions. He enables them by suggesting a way of access for the project of rereading the Judaic, namely, to take a negative and privative description within a hierarchical opposition, radicalize a possibility inherent in it, and reinscribe it as no longer privative but anterior to the opposition.

The implications and the rigor of Levinas's way of access for the rereading of the Judaic can be summarized as follows. There is no rereading without unreading. There is no rereading of the Judaic without an unreading of its (privative and negative) in-terpretation in the Greco-Christian scheme. There is thus no immediate access to Judaism. For we do not have access to the Judaic tradition apart from the Greco-Christian filter of our historically situated understanding. The return to Judaism that this reinscription offers is *difficult*. It is not a nostalgic return: it is irreducibly *mediated*. The return to Judaism in Levinas's work cannot easily be appropriated in a literary critical or phil-osophical neoorthodoxy. Thus, when we would include Levinas in a tradition of Jewish philosophy, we cannot take for granted that we know what we mean by "Jewish." Because Levinas's rereading of the Hebrew tradition is its reinscription, Hebrew no longer means what it did in its dyadic and symmetrical op-position to Greek or Christian. The Greek tradition—which includes an interpretation of and opposition to the Hebrew tradition—would now have to be opposed to a "Hebrew" tra-dition.

But what do "Greek" and "Hebrew" mean in this context? The governing, indeed paradigmatic, opposition between Greek and Hebrew in Levinas's work is not primarily historical, or it lies at what Derrida calls "a historical depth which the sciences and philosophies of history can only presuppose" (VM, 82). As Derrida reminds us, when Levinas speaks of the "Greek" the two "Greeks" that he has above all in mind are Husserl and Heidegger (VM, 83). "Greek" means a way of philosophizing; it means the way in which both Husserl and Heidegger recall us to the irreducible relation of "Greek" to philosophy. Derrida warns us against historicist misreadings of the "Greek" source of philosophy: "Philosophy is something which first of all determines the existence of the Greek world" (VM, 312). He cites Heidegger: "Greek in this instance means that in origin the nature of philosophy is of such a kind that it first appropriated the Greek world, and only it, in order to unfold" (VM, 312). Thus, if "Greek" is not primarily historical in the Greek/Hebrew opposition (as "Christian" would not be primarily historical in its opposition to "Hebrew" but would be, for example, according to our analysis in Chapter 1, a figure for an attempted textual totalization that excludes its radical outside, its referral to other), then "Hebrew" is not historical either.[22] Again, the reinscribed "Hebrew" tradition is in asymmetrical opposition to a "Greek" tradition which itself includes the dyadic opposition between Greek and Hebrew. Or, to mark this diacritically, Greek includes Greek/Hebrew, and Hebrew becomes "Hebrew"; "Greek" includes "Greek/Hebrew"; "Hebrew" becomes "*Hebrew*"—one needs an infinity of diacritical marks here. But this problem of marking conveys the sense in which to call what Levinas returns us to "Judaism" may be too Greek. Judaism would be, for example, a figure for the nonphilosophical source of philosophical reflection.[23] The interplay between its status as figure and as a historical or positive religion would remain to be interrogated.

If "Greek" in Levinas's work is not to be taken in a historicist sense, then Levinas's characterizations of the Odyssean journey as "adventures which are but the accidents of a return," the "security," the calm of this journey, its lack of surprise, its anticipation of the return—in short, all of what Derrida calls "the security in the Greek element"—should also not be misunderstood. This "security in the Greek element," Derrida explains, is not the experience of being comfortable or free from care: it is that which "permits us to experience torment or distress in general" (VM, 82). Beyond any psychological or existential notion of security, our "security in the Greek element" is a more essential security; it is the condition, if you will, of both security *and* insecurity. In this sense, our immersion in the Greek element is total. It is, as Derrida writes, "the possibility of our language and the nexus of our world" (VM, 82). "Greek" is a language, or—as Levinas refers to it in his work—the language of philosophy. The opposition between Greek and Hebrew in his work describes a problem of language: speaking Greek versus speaking Hebrew. This somewhat absolutized metaphor of "speaking Greek," in which the status of "speaking" is at least as metaphorical as "Greek," presupposes the inseparability of language and thought. It signifies that our conceptual structures are Greek. We have access to the Hebrew tradition only by way of a Greek conceptuality which may be inapplicable to and incommensurable with it. How to speak Hebrew ethics in a philosophical language that is Greek? How to speak (to) exteriority in the Greek language, a language which, as Derrida suggests, is characterized by a fundamental "autism" (VM, 152)? For there is an autism to the Greek language, an absorption in the self-same, a withdrawal from and refusal of exteriority. This introverted daydream, this autism (from the Greek *autos*, "self, same") is not a withdrawal from or loss of language, not an aphasia; it is speech itself. It is the Greek language, the language of a shut-in. How to speak (to) the other in this Greek language? How (not) to speak Hebrew ethics in a philosophical language that is Greek? In short, what language can, does, Levinas speak?

In "Violence and Metaphysics," Derrida suggests that Levinas *feigns* to speak Greek, thereby allowing us "to *dream* of an inconceivable process of dismantling and dispossession" (VM, 82). In *Time and the Other* (1948), Levinas had exhorted us to a parricide, to a break with Parmenides, in order to approach a pluralism that does not fuse into unity. Derrida writes:

This is what a Greek—Plato—could never resolve to do, deferring the act into a hallucinatory murder. A hallucination within the hallucination that is already speech. But will a non-Greek ever succeed in doing what a Greek in this case could not do, except by disguising himself as a Greek, by *speaking* Greek, by feigning to speak Greek in order to get near the king? And since it is a question of killing a speech, will we ever know who is the last victim of this strategem? Can one feign speaking a language? (VM, 89)

If the inability to speak beyond Parmenides turns Plato into a hallucinatory murderer and a Greek Hamlet and turns his speech into a double hallucination, then the speech of Levinas, the non-Greek, is also, at the very least, doubled. His is a strategic double speaking, a double talk. When Levinas by necessity "lodges himself within a traditional conceptuality in order to destroy it" (VM, 111), he does not merely feign or simulate speaking Greek, that is, engage in a pretense of what is not the case. According to Derrida's metaphor, he "disguises himself as a Greek," that is, he dissimulates: he conceals or hides what is in fact the case—that he speaks Hebrew *under* a feigned appearance of speaking Greek.

This dissimulation is a strategy for dispossession and parricide that acknowledges its own difficulty and necessity—how not to speak Greek? But the necessity for this dissimulating strategy is also its potential undoing. Certainly the strategy risks turning on him who would assume this dissimulation as the initiative of a subject. The subject of dissimulation is himself subjected to dissimulation; if Levinas believes that under a feigned appearance of speaking Greek he really speaks Hebrew, there is no guarantee that people will hear him speaking anything but Greek. Is the dissimulation then an involuntary assimilation? This is no doubt a constitutive risk of "Jewish philosophy." In what might be a parable of this dilemma, Franz Rosenzweig recounts the following anecdote:

When Hermann Cohen was in Marburg, he once expounded *[setzte er . . . auseinander]* the God-idea of his ethics to an old Jew of that city. The Jew listened with reverent attention, but when Cohen was through, he asked, "And where is the *bore olam* [Creator of the universe]?" Cohen had no answer to this and he broke into tears *[Da antwortete Cohen nichts und brach in Tränen aus]*.[24]

These are the tears and the bewilderment of a subject who, as it were, "finds himself" to *be* the hallucination, who is recalled to his "own" autism (just when he thought he was speaking the language of exteriority), recalled to it as never having departed from it, recognizing his "own" language in withdrawal, a language at once his own and not his own. This is the situation of Hermann Cohen, the neo-Kantian who, as it were, translates Hebrew ideas into Greek, into the universal—Hebrew ideas which are no longer recognizable to a pious Jew, no longer understood by the other whose experience Cohen would name. For the Marburger Jew's question is phrased, as Nahum Glatzer remarks, in the language of "a pious Jew's intimate appellation for God." Rosenzweig himself explains: "The *bore olam*, the Creator of the universe, does not mean something remote *[etwas Fernes]*, as the content of the words seems to indicate. On the contrary, in popular speech the words are fraught with emotion, they are something near *[im Volksmunde ein ganz gefühlsnahes Wort]*."[25] The pious Jew's question is thus phrased in the language of "popular speech," in the vernacular *(im Volksmunde)*, or, more literally, in the mouth of the people. Cohen does not answer the pious Jew's question; he breaks into tears. Is this break in speech privative, a loss of speech (a speech that was already a dream within a dream), or is it ever garrulous and of the same? And what do the tears speak on the part of a philosopher who, according to Julius Guttmann, sought to find a place for feeling in his ethics?[26] Perhaps they are an opaque recognition of the hallucinatory quality of this would-be exchange, of this *Auseineindersetzung*.

But the pathos of this anecdote—the despair, even the madness, in which dissimulation has become assimilation—is not simply the pathos, madness, or despair of a subject. The madness of assimilation is not psychological; its facticity is linguistic. It is the linguistic and discursive situation of one who, in trying to dissimulate speaking Hebrew under the feigned appearance of speaking Greek, "discovers" that there is, *properly speaking*, no speaking Hebrew. For the *Greek* language dissimulates and encloses the Hebrew. And if *one*, a subject, cannot dissimulate speaking Hebrew under the feigned appearance of speaking Greek, that is because the Greek *language* dissimulates and encloses the Hebrew, beyond the power of a subject to dissimulate, beyond the notion of one's "own" language. How not to speak Greek—and *who* asks this? And what of Levinas's project of speaking Greek, specifically the language of Husserl and Heidegger, in order to indicate a Hebrew ethics that is anterior to Greek phenomenology and ontology? Does it have to come to grief?[27]

This question—or a version of it—has been posed by Derrida and prolonged in its full complexity by Robert Bernasconi.[28]

The question is difficult because Levinas's discourse, while implicitly a (negative) indication of the Judaic, is explicitly a transcendental analysis in the manner of Heidegger. That is, it is a description of the fundamental ethical structures conditioning the existent.[29] Levinas explicitly indicates his indebtedness to Husserl and Heidegger and the necessity of using a post-Husserlian, post-Heideggerian vocabulary.[30] He is not even interested in contesting Husserl's and Heidegger's claims (whose contributions, he insists, should not be denied). Rather he would indicate what is repressed by and anterior to their discourses. In this way, he maintains what Derrida calls "a respect for the zone or layer of traditional truth. . . . It is a question simply of revealing beneath this truth, as that which founds it and is dissimulated within it" (VM, 88), the ethical structures and/or the heteronomous experience that are anterior to it.

There is, however, a peculiar feature to Levinas's claim to indicate a Hebrew ethics that is anterior to Greek (i.e., Heideggerian) ontology. Since Levinas's discourse is post-Heideggerian, the articulation of his claim to an anterior ethics is necessarily posterior. This posteriority of the anterior does not trouble Levinas. He refers to it in another context as "an inversion logically absurd . . . but it must precisely be interpreted as a revolution in being" (TI, 54). In this case, it is the necessary discursive metalepsis—reversal of early and late—of any "post-Heideggerian" discourse that would claim anteriority to Heidegger's claims. But how do we evaluate the status of Levinas's claims about the ethical in relation to Heidegger's claims about fundamental ontology? To the extent that Levinas's is a transcendental claim, it tends to exclude every other transcendental claim. Is the priority each would claim for his description "the same"? How are we to think the relation of the question of the ethical to the question of the meaning of Being?

In the introduction to *Otherwise than Being or Beyond Essence*, Levinas suggests a certain analogy between the two inquiries: "To understand/hear [*entendre*] a God not contaminated by being is a human possibility no less important and no less precarious than to bring Being out of the oblivion into which it is said to have fallen in metaphysics and in ontotheology" (OB, xlii). Thus: just as Heidegger wants to bring the

question of the meaning of Being out of its oblivion in the
tradition of Western metaphysics, out of the particular determinations that cover it up, out of its interpretations as the being
God of God, as most excellent being (i.e., as ontotheology), as
first cause, as full presence, and so on, so too Levinas wants to
understand a God not contaminated by being. This will require,
analogously, detaching this God from the derivative, "contaminating" interpretations which impose on him an inapplicable
ontology, an essence, in the ontotheological tradition of Western metaphysics. This "God not contaminated by being" necessarily functions by "synecdoche" for the ethical and for the
(reinscribed) Hebrew tradition as a whole. It stands for the
possibility and difficulty of rethinking that tradition. For the
Hebrew God "may be" beyond being. (In *Humanisme de
l'autre homme,* Levinas asserts, within a heterogeneous context:
"The invisible of the Bible is the idea of the good beyond
being" [HAH, 78].) The Hebrew God, accessible neither as a
phenomenon nor as a being, may escape all the categories of
Greek conceptuality. Like Being, the Hebrew God "may be"
prior to the ontotheological tradition of Western metaphysics.
But this Hebrew God is hard to think, as hard to think as Being.

We can only let resonate the enormous question of the
possibility of a Judaic nonontotheological theology and the difficult sense in which the space toward which Heidegger is
pointing resembles this Judaic nonontotheological theology.
(What would this resemblance mean?)[31] Let us remark simply
that the analogy that Levinas suggests is not strictly proportional. For Levinas's project—to understand a God not contaminated by being—is also directed against Heidegger (against
both ontotheology and fundamental ontology). He states his
"profound need to depart from the climate of Heideggerian
philosophy" (EE, 19). He wants (always at the risk of a certain
incoherency) to contest the primacy, the ultimacy of Being
which as an inquiry itself covers up the question of the ethical.[32]
Thus: just as Heidegger wants to bring Being out of its oblivion
in metaphysics and ontotheology, so too Levinas wants to bring
the ethical out of its oblivion in metaphysics and ontotheology.
And so also: Levinas wants to bring the ethical out of its oblivion in Heideggerian ontology. (This asymmetry or imbalance

within the analogy is barely noticeable; it *is* not.) Thanks to and in spite of the certain analogy between the two inquiries, Levinas would think the Hebrew God *before* what Heidegger calls Being.

But if the analogy with Heidegger makes Levinas's question possible, it also makes it impossible. In re-posing the question of the ethical, Levinas is up against the problem of, as Derrida puts it, "a question which cannot be stated except by being forgotten in the language of the Greeks and a question that cannot be stated *as forgotten* except in the language of the Greeks" (VM, 133). This means, first of all, that the question of the Hebrew ethical tradition must be posed in a Greek and Heideggerian *language* that covers it up, a language in which the question of the ethical reposes. It thus requires the hermeneutic labor of bringing it out of its repose. But the Greek and Heideggerian *language* in which the question of the ethical reposes is the only language possible in which to re-pose the question. That is why to re-pose the question of the ethical, Levinas must at once bring it out of its repose and retain it in its repose. We have to do here with an essential repose. But Levinas's project does *not* differ from Heidegger's in this respect.

For Heidegger, as Rodolphe Gasché has shown, the question of the meaning of Being determined the history of Western thought to the extent that from the moment the question was posed it was immediately dissimulated and forgotten.[33] The question of the meaning of Being is dissimulated in Western metaphysics not in the simple sense (the sense we used earlier) of something whose disguise can be unveiled or uncovered. The recovery of the question of the meaning of Being is its re-covering. Thus the question of Being, which cannot be stated except by being dissimulated in the language of metaphysics, can only be stated *as* dissimulated in the language of metaphysics, in the language of the "as such." There is thus an essential dissimulation of the question of the meaning of Being, a dissimulation *of* dissimulation. The "as" is another dissimulation; it marks the double dissimulation. For Being "is" nothing outside the existent which dissimulates it. As Gasché puts it, "being cannot 'be' itself, it cannot be 'as such.'"[34] Similarly then, to pursue the analogy that Levinas suggests, there is an essential dissimulation of the question of the ethical, of the Hebrew ethical tradition, of Judaism. Even the most rigorous description—phenomenological or ontological—of Judaism "as it is" (e.g., as beyond being), or "as such," is a dissimulation, because this "as such" still dissimulates the extent to which Judaism *escapes* Greek metaphysics, including phenomenology and ontology. There would be thus a double dissimulation of Judaism. (Levinas writes, "The invisible of the Bible is beyond being," only after he has crossed out the verb "to be.") Judaism, finally, cannot be evoked "as such" and can only be evoked "as such." Even if it is evoked *as* itself, it is evoked *as* something that it is not (as is the case with Being in the Heideggerian analysis of the nothing).[35] Since what Levinas would re-cover as the experience of the infinitely other or as Hebrew ethics must "occur *as* logos" (VM, 152), as Greek, as essentially dissimulated, indeed *to call* this experience of the infinitely other in Levinas's work "Judaism" would be too Greek. Again, in terms of the question of the language that Levinas can speak, "we" find that there is, properly speaking, no speaking Hebrew.

Of course, there is an equivocalness in insisting on this analogy between "a God not contaminated by being" (as a "synecdoche" for Judaism) and Heideggerian Being. Part of this equivocalness is due to using Heideggerian categories to describe this resemblance, the sense in which they are "the same." But the difficulty, the *precariousness,* of the two inquiries is "the same." Or, as Levinas puts it, "To understand a God not contaminated by being is a human possibility *no less important* and *no less precarious* than to bring Being out of the oblivion into which it has fallen in metaphysics and in ontotheology" (OB, xlii). In saying that his inquiry is "no less important" and "no less precarious" than Heidegger's, he asserts by understatement an analogical importance and precariousness of the two inquiries, but he also leaves open the possibility that his inquiry into the ethical may be "more" important, "more" precarious, thereby unbalancing the proportional analogy. Levinas's singular syntax makes it possible to think the "analogy" between his and Heidegger's projects in a conceptuality other than Heidegger's.

We find another example of this singular syntax or rhetoric[36] later on in *Otherwise than Being,* when Levinas asks in effect if his entire description of an otherwise than being does not collapse into an ethical aspect *of* being, into a being otherwise. He concludes by saying, "But it is absolutely necessary to ask if in it [this description of ethical substitution] a voice cannot be heard coming from horizons *at least as vast* as those in which ontology is situated" (OB, 140). Horizons "at least as vast," a possibility "no less important" and "no less precarious." There is a singular tentativeness, indeed an unobtrusiveness, of these comparisons.[37] They are figures of comparison that do not claim to know what they are comparing and then to analogize on the basis of their known resemblance. In comparing what only "may be" compared (or may not "be" comparable), they mark a certain departure from the ontological. The tentativeness of these formulations is strategic. It is how Levinas maintains a *specificity* to the ethical that is not completely absorbed by Heideggerian ontology. These formulations make no explicit reference to the anteriority of the ethical, yet they leave open the possibility that the nature of the priority Levinas would claim for the ethical may be not "the same" as Heidegger's, that it "may be" otherwise. They mark the way in which speaking Greek to say "Hebrew," applying a Greek language to a Hebrew experience that is incommensurable with it, does not happen without transforming the Greek language. Perhaps this transformation "is"—maybe.[38] Levinas's saying otherwise strains against its own impossibility. For the certain departure from the ontological is, within all the categories of Western logic, no departure at all.

Thus Levinas's translation project—the encounter between Judaism and philosophy, the "translation of biblical wisdom into Greek" ("The invisible of the Bible is the good beyond being"), speaking the Greek language of phenomenology and ontology in order to indicate a Hebrew ethics anterior to it—does, in a certain sense, come to grief in its encounter with Heidegger. But what is the sense of this grief? The perils of this translation project—either for a subject who would dissimulate speaking Greek or in the face of a more essential dissimulation—have become abundantly clear. "The translation of biblical wisdom into Greek," namely, the Septuagint in the making, is characterized by a constitutive impossibility, an inability to "go over." Or, as Rosenzweig's anecdote about Hermann Cohen suggests, if it does "go over," it cannot necessarily "come back." But is Levinas's project "to understand a God not contaminated by being" in fact Septuagintal, simply a matter of translation from Hebrew into Greek? What kind of translation would such a project require?

Contamination implies contact, which violates the absolute separation between the Same and the Other. To think God (either contaminated *or* not contaminated by being) is always to think that God first of all in a Greek language that dissimulates his "beyond being," in a Greek language that contaminates not only by the derivative ontologies and interpretations but also by the very question of being that all thinking, discourse, propositions about God presuppose. Ontological contamination is inseparable from thinking the Hebrew God, because it is inseparable from thinking itself.

Is it different to try to *hear* a God not contaminated by being? There, too, it is necessary first of all to hear the Hebrew God in a Greek language that contaminates the Hebrew, or else in a Hebrew language that has been contaminated by Greek. We deliberately multiply our metaphors for Levinas's language in asking: is it possible that rather than dissimulating speaking Greek, or translating into Greek, Levinas speaks and hears a Hebrew that has been *contaminated* by Greek? If there is, properly speaking, no speaking Hebrew, is there an improper speaking of Hebrew, a taking up of a contaminated language? Or is there, for that matter, an improper hearing? Perhaps it is Levinas's *hearing* of the Hebrew that has been contaminated; he could be a man of uncircumcised ears. If we have to do with the contamination of a language here, to hear a Hebrew God not contaminated by the Greek language of being will require a singular decontamination of the Hebrew language. It will require not only detaching that God from his derivative onto-theological determinations, in an activity analogous to the Heideggerian destruction of the history of ontology, but also (and this analogy is "no less" close) reverting a contaminating Greek back into Hebrew, or reverting a Hebrew that has been contaminated by Greek (a contaminated Hebrew/Greek) back into Hebrew. It will require not a translation from Hebrew into Greek, not a Septuagint in the making, but its translation in reverse, its retroversion, or translation from Greek back into Hebrew.

How would such a retroversion happen? Here it may be useful to set Levinas's attempt against the backdrop of André Chouraqui's project to translate the Book of Revelation back into its nonexistent Hebrew "original."[39] In the course of what is a translation of the New Testament from Greek into French, Chouraqui proposes "to search out the semitic substratum under the Greek text." The reasons for this essentially midrashic (*darash*, "to search out") procedure are philological, insofar as they concern the semiticisms in the Greek text, the "Hebraic *logia* that can be rediscovered under their Greek expressions," and historical, because of the semitic context and milieu in which Jesus lived and died and the probability that Jesus spoke in Gallilean-Aramaic. They are also hermeneutical, a reflection on the way in which the Bible (in this case the New Testament) reads, exegetes, and ultimately refers to itself. Chouraqui writes: "Even if the text expresses itself in Greek, and, in the case of Jesus' utterances, is founded on an Aramaic or Hebrew (mishnaic, rabbinic, or Qumranic) the traces of which have disappeared, the thought of the Gospel writers and the apostles has, for its ultimate point of reference, the word of Yahweh, that is the whole Bible." Thus, when translating the Greek New Testament (or Revelation) into French, Chouraqui passes through "an Aramaic or Hebrew retroversion" and "returns" to the Greek now "enriched by a new substance" before passing to the French.[40] This Hebrew or Aramaic retroversion that Chouraqui passes through is a phantom text; it is a reconstituted "original." As a re- or de-translation to the "original" language of a text that never was, that *is* not, retroversion is impossible. This impossibility does not stop the translator. In biblical studies—for example, in the text critical use of the Septuagint—there have been numerous attempts to retrovert the Greek translation of the Hebrew Bible to a missing or absent manuscript tradition that is presumed to differ from the (canonical) masoretic text. In a sense, retroversion is a rigorous taking up of the impossibility of all translations. Retroversion is impossible, but no more impossible than any version. Translations are necessary and possible because of the constitutive impossibility of going over (or coming back).[41]

Retroversion—a reverse translation, a translation turned or directed backward—also goes against the chronological order. But the true hermeneutical order is not the chronological order. To hear a God not contaminated by being is necessarily to *first* hear a God through the contaminating Greek filter or conceptual structures of one's historically—at a depth—situated understanding. To read the Hebrew Bible is necessarily to read (and unread) the New Testament *first*.[42] To read the Hebrew Bible is always already to read a Septuagint translated back to its nonexistent original.

To read, as Levinas does, the talmudic tradition or biblical ethics, the privileged text for the re-posing of the question of the ethical, the third precedent for the unheard-of escape from the domination of the Same, is thus to engage in *both* a version *and* a retroversion. On the one hand Levinas translates biblical and talmudic wisdom into philosophy, renders it explicit, such as in the formulation "the invisible of the Bible is beyond being." He translates Hebrew into Greek, in accordance with his reading model of a Septuagint in the making. But as the translator can only *hear* this Hebrew through the contaminating Greek filter (through contaminated ears), the translating *forward* from Hebrew into Greek is also a translating *back,* a decontamination and a retroversion from hearing Hebrew *as* Greek to hearing it as "Hebrew," from Greek/Hebrew to "Hebrew."

However, even the "Hebrew" that he would then translate forward is not simply "Hebrew," for the Talmud, in Levinas's description, is already marked by translation. Levinas had said that the Talmud has "a philosophical prolongation often *dissimulated* beneath problems concerning positive and negative commandments," that is, beneath its apparent preoccupation with ritual observance. The Talmud is thus constituted by an internal movement of translation, by a translation/dissimulation of its wisdom. Written in "Hebrew," the language of religion, the Talmud dissimulates the extent to which it is already philosophical, "underwritten" in Greek. It dissimulates the extent to which it is already a translation from philosophy to religion, already a translation from Greek to "Hebrew," already and "originally" a retroverted Septuagint of sorts. Thus, once again: when Levinas reads the Talmud, he translates it *forward,* projects Greek conceptual structures onto a Hebrew which he hears *as* Greek, and translates it *back,* retroverts it to "Hebrew," a "Hebrew" that he in turn translates again, renders explicit, renders philosophical, renders into Greek. The talmudic "Hebrew" that he is translating not only appears *as* a Greek marked by its suppression of the Hebrew, which is what necessitates a forward and backward translation, a projective retroversion (or reductive construction),[43] but is itself "originally" marked and contaminated by a Greek from which it has translated itself and which it dissimulates. What do this contamination and this dissimulation mean?

To describe talmudic "Hebrew" as contaminated by Greek does not in this case presuppose the purity of a language: the contamination here is originary. Just as the New Testament Greek that Chouraqui translates is a Greek marked by its suppression of the Hebrew, or a Greek that silently translates Hebrew tropes, figures, and conceptual structures, a Greek haunted by Hebrew names, so too the talmudic "Hebrew" that Levinas translates is an irreducible mixture of Greek and Hebrew, at once Greek and Hebrew and neither (Is there in the Talmud "neither Jew nor Greek" [Gal. 3:28])? In the case of both Chouraqui's and Levinas's translation projects, the difficulty of talking about a text's "original language" is evident.

That the Talmud dissimulates is an event (an event which does not happen) whose implications we can only partially indicate. First of all, the Talmud's dissimulation of Greek *under* the feigned appearance of Hebrew is not a hermeneutic structure in the derived sense; it does not conceal a meaning that can be unveiled. To the extent that it dissimulates Greek *under* Hebrew, it is not a Greek we can get to except *as* a Hebrew that is dissimulated *as* a Greek that dissimulates the Hebrew. This double dissimulation is originary. There is nothing under this veil (except perhaps the nothing).[44]

Moreover, dissimulation, in the diverse senses that we have

encountered and in the slippage between these senses, may be caught up with the question of "Jewish philosophy" in an important way. This is certainly the case in Levinas's work. Again, he refers to the Talmud as "the difficult exegesis that dissimulates itself behind the apparent naiveté of an archaic commentary" (DL, 11). His review of S. Zac's Spinoza book begins with the (rhetorical) question: "Did Spinoza dissimulate his veritable thought . . . in the *Theologico-Political Treatise?*" (DL, 148). Ultimately this never refers to the dissimulation of a subject (it is a reinscription, if you will, of the negative and stereotypical interpretation of the crafty, deceitful Jew with a secret language). It refers to the linguistic facticity of assimilation and to the dissimulation of a language. In Levinas's work, dissimulation is a trope of the ethical as well. As he exposits it in *Totality and Infinity*, the face of the other "dissimulates" itself as a phenomenon, as a theme for the phenomenological gaze. But the face is defined as precisely that which in the other exceeds phenomenological presentation.

In summary, the return to "Judaism" that Levinas's work offers is complex, peculiar, and mediated. It is not the recapturing of a former self or even a former faith in an allegory of personal salvation. Following Rosenzweig's precedent this retroversion to "Judaism," if you will, does not produce a narrative of the self. When Rosenzweig, on the eve of his intended conversion to Christianity, turned back to Judaism, his only narrative references to his experience were: "I have taken back my decision" *(meinen Entschluß zurückzunehmen)* and "I hope to have found the way back" *(ich hoffe den Rückweg gefunden zu haben),* the latter written on a postcard to his less than pleased parents.[45] He did not write a narrative of conversion (or retroversion). He wrote *The Star of Redemption* instead.

But to what (Judaism), we have to ask, does Levinas revert? His retroversion is always to a voice. Levinas seeks "to *hear* a God not contaminated by being." He asks "*if a voice cannot be heard* from horizons at least as vast as those in which fundamental ontology is situated." A reading of the privileged experience of voiced otherness in Levinas's work could begin here. To give only a few indications: In Levinas's descriptions, the face, although it is given to vision, is not primarily a thing seen. In a

repeated figural transfer (that resembles a synesthesia, a crossing of sensory attributes), the face *(le visage)* turns from a thing
seen or intended *(visée)* to a voice which speaks:

Form—incessantly betraying its own manifestation—congealing into
plastic form, since it is adequate to the Same, alienates the exteriority of
the other. The face is a living presence, it is expression. The life of
expression consists in undoing the form in which the existent, exposing
himself as a theme, in this way dissimulates itself. The face speaks *[Le
visage parle].* (TI, 66)

Here the gaze, which would grasp the face as "form," as
"theme," becomes a hearing of the other's voice, an encounter
with a speaking face. Because vision is a violence and an adequation, the figural transfer from vision to voice is also an ethical
transfer and an ethical exigency. Levinas takes seriously the pro-
hibition against images. It is necessary to turn away from seeing. This necessity is a responsibility imposed on the self in the
encounter with the face of the other.[46] But in the crucial ambiguity of the face's self-presentation, in which the face at once
dissimulates itself as a phenomenon and is also beyond the phenomenon, resides the entire possibility of violence as well as
ethical responsibility. In the vision of the face, the temptation
of murder is inscribed:

The face, it is inviolable; these eyes absolutely without protection, the
most naked part of the human body, offer, nevertheless, an absolute
resistance to possession, an absolute resistance in which the temptation
of murder is inscribed. . . . This temptation of murder and this impossibility of murder constitute the very vision of the face. To see a face is
already to hear: "Thou shalt not kill" *[Voir un visage, c'est déjà entendre: "Tu ne tueras point"].* (DL, 20–21)

Here, just as with the formulation "the face speaks," Levinas
gives a face and defaces it, that is, he gives the face as figure,
gives it as voice. This is once again the figural and ethical transfer, the turn from vision (seeing a face) to voice (hearing a
voice). But here the temporality of this transfer is peculiar. The
encounter with the face of the other is not a simultaneous seeing the face and hearing the voice. Vision does not become
voice; it is *already* voice: "To see a face is *already* to hear, 'Thou

shalt not kill.'" Hearing the voice is "older" than seeing—that is, if there is hearing the voice.

At the foot of Mt. Sinai, during the theophany that resembles a thunderstorm and immediately after the revelation of the Decalogue, we read: "And the people saw the thunderings [literally "voice," "sound"] and the flaming torches, and the sound [literally "voice"] of the shofar" (Exod. 20:15). Textual editors find this figure ("seeing the voice") alternately described as a synesthesia, a zeugma, or a catechresis—disturbing and distracting. They would emend the text. Should "saw the voice" be "heard the voice"? Rashi says, after the *Mekilta*: they saw the voice ("They saw that which should be heard—something which is impossible to see on any other occasion.")[47] The *Mekilta* says: "they saw what was visible and heard what was audible." The *Mekilta* also says, in effect, that they *neither* saw *nor* heard, they saw the writing on the tablets ("They saw the fiery word coming out from the mouth of the Almighty as it was struck upon the tablets, as it is said, 'The voice of the Lord hewed out flames of fire' [Ps. 29:7]").[48]

Thus, in the retroversion to a voice, in the ethico-figural turn from vision to voice, it may even be necessary to turn away from voice, to "veil the voice,"[49] to do before hearing, not to hear (not to render to oneself) the "do not render" of the gift. As Lyotard remarks, perhaps there is too much to see even in the voice.[50] "The people saw the voice," that is, they saw the writing on the tablets. This progressive dephenomenalization— from vision to voice to writing—suggests precisely that what they experienced was not phenomenally accessible. They saw writing on stone (God's "hewing" word); in other words, they were referred to the giving of the law and also implicitly to the activity of study which is given in advance there (and of course in which the *Mekilta*'s commentators are themselves engaged). They were referred to an arche-writing, in the structure of which even Heidegger's thought is inscribed. Is not this arche-writing the heteronomous experience to which Levinas refers?

To ask about the place of the Judaic in literary criticism, is this not also to ask about the place of literary criticism in the Judaic? Or, to rephrase this, since it is not a question of a too

easy symmetrical chiasmus, is it enough to imply that the "figural logic" of Talmud and midrash could be called "deconstruction," "protodeconstruction," or "ethics," or is this "logic"—
which is in fact an "illogic," against all (sensible and intelligible)
sense—larger than the discourse in which it would be a possible
object? Does the figural logic of Talmud perhaps condition
deconstruction as an always possible becoming-talmudic of the
literary critical discourse?[51] To ask about the place of the Judaic
in literary criticism, is this not to place literary criticism in the
Judaic? But where is this place? "It is not far from you. It is not
in heaven that you should say, 'Who will go up for us to heaven
and bring it to us that we may hear it and do it?' . . . Rather, it
is very near to you, in your mouth" (Deut. 30:11–14).

Conclusion: Versions of the Other

As Peter Brown stresses in his biography of Augustine, Augustine had many friends. He was surrounded by friends during his boyhood at Thagaste, during his student and teacher days at Carthage, Rome, and Milan, and finally in his capacity as Bishop of Hippo. Brown writes: "Having read the life of this extremely inward-looking man, we suddenly realize, to our surprise, that he has hardly ever been alone. There have always been friends around him."[1] The reasons for this range from Augustine's being a "naturally expansive man" to his youthful adherence to a classical ideal of friendship, conceived of as a "complete harmony of minds and purpose."[2] There is theological significance to this gregariousness as well: Augustine has hope in a Christian fellowship or community.[3] To a certain extent the *Confessions* is a *record* of Augustine's friendships, from the boyhood friend who died in book IV to the cultivated Nebridius, who followed Augustine from Carthage to Milan in book VI, to the loyal Alypius, who followed him into the garden of his conversion. Indeed, in addition to being a record of friendships the *Confessions* was, according to Brown, an attempt on Augustine's part to *widen* his circle of friends, to introduce himself to those fellow Christians, "spiritual men to whose acquaintance [he] felt entitled."[4] Thus the *Confessions,* which is addressed to God, takes on the additional performative dimension of an address of friendship, an address to the other. In what follows, I will consider these diverse pragmatic and performative, theoretical and theological, registers of friendship in

133

Augustine's work in order to ask: What is the Augustinian model of friendship? What is his version of the other? I will conclude with a consideration of the notion of friendship as it pertains to Levinas's ethical discourse and his description of the alterity of the other.

In book IV of the *Confessions,* Augustine's narrator recounts his grief at the death of a boyhood friend, who is never named but whom he had called, citing Horace, "half of my soul."[5] (The eloquent discussion of friendship in general that follows in book IV would thus be an example of what Jacques Derrida has called "the great canonical meditations on friendship [that] are linked to the experience of mourning, to the moment of loss.")[6] His grief was extreme and was a primary reason he left his native town of Thagaste. As he recounts it, he was consoled only by time and by the company of new friends in Carthage, which he describes as follows:

All kinds of things captivated my soul in their company—to talk and laugh and to do each other kindnesses; to read pleasant books together; to make jokes together and then talk seriously together; sometimes to disagree, but without any ill feeling, just as a man might disagree with himself *[dissentire . . . tamquam ipse homo secum],* and to find that these very rare disagreements made our general agreement all the sweeter; to be sometimes teaching and sometimes learning; to long impatiently for the absent and to welcome them with joy when they returned to us. These and other similar signs *[signis],* which proceed from the hearts of those who love and are loved in return, and are revealed in the face, the voice, the eyes, and in a thousand charming ways *[a corde . . . procedentibus per os, per linguam, per oculos et mille motus gratissimos],* were like a kindling fire to melt our souls together and out of many to make us one *[ex pluribus unum facere].* It is this which we love in our friends.[7]

The narrator describes the joys of friendship in terms of symmetry and reciprocity. Even the disagreements between friends are ultimately a form of agreement: a privilege of friendship is to disagree without rancor, "just as a man may disagree with himself" *(dissentire . . . tamquam ipse homo secum).* In the narrator's formulation, one that recurs throughout Augustine's work, the relationship with the friend is like the relationship with oneself, with one's other self, or other half. A classical—specifically Ciceronian—conception of friendship pervades both Augustine's

theoretical statements on friendship and the youthful friendships he describes.[8]

One might also remark that in this description the *face* of the
friend is found to signify in a distinctive way. (And by what
exigency is the discourse of the friend or other linked to that of
the *face?*) The narrator describes "the signs which proceed from
the heart . . . and are revealed in the face, the voice, the eyes,"
(signis a corde . . . procedentibus per os, per linguam, per oculos).
In other words, he describes signs that have a necessary rather
than arbitrary link to their referent because of the coincidence
between the movement of the heart and the movement of the
facial expression. The pleasure, the warmth, indeed the confla-
gration, that the narrator recounts in beholding the face of a
friend derives from this perceived coincidence. Here the face is
a totalizing figure which mediates between opposites, such as
soul and body, inside and outside.[9] It also mediates between
persons, producing a commingling, a fusion, a communion of
souls *(e pluribus unum facere).*

The break that marks Augustine's conversion, however, also
marks a rupture in his conception of friendship. Later in life and
at the time of the writing of the *Confessions,* Augustine will look
back on these earlier attachments and repudiate them. They are
too tied to love for mortal things; they smack of the physical;
they have the human as their term. He discredits his earlier
affections, introducing a regulative distinction between true
and false friendship: "There can be no true friendship unless
those who cling to each other are welded together by you
[God] in that love *[caritate]* which is spread throughout our
hearts by the holy spirit which is given us."[10]

Of course, in Augustine's mature Christian thought, *caritas*
is a central notion whose significance is too wide to be fully
addressed here. Etienne Gilson comments that, for Augustine,
caritas is not just a virtue but the consummation of the virtues,
"the happiness and the goal of the whole moral life." It is "not
only the means whereby we shall obtain God; it is God already
possessed, obtained and circulating, so to speak, within us
through the gift He has made of Himself."[11] Thus, when Augustine speaks of true friendship in love *(caritate),* he alludes to
a Christian community in which persons are united by a common love for God, an idea that will culminate in his vision of

the City of God. Here, suffice it to note one of the important differences between Augustine's Christian and classical models of friendship: the relationship between friends now requires a third party, God.

God underwrites the privileged figure of fraternity that begins to emerge in Augustine's theologized conception of friendship, his Christian community. Yet even in this theological context, the concrete experience of friendship seems irreducible for him. Brown refers us to the beginning of Augustine's discussion of the double precept of charity—love of God and of the neighbor—in *On Christian Doctrine*. There, as Brown says, the "discussion of love of one's neighbor begins, with Augustine, in terms of a relationship to a friend."[12]

In this passage from *On Christian Doctrine*, Augustine is considering "whether man is to be loved by man for his own sake or for the sake of something else."[13] (The passage follows, and intersects with, the important distinction between use and enjoyment: "Some things are to be enjoyed, others to be used. . . . To enjoy something is to cling to it with love for its own sake. To use something, however, is to employ it in obtaining that which you love." Augustine will specify that the only thing which is to be enjoyed is God; every other thing in the world is to be used.)[14] The passage in question—"whether man is to be loved by man for his own sake or for the sake of something else"—is instructive, because Augustine will in fact conclude that man should *not* be loved for his own sake (that is, not enjoyed) but loved for the sake of God (or used). Loving man for his own sake falls into an idolatry of friendship (the error to which Augustine's classical ideal of friendship was liable) by coming to rest in what should merely be a vehicle to God.[15] Loving man for his own sake elides the eternal God in favor of his transitory creature. Thus man should be loved not for his own sake but only for the sake of God: loving man is a means to loving God.

Here one might remark that Kierkegaard, examining the same problem in *Fear and Trembling*, comes to the opposite conclusion. His pseudonymous author Johannes de Silentio argues that loving the neighbor for the sake of God (or what for Augustine would be a salutary "use" of the neighbor) is in fact impossible. He writes:

In the duty [to love one's neighbor] I enter into relation not to God but to the neighbor I love. If in this connection I then say that it is my duty to love God, I am actually pronouncing only a tautology, inasmuch as "God" in a totally abstract sense is here understood as the divine—that is, the universal, that is, the duty.[16]

In de Silentio's understanding of the relation between man, the neighbor, and God, by loving the neighbor I cannot come into relation with God. (It is only by a private and absolute relation to the absolute that I can do so, as does Abraham, the knight of faith.) Loving the neighbor leaves one, rather disappointingly, with the neighbor alone. De Silentio has, as it were, pointed out a flaw in a too-easy conception of Christian ethics. A radical understanding would show that loving man cannot be a means to loving God and would thus show the impossibility of performing *God's* commandment to "love thy neighbor." For, according to de Silentio, in the performance of such a commandment, God drops out of the equation, just as for Augustine, ultimately, in the performance of the same commandment, the neighbor drops out of the equation.

Even though Augustine and Kierkegaard come to opposite conclusions here, they share the premise that the encounter with the friend or neighbor goes by way of the universal. They also share, as Emil Fackenheim argues in relation to Kierkegaard, a dichotomous terminology, an understanding of ethics as a two-term relationship that cannot do justice to the richness and complexity of a revealed ethics. It is a terminology which, for Fackenheim, specifically ignores the revealed morality of Judaism, in which there is what he calls an "internal and necessary" relation between three terms, *God, man,* and *the neighbor:* "God confronts man with the demand to turn to his human neighbor *and in doing so,* turn back to God himself."[17] Levinas will express a similar understanding of Judaic ethics: "'Going towards God' is meaningless unless seen in terms of my primary going towards the other person. I can *only* go towards God by being ethically concerned by and for the other person."[18] I will return to this question of a specifically Judaic ethics.

While Augustine's theoretical statements about friendship are indeed significant, his relationship to his friend Alypius, who is described in the *Confessions* as the "brother of my heart"

(frater cordis mei), assumes particular importance. It is in this
relationship that the personal, professional, theological, and
even the literary dimensions of friendship seem to converge.
The loyal Alypius had followed Augustine from their native
Thagaste to Carthage, Rome, Milan, and even into the garden
where Augustine converted. After Augustine read the scriptural
verse that converted him, Alypius read the subsequent scriptural
verse that converted him. In chapter 1, I analyzed this scene as
an instance of "the contagion of example."[19] In demonstrating
such an intensely personal relationship to a scriptural verse and
in converting by reading, Augustine *already* follows the example of others (Anthony and the *agentes in rebus*). He follows
them in a fever of imitation. As Romano Guardini explains this
occurrence, the example of others renders concrete a divine
truth that had previously been abstract. The other person is
here, in Guardini's phrase, "a concrete embodiment of the
truth of God's revelation."[20] According to this model the other
is either apprehended through or allows the apprehension of a
universalist proclamation. Again, the encounter with the other
goes by way of the universal.

But this structure of exemplarity has additional significance.
Augustine not only follows the example of others, he also becomes an example to be followed. As John Freccero has argued,
when Augustine passes the book to Alypius he suggests "that
his own text is to be applied metaleptically to the reader himself
as part of the continual unfolding of God's Word in time."[21]
The relationship between Augustine and Alypius thus suggests
the proselytizing, indeed the performative function of a narrative of conversion. (And here the performative aspect of the
Confessions—its address to the other—widens from Augustine's
attempt merely to enlarge his circle of friends—many of whom,
like Jerome and Paulinus of Nola, are already converted and do
not need to convert by reading—to include the whole human
community or Christian brotherhood, the community of the
Confessions' future readers.) When Alypius converts as he does,
he figures the reader of the *Confessions,* who, it is hoped, will
read, convert, and pass the book on to another who will read,
convert, and pass it on, and so on.

But perhaps there is a reader who would stop, who would fail
to convert, who would not pass the book on, thereby rendering

the Christian performative infelicitous. Here neither Augustine's personal nor his professional generosity would suffice to prevent the suppression of this other (reader) in his text. In fact, as I have shown, such a suppression of the other, in the figure of the elder brother, is essential to the proclamation that Augustine would share (and that he has internalized for the writing of his Christian autobiography). The elder brother of the prodigal son stands *outside* the celebration of the prodigal's return, blind, hard of heart, and unredeemed. He figures what Jean Starobinski identifies as a *necessary* resistance to the proclamation. Starobinski writes: It "is a matter of a narrative that would dry up if new tests did not reappear progressively. The residue of opposition . . . provokes the continuation of the narrative."²² (Ultimately, in Starobinski's argument, this "residue of opposition" is essential to the economy of the passion narrative as a whole.) But Starobinski's formal insight can be filled in as to a particular content. The elder brother figures the text of Judaism that Augustine would go through and beyond. As the Judaic other, he falls outside Augustine's theologized conception of friendship and Christian fraternity. Despite the wording of his angry complaint to the father, "You never gave me so much as a kid that I might make merry with *my* friends," it is clear that the elder brother has no friends, in the Augustinian sense. Who are these friends to which he refers and with whom he wishes, quite incongruously, "to make merry"? In the figure of this quintessentially other brother another version of fraternity begins to emerge, and perhaps another version of the other as well.

For it can be shown that Augustine's conception*s* of friendship cannot do justice to the alterity of the other; they threaten to absorb it, to reduce it to the same. In communion or contagion (or even united by a common love for God), they blur the self and the other. They ignore what Levinas describes as "the fundamental asymmetry" between oneself and the other, the distance and the absolute separation that characterizes the relation. In short, despite the profound differences between the classical and Christian models of friendship that Augustine takes up, they have in common what they seek to exclude.

In the case of the classical model (which Augustine perhaps never entirely abandons) and where the friend is proposed as

other self or other half, the relationship to the other is nostalgi-
cally formulated as a desire for a lost unity. In Levinasian terms,
such a relationship is characterized by need (based on a lack)
rather than desire (which relates to what is infinite and which is
a surplus). Similarly, when Augustine asserts that there is an
analogy between the relationship with a friend and the relationship with oneself (with a friend one may "disagree, but without
any ill feeling, *just as* a man might disagree with himself"), he
describes the relation to the other as a relation to a finite alterity.

The model of Christian friendship suggested in *On Christian Doctrine* is more ambitious: it proposes the other as a
conduit to God. Similarly, in the *Confessions,* which describes a
proselytic contagion in which persons are impelled to feverish
imitation of the Christian example, the other is understood
either as an embodiment of the universal truth of God's proclamation or as that which permits the apprehension of a universalist proclamation. But by insisting on a third term—*God,
truth, the universal*—that regulates the relationship to the other
in Christian friendship, such a model threatens to neutralize
that which in the other is radically singular and resistant to all
categories. It ignores the approach *of* the singular which is, for
Levinas, revealed when one encounters the other face-to-face.
Thus contagion would be just another form of what Levinas
identifies in the West as an "allergy" to the other. It would be
an attempt to convert the other to the self(same).[23]

What kind of friendship, what kind of relationship to the
other would *not* return to self and same? What kind of relationship to the other would do justice to his alterity? Is such a model
provided by what Levinas, Fackenheim, and (in the preceding
pages) I—each no doubt differently—call "Judaism"? If so, it
cannot be the Judaism to which Augustine refers—negatively
and privatively. It will be, for example, a reread and reinscribed
Judaism, in the distinctive intonation that Levinas gives the
term.

For Levinas, a relationship to the other which would respect
his alterity permits neither reciprocity nor contact; it is characterized by asymmetry and distance. It allows for a fundamental
opacity (an opacity that Kierkegaard in fact observes when he
argues that there is no going through the other to God). The
relationship between oneself and the other, writes Levinas, is

"not a simple correlation in which the two terms would complete one another in a system visible from the outside."[24] (That is why the relation to the other is not even, strictly speaking, a relation.) The asymmetry denotes "the radical impossibility . . . of speaking in the same sense of oneself and the other and consequently the impossibility of totalization" (TI, 53).

"The alterity of the other," writes Levinas, "is not 'other' like the bread I eat, the land in which I dwell, like, sometimes, myself for myself" (TI, 33). A relation to this latter, finite alterity characterizes what Levinas calls the work of identification, that is, my ability to absorb otherness "into my identity as thinker or possessor" (TI, 33). (He also calls it the economy of the Same, and it refers to the habitual exchanges that make up the self's concrete relationship with the world.) But the alterity of the other is *infinite*. Encountered neither as a phenomenon nor as a being, the other is encountered as a face.

It is this encounter with the face of the other *(le visage d'Autrui)* which reveals his infinite alterity. Why is the face privileged for the revelation of alterity? It is privileged because something about the face resists my powers absolutely. The face stops the *look* that would reduce it to a thing seen, that would make it a theme, that would try to grasp it or possess it. In this way, the face checks my habitual economy; it checks my tendency to conceive of the world as a space of possibilities and power *(pouvoir)*. It interrupts the play of the same.

For the presence before the face, my orientation toward the Other can lose the avidity of the gaze only by turning into generosity, incapable of approaching the other with empty hands. This relationship, over the things hereafter possibly common, that is, susceptible of being said, is the relationship of discourse *[discours]*. The way in which the other presents himself, exceeding the idea of the other in me, we here name face *[nous l'appelons visage]*. (TI, 50)

The mutation described here—the gaze "turning into generosity"—is emblematic of the ethical movement as Levinas describes it; it is the very birth of ethics or responsibility. At times he calls it a "conversion or reversal of our nature."[25] It is a description in which vision—which is "avid," violent, because it is a form of adequation, which is even "by essence murderous"—turns into something else. Vision turns into generosity

and language, relationships of nonadequation. The nontotalizing relation to the face of the other is accomplished "in a discourse, in a conversation [entre-tien] which proposes the world.
This proposition is held between [se tien entre] two points
which do not constitute a system, a cosmos, a totality" (TI, 96).
This conversation is utterly asymmetrical. As Maurice Blanchot
says, it does not resemble a "tranquil humanistic speaking."[26] It
has none of the give-and-take, the reciprocity of most hermeneutic models of conversation. In fact the founding conversation that Levinas describes is precisely presupposed by such
hermeneutic models. This is a conversation that, rather than
being a searching together for consensus, makes possible the
difference between consensus and agreement; it makes *lieux
communs* possible. Thus, like generosity, discourse is a primordial relatedness to the other. The relationship to the other, says
Levinas, is always in the dative or in the vocative.

Moreover, the mutation that Levinas describes, the transformation from the "avid" gaze to generosity and language, does
not come about as a result of *my* initiative. It is a response *to* the
face, to a speaking face in particular. The face, as Levinas argues,
is not reducible to a phenomenon, for it breaks out of phenomenological presentation. It does so with a distinctive mode of
signification that Levinas identifies as expression, namely, that
which signifies only relative to itself: "The life of expression
consists of undoing the form in which the existent, exposing
itself as a theme, in this way dissimulates itself. The face speaks
[Le visage parle]" (TI, 66). Levinas's difficult discussion of
expression *kath 'auto*, "according to itself," which he identifies
as a "coincidence of the expresser and the expressed," resembles
in many ways Augustine's account of facial expression as a self-
coincidence. An important difference, however, is that the
Levinasian "expression" is not pleasing to the gaze that would
encompass it; in fact the content of the expression is negative.
It does not result in communion, nor does it totalize. It inaugurates an asymmetrical and heterological relationship with
what is infinitely other. It delivers an imperative.

The other, faced with my murderous powers, "opposes to me
the infinity of his transcendence": "This infinity, stronger than
murder, already resists us in his face, is his face, is the primordial
expression, is the first word: 'thou shalt not kill'" (TI, 199).

The imperative or commandment is necessitated by the very ambiguity of the face's presentation. To the extent that the face *does* present or dissimulate itself as a phenomenon, it is absolutely vulnerable, exposed to violence, and the temptation of murder is inscribed there. Murder aims at the sensible, says Levinas, and no doubt it effects an annihilation of the other in his being. But in murdering the other, one misses him, one misses his genuine alterity, that which in him goes beyond the sensible, escapes or exceeds the phenomenon (and that which in him is beyond or before being). Thus, to the extent that the face *breaks out of* the phenomenon, *speaks, is voice,* murder always misses its mark. That is why while murder is a real possibility, it is an ethical impossibility.

The face, it is inviolable; these eyes absolutely without protection, the most naked part of the human body, offer, nevertheless, an absolute resistance to possession, an absolute resistance in which the temptation of murder is inscribed: the temptation of an absolute negation. The Other is the sole being that one can be tempted to kill. This temptation of murder and this impossibility of murder constitute the very vision of the face. To see a face is already to hear: "Thou shalt not kill."[27]

Here the face of the other speaks God's word and reveals the law to me. Levinas radicalizes a certain relationship to the law in Judaism, which is his version of what Fackenheim calls the three-term relationship between man, his neighbor, and God. "The Torah," writes Levinas at the end of his reading of the talmudic treatise *Shabbath* 88a–88b, "is given in the light of a face" (QLT, 103). Yet these assertions should not be misunderstood. The experience to which Levinas refers is both Judaism and something other: "We propose to call religion the bond that is established between the same and the other without constituting a totality" (TI, 40). The face speaks, and it obligates me infinitely.

The face speaks to me from a height and also in utter destitution. As Blanchot explains this doubleness, the description of the face's height proceeds from me to the other, the description of the face's destitution from the other to me.[28] In either case, there is an asymmetrical relationship to an absolute singularity. Yet, despite Levinas's insistence on this point, we do not get away from the universal altogether. As Derrida reminds us, in

Levinas's descriptions, "the relation to the other also passes through the universality of law."[29] In *Totality and Infinity,* Levinas writes: "The third party looks at me in the eyes of the Other, language is justice" (TI, 213); and also, "The presence of the face, the infinity of the other is a destituteness, a presence of the third party, that is the whole of humanity which looks at us" (TI, 213); and finally, "The Other qua Other is situated in a dimension of height and of abasement—glorious abasement, he has the face of the poor, the stranger, the widow and the orphan. . . . This inequality does not appear to the third party who would count us. It precisely signifies the absence of a third party capable of taking in me and the other" (TI, 251).

The *fact* of my relationship to the speaking face is irreducible. The face speaks, and it in turn demands a response, an originary response. That is my responsibility (from the Latin *respondere*). Moreover, the responsibility in which "I" find myself with respect to the speaking face is not part of the initiative of a subject. Responsibility is not a response-ability, for such ability would leave the subject's mastery intact. There is an *in*ability there.[30]

That is why Levinas describes the subject as subjected to the imperative to be responsible to the other. In an interview, Levinas states: "It is I who support the other and am responsible for him. One thus sees in the human subject, at the same time as a total subjection, that my primogeniture manifests itself."[31] The subjection to the other of which Levinas speaks does not designate the subject's fall from some prior condition of sovereignty. The subjection to the other is the most fundamental description of the self: the self *is* this subjection. This subjection is "older" than the subject, not in the sense of mere temporal succession but in the sense of prior to it, conditioning of it. This is the self's firstborn, first-begotten responsibility, its primogeniture.

Notes

Introduction: Figurations of the Judaic

1. Some notable recent examples are Kenneth Burke on Augustine, John Freccero on Dante, and Frank Kermode on the New Testament. See Burke, *The Rhetoric of Religion* (1961; repr. Berkeley: University of California Press, 1970); Freccero, *Dante: The Poetics of Conversion,* ed. Rachel Jacoff (Cambridge, Mass.: Harvard University Press, 1986); Kermode, *The Genesis of Secrecy: On the Interpretation of Narrative* (Cambridge, Mass.: Harvard University Press, 1979).

2. Augustine, *The First Catechetical Instruction* IV.8, trans. Joseph P. Christopher (Westminster, Md.: Newman Press, 1962). The Latin text is from *Oeuvres de Saint Augustin,* vol. 11 (Paris: Desclée de Brouwer, 1949).

3. Harold Bloom, "'Before Moses Was, I Am': The Original and the Belated Testaments," in *Notebooks in Cultural Analysis,* vol. 1, eds. Norman F. Cantor and Nathalia King (Durham, N.C.: Duke University Press, 1984), 3.

4. Erich Auerbach, "Figura," trans. Ralph Mannheim, in *Scenes from the Drama of European Literature* (Minneapolis: University of Minnesota Press, 1984), 34.

5. Mark C. Taylor, *Erring: A Postmodern A/theology* (Chicago: University of Chicago Press, 1984), chap. 3.

6. Taylor discusses "the close relation between type and trope" in *Erring,* 56–57.

7. Auerbach, "Figura," 12.

8. Paul Ricoeur, "Preface to Bultmann," trans. Peter McCormick, in *The Conflict of Interpretations: Essays in Hermeneutics* (Evanston, Ill.: Northwestern University Press, 1974), 385.

9. Augustine, *City of God* XX.4, trans. (modified) Henry Bettenson

(Baltimore: Penguin Books, 1976). The Latin text is from *Oeuvres de Saint Augustin*, vols. 33–37 (Paris: Desclée de Brouwer, 1959).

10. Wayne A. Meeks, ed., *The Writings of Saint Paul* (New York: W. W. Norton, 1972).

11. Technically this is an allegory, as Paul himself says in what is a seminal usage for Christian hermeneutics. There are important differences between allegory, which substitutes term for term, and *figura*, which retains the historicity of both terms. Auerbach is at pains to distinguish "abstract" allegory from "living" *figura*. Yet, despite these differences, the figural claim about the prefigural status of the Genesis passage remains the same.

12. Augustine, *City of God* XV.2.

13. Rosemary Reuther, *Faith and Fratricide: The Theological Roots of Anti-Semitism* (New York: Seabury Press, 1979), 132.

14. The term is Jacques Derrida's from "Violence and Metaphysics," in *Writing and Difference*, trans. Alan Bass (Chicago: University of Chicago Press, 1978), 90.

15. This privative interpretation is the risk inherent even in Auerbach's characterization of the Old Testament in "Odysseus' Scar": it is "dark, unexpressed, incomplete." Despite Auerbach's privileging of Hebrew narrative over the Homeric, ultimately the Hebrew narrative is privileged only to the extent that it anticipates Christian realism. In other words, for his thesis, Auerbach's Hebrew Bible is, and must be, an Old Testament. Yet one must also acknowledge that insofar as Auerbach's overall characterization of Hebrew narrative is correct, the risk of this negative and privative interpretation is intrinsic to the Hebrew narrative itself. The very narrative features which "demand interpretation," and from which the narrative derives its "claim to absolute authority," also "force[s] it to a constant interpretive change," that is, render possible transgressive interpretations which would deny the narrative its authority. See *Mimesis: The Representation of Reality in Western Literature*, trans. Willard R. Trask (Princeton, N.J.: Princeton University Press, 1953), especially 15–16.

16. *In quali ergo opprobrio sunt Judaei? Codicem portat Judaeus, unde credat christianus. Librarii nostri facti sunt, quomodo solent servi post dominos codices ferre, ut illi portando deficiant, illi legendo proficiant. In tale opprobrium dati sunt Judaei; et impletum est quod tanto ante praedictum est: "Dedit in opprobrium conculcantes me." Quale autem opprobrium est, fratres, ut hunc versum legant, et ipsi caeci adtendant ad speculum suum? Sic enim apparent Judaei de scriptura sancta quam portant, quomodo apparet facies caeci de speculo: ab aliis videtur, ab ipso non videtur. "Dedit in opprobrium conculcantes me."* Augustine, *Expositions on the Psalms* LVI.9, translation mine. The Latin

text is from *Corpus Christianorum: Series Latina,* vol. 39 (Turnholti, 1956). Thanks to John Peradotto for his help in translating this passage.

17. Bernhard Blumenkranz, "Augustin et les juifs," *Recherches Augustiniennes* 1 (1958).

18. For a reading of the rhetorical or figurative structure of Auerbach's *figura,* see Timothy Bahti, "Auerbach's *Mimesis:* Figural Structure and Historical Narrative," in *After Strange Texts: The Role of Theory in the Study of Literature,* ed. Gregory S. Jay and David L. Miller (University, Ala.: University of Alabama Press, 1985), 124-45.

19. Ricoeur, "Preface to Bultmann," 383-84.

20. Although the links between the biblical and philosophical disciplines of hermeneutics cannot be taken for granted, here Ricoeur identifies the role of understanding as a feature common both to patristic interpretation and to the post-Heideggerian hermeneutics that he and Hans-Georg Gadamer represent.

21. *International Critical Commentary* (Edinburgh: T. and T. Clark, 1901), 371.

22. Jean Starobinski's analysis of Mark's Gospel narrative has been especially helpful in mapping out the figure of the outside in New Testament discourse. See "The Struggle with Legion: A Literary Analysis of Mark 5:1-20," trans. Dan Via, Jr., *New Literary History* 4 (1973). "Le combat avec Légion," in *Trois fureurs* (Paris: Gallimard, 1974).

23. Friedrich Nietzsche, *Morgenröte* (Aphorism 84) in *Werke,* ed. Karl Schlechta, I, 1067ff., cited by Hans Joachim Schoeps in *Paul: The Theology of the Apostle in the Light of Jewish Religious History,* trans. Harold Knight (Philadelphia: Westminster Press, 1959), 235.

24. See James Kugel, "Two Introductions to Midrash," in *Midrash and Literature,* ed. Geoffrey H. Hartman and Sanford Budick (New Haven, Conn.: Yale University Press, 1986), originally published in *Prooftexts* 3 (1983). Other important introductions to midrash from which I have benefited include Renée Bloch, "Midrash," in *Approaches to Ancient Judaism: Theory and Practice,* ed. William Scott Green (Missoula, Mont.: Scholars Press, 1978); Judah Goldin, "From Text to Interpretation and from Experience to the Interpreted Text," *Prooftexts* 3 (1983); Geza Vermes, "Bible and Midrash: Early Old Testament Exegesis," in *The Cambridge History of the Bible,* vol. 1 (Cambridge: Cambridge University Press, 1970); John Bowker, *The Targums and Rabbinic Literature: An Introduction to Jewish Interpretations of Scripture* (Cambridge: Cambridge University Press, 1969); David Stern, "Rhetoric and Midrash: The Case of the Mashal," *Prooftexts* 1 (1981). See also the works by Daniel Boyarin and David Stern cited in note 28.

25. Kugel, "Two Introductions," 84–90. Daniel Patte, *Early Jewish Hermeneutic in Palestine* (Missoula, Mont.: Scholars Press, 1975), 21–27.

26. Kugel, "Two Introductions," 93.

27. Goldin, "From Text to Interpretation," 159.

28. For the resemblances between midrash and contemporary literary criticism, see Hartman and Budick, *Midrash and Literature;* Susan Handelman, *The Slayers of Moses: The Emergence of Rabbinic Interpretation in Literary Theory* (Albany: State University of New York Press, 1982); Gerald L. Bruns, "Midrash and Allegory," in *The Literary Guide to the Bible,* eds. Robert Alter and Frank Kermode (Cambridge, Mass.: Harvard University Press, 1987); David Stern, "Midrash and Indeterminacy," *Critical Inquiry* 15 (1988); and a recent study by Daniel Boyarin, *Intertextuality and the Reading of Midrash* (Bloomington: University of Indiana Press, 1990). Boyarin's book, a rigorous description of midrash that is informed by contemporary literary theoretical developments, will prove indispensable to future debates within this field.

29. Handelman, *The Slayers of Moses,* 31.

30. Maurice Blanchot, "La lecture de Kafka," in *La part du feu* (Paris: Gallimard, 1949), trans. Glen W. Most in *Twentieth-Century Interpretations of the Trial,* ed. James Rolleston (Englewood Cliffs, N.J.: Prentice Hall, 1976), 12.

31. This at times resembles imaginative retelling. Such a resemblance is deceptive because a midrashic remark is never detached from its (exegetical) starting point in the scriptural verse.

32. Geoffrey H. Hartman, "The Realism of Numbers: The Magic of Numbers," in *Congregation: Contemporary Writers Read the Jewish Bible,* ed. David Rosenberg (New York: Harcourt Brace Jovanovich, 1987), 44.

33. Hartman and Budick, *Midrash and Literature,* xi.

34. In an important essay, "Midrash and Indeterminacy," David Stern argues that contemporary literary critical categories such as "indeterminacy" bear little connection to the midrashic phenomenon of multiple interpretation, a phenomenon which may itself be a misleading effect of the midrash's redactional form. "Nonetheless," he writes, "indeterminacy may still remain a significant category for understanding our own reading of midrashic discourse" (pp. 132–61). Stern warns literary critics against anachronistic determinations of midrash, in effect against projecting our own historically situated prejudices onto midrash. Yet such a projection is not only inevitable but an indispensable part of the encounter between past and present, or any act of historical understanding in the sense that Gadamer would give it. We would simply want to make our own historical filter, say, the literary critical

"moment" in the apprehension of midrash, as explicit as possible. Stern is well aware of this when he describes the literary critic's encounter with midrash as an occasion for understanding his own understanding, however negative or lacking. He writes that the "lack of equivalence between midrash and the theoretical categories we use to read it . . . may help us see a little more clearly the very conditions of our own theorizing" (p. 135). Moreover, in my own discourse, if what I am calling midrash at times seems in fact to be "deconstruction" or "poststructuralism," this misnomer may be referred to the problematic status of the assertions that midrash is a recovered source of our herme- neutical practices or is an alternative to Western logocentrism.

35. Martin Buber, *Two Types of Faith,* trans. Norman P. Goldhawk (New York: Harper Torchbook, 1961).

36. Jean-François Lyotard and Jean-Loup Thebaud, *Just Gaming,* trans. Wlad Godzich (Minneapolis: University of Minnesota Press, 1985), 65.

37. Derrida, "Violence and Metaphysics" (cited in note 14 above).

38. Emmanuel Levinas, "Signature," ed. and annotated by Adriaan Peperzak, trans. M. E. Petrisko, *Research in Phenomenology* 8 (1978), 175–89.

39. A rigorous historical analysis could well discover as many simi- larities as differences. See, for example, Kugel, "Two Introductions."

40. See Emmanuel Levinas's formulation about the way in which the other presents himself at the close of "Phenomenon and Enigma," trans. Alphonso Lingis, in *Collected Philosophical Papers* (Dordrecht: Martinus Nijhoff, 1987).

1 / Prodigal Son and Elder Brother

1. Augustine, *The Confessions* VIII.3, emphasis original. English translation by Rex Warner (New York: New American Library, 1963), with occasional modifications of my own. Latin quotations are from the Skutella edition published by A. Solignac, *Oeuvres de Saint Augustin,* vols. 13–14 (Paris: Desclée de Brouwer, 1962). All subsequent refer- ences will be given in the text.

2. A. Solignac and Paul L. Jay have noted the identification be- tween Augustine's sinner and the prodigal son. John Freccero, Pierre Courcelle, and William Spengemann mention the adaptation of the parable to certain spiritual dilemmas. None has given this relationship more than the briefest attention. See Solignac, *Oeuvres de Saint Au- gustin;* Jay, "Being in the Text: Autobiography and the Problem of the Subject," *Modern Language Notes* 95 (1982); Freccero, *Dante: The Poetics of Conversion,* ed. Rachel Jacoff (Cambridge, Mass.: Harvard

University Press, 1986), chap. 1 ("The Prologue Scene"); Courcelle, *Recherches sur les Confessions de Saint Augustin* (Paris: Éditions de Boccard, 1950); Spengemann, *The Forms of Autobiography* (New Haven, Conn.: Yale University Press, 1980).

3. For the influence of Ambrose's sermons on Augustine's particular use of Plotinus here, see Courcelle, *Recherches sur les Confessions.*

4. John Gibb and William Montgomery, eds., *The Confessions of Augustine* (London: Cambridge University Press, 1927), 51.

5. Gibb and Montgomery, *The Confessions,* 64.

6. See the discussion by Solignac in his notes, *Oeuvres de Saint Augustin,* 689–93; and by Etienne Gilson, *Philosophie et incarnation selon Saint Augustin* (Montreal: Institut d'études médiévales Albert-le-Grand de l'Université de Montréal, 1947).

7. On the problematics of conversion, see works by John Freccero: *Dante,* esp., chap. 1 ("The Prologue Scene") and chap. 7 ("Medusa: The Letter and the Spirit"); "Logology: Burke on St. Augustine," in *Representing Kenneth Burke: Selected Papers from the English Institute,* New Series, no. 6, ed. Hayden White and Margaret Brose (Baltimore: Johns Hopkins University Press, 1982); "The Fig Tree and the Laurel: Petrarch's Poetics," *Diacritics* 5 (1975). I have also benefited from the work of Eugene Vance: *Mervelous Signals: Poetics and Sign Theory in the Middle Ages* (Lincoln: University of Nebraska Press, 1986), and "Augustine's *Confessions* and the Grammar of Selfhood," *Genre* 6 (1973), 1–28.

8. Kenneth Burke, *The Rhetoric of Religion* (1961; repr. Berkeley: University of California Press, 1970), 94.

9. Burke, *The Rhetoric,* 94.

10. Solignac, *Oeuvres de Saint Augustin,* introduction.

11. Spengemann, *The Forms,* 25–26.

12. Burke, *The Rhetoric,* 100.

13. See Jean-Marie le Blond, *Les conversions de Saint Augustin* (Paris: Aubier, Éditions Montaigne, 1950), and Courcelle, *Recherches sur les Confessions,* 7–12. At issue in Courcelle's discussion is the historicity of Augustine's conversion, a problem that also arises between the Augustine of the *Confessions* and the Augustine of the *Dialogues.*

14. Freccero, *Dante,* chap. 1 ("The Prologue Scene").

15. Labriolle uses the phrase as a subtitle of his translation of book VIII. *Confessions* (Paris: Société d'Édition 'Les Belles Lettres,' 1947).

16. Romano Guardini, *The Conversion of Augustine* (Westminster, Md.: Newman Press, 1960), 229–30.

17. One rabbinic reading has it that the "back" which Moses saw from the cavity of the rock "was only the knot of the cords of the phylacteries on the divine neck." *Berakoth* 7a, cited by Emmanuel

Levinas, "La révélation dans la tradition juive," in *La révélation,* ed. Paul Ricoeur et al. (Brussels: Facultés Universitaires Saint-Louis, 1977). Reprinted in Emmanuel Levinas, *L'au-delà du verset: Lectures et discours talmudiques* (Paris: Minuit, 1982).

18. Spengemann, *The Forms,* 15.

19. Translation (modified) from the Jerusalem Bible. Latin from *Biblia Vulgata* (Madrid: Biblioteca de Autores Christianos, 1977). Of course, Augustine used a Latin version of the Bible anterior to Jerome's. See Henri-Irénée Marrou, *Saint Augustin et la fin de la culture antique* (1958; repr. Paris: Éditions de Boccard, 1983), 475.

20. Joachim Jeremias, *The Parables of Jesus* (1954; repr. New York: Charles Scribner's Sons, 1972), 128.

21. The Entrevernes Group, *Signs and Parables: Semiotics and Gospel Texts,* trans. Gary Phillips (Pittsburgh: Pickwick Press, 1978), 134–35.

22. Entrevernes Group, *Signs and Parables,* 138.

23. Jeremias, *The Parables,* 130.

24. Augustine, *Quaestiones Evangeliorum.* The Latin text is from *Corpus Christianorum: Series Latina,* vol. 44 (Turnholti, 1953), lines 25–30, emphasis original, translation mine. Erich Auerbach's remark that Augustine "favored a living, figural interpretation, for his thinking was far too concrete and historical to content itself with pure abstract allegory" should be read in the light of C. H. Dodd's comment on Augustine's "allegorical method" in this collection, "in which each term stood as a cryptogram for an idea, so that the whole had to be de-coded term by term." See Auerbach, "Figura," trans. Ralph Mannheim, in *Scenes from the Drama of European Literature* (Minneapolis: University of Minnesota Press, 1984), 37; Dodd, *The Parables of the Kingdom* (New York: Charles Scribner's Sons, 1961), 1. Line numbers cited in the next three paragraphs of text will refer to Augustine, *Quaestiones Evangeliorum.*

25. Jeremias, *The Parables,* 130.

26. *The Interpreter's Bible,* vol. 8 (New York: Abingdon, 1952), 280.

27. Dan Via, Jr., *The Parables: Their Literary and Existential Dimension* (Philadelphia: Fortress Press, 1967), 174.

28. Jeremias, *The Parables,* 132.

29. *International Critical Commentary* (Edinburgh: T. and T. Clark, 1901), 378.

30. Via, *Parables,* 171.

31. *International Critical Commentary,* 378.

32. *The Interpreter's Bible,* vol. 8, 271.

33. Holy Bible: King James Version and *Biblia Vulgata.*

34. *International Critical Commentary,* 371.

35. See Jean Starobinski, "The Struggle with Legion: A Literary Analysis of Mark 5:1–20," trans. Dan Via, Jr., *New Literary History* 4 (1973), originally published as "Le combat avec Légion," in *Trois fureurs* (Paris: Gallimard, 1974); Frank Kermode, *The Genesis of Secrecy: On the Interpretation of Narrative* (Cambridge, Mass.: Harvard University Press, 1979).

36. Jeremias, *The Parables,* 131.

37. John Ruskin, *Praeterita: The Autobiography of John Ruskin* (Oxford: Oxford University Press, 1978; first published between 1885 and 1889), 455.

38. Cited by J. M. Creed, *The Gospel According to St. Luke* (London: Macmillan, 1930), 197.

39. Via, *Parables,* 163–64. Those critics who want to keep the elder brother in the parable end up getting rid of him anyway, by arguing that the prodigal son's itinerary includes—that is, goes through and beyond—the stance of the elder brother. For a recent example, see David Wyatt, *Prodigal Sons: A Study in Authorship and Authority* (Baltimore: Johns Hopkins University Press, 1980).

40. Rosemary Reuther argues that when contemporary Christianity interprets the Pharisee as the Jew, it deprives itself "of the tradition of prophetic self-criticism." Reuther, *Faith and Fratricide: The Theological Roots of Anti-Semitism* (New York: Seabury Press, 1979), 228–32.

41. Augustine, *Quaestiones,* lines 106–13.

42. Augustine, *Contra Faustum Manichaeum,* chap. XI in *Oeuvres complètes,* vol. 25 (Paris: Librairie de Louis Vivès, 1870).

43. Augustine, *Quaestiones,* lines 131–32.

44. Augustine, *Tractatus adversus Judaeos,* chap. VII, para. 9. The English translation (modified) is by Sister Marie Liguori in Augustine, *Treatises on Marriage and Other Subjects* (New York: Fathers of the Church, 1955), vol. 27.

45. Augustine, *Tractatus,* chap. VII.

46. Augustine, *City of God* XVIII.46, trans. Henry Bettenson (Baltimore: Penguin Books, 1976).

47. Bernhard Blumenkranz, "Augustin et les juifs," *Recherches Augustiniennes* 1 (1958).

48. Emmanuel Levinas, "The Trace of the Other," trans. Alphonso Lingis, in *Deconstruction in Context,* ed. Mark C. Taylor (Chicago: University of Chicago Press, 1986), 348. "La trace de l'autre," *Tijdscrift voor Filosofie* 3 (1963); repr. in *En découvrant l'existence avec Husserl et Heidegger,* 2d. ed. (Paris: Vrin, 1967, 1974), 191.

49. Augustine, *City of God* XV.7–8.

50. As Freccero notes, paradigmatic for proselytism is the moment

when the newly converted Augustine "passes the Bible to Alypius, thereby suggesting that his own text is to be applied metaleptically to the reader himself as the continual unfolding of God's word in time." Freccero, "The Fig Tree," 37.

51. Richard A. Lanham, *A Handlist of Rhetorical Terms* (Berkeley: University of California Press, 1969), 67.

52. King James Version and *Biblia Vulgata.*

53. The word in Hebrew *(lakah)* means "take." I follow the Vulgate in rendering "seize."

54. Augustine's "quoting" here is not to be taken as a conscious (or unconscious—conceived in phenomenological terms) echo or allusion. In using the word *arripere* (in itself a common word), he "quotes" only on the level of the letter, and in doing so he not only (1) quotes and allegorizes the Old Testament (as prefiguring the New) but also (2) is quoted and (re)allegorized by the Hebrew Bible.

55. Augustine, *De beata vita,* trans. (slightly modified) Ruth Allison Brown (Washington, D.C.: Catholic University of America Press, 1945). The Latin text is from Augustine, *De beata vita* II.7, ed. R. Jolivet, in *Oeuvres de Saint Augustin,* vol. 4 (Paris: Desclée de Brouwer, 1948).

2/ Petrarch Reading Augustine

1. Francesco Petrarca, "The Ascent of Mont Ventoux," trans. Hans Nachod (with occasional modifications of my own), in *The Renaissance Philosophy of Man,* eds. Ernst Cassirer, Paul Oskar Kristeller, and John Randall, Jr. (Chicago: University of Chicago Press, 1971), 46. All subsequent references will be given in the text. The Latin text of this letter, *Rerum Familiarium* IV.1, is from Francesco Petrarca, *Opere* (Florence: Sansoni, 1975). This edition follows the text of *Le familiari,* ed. Vittorio Rossi and Umberto Bosco, in *Edizione nazionale delle opere di Francesco Petrarca,* vols. X–XIII (Florence: Sansoni, 1933–42).

2. Recounted by Hans Baron, *From Petrarch to Leonardo Bruni: Studies in Humanist and Political Literature* (Chicago: University of Chicago Press, 1968), 17–23.

3. Giuseppe Billanovich, "Petrarca e il Ventoso," *Italia Medioevale e Umanistica* 9 (1966), 349–401.

4. A. von Martin, "Petrarca und Augustin," *Archiv für Kulturgeschichte* 18 (1928), 59; G. Voigt, *Die Wiederbelebung des classischen Altertums,* vol. 1, 3d edition (Berlin, 1893), 131. Cited by Pierre Courcelle in *Les Confessions de Saint Augustin dans la tradition littéraire* (Paris: Études Augustiniennes, 1963), 341.

5. Baron, *From Petrarch to Leonardo Bruni,* 19. See also E. H.

Wilkins, *The Making of the "Canzoniere" and Other Petrarchan Studies* (Rome: Edizioni di storia e letteratura, 1951).

6. Michael O'Connell, "Authority and the Truth of Experience in Petrarch's "Ascent of Mont Ventoux," *Philological Quarterly* 62 (1983). Each of Petrarch's critics produces a verdict on the veracity of his account. Is this juridical role a response to topics introduced within the letter—such as questions about the status of the Livy rumor, the letter's own claim to spontaneity and authenticity, even Petrarch's stated fear that his desire to write might evaporate—or is it rather a function of its direction and address to Petrarch's father confessor? Generations of critics would seem to be troping on this role.

7. Hans Nachod's introduction to "The Ascent of Mont Ventoux," 28.

8. Augustine, *The Confessions* X.34, trans. Rex Warner (New York: New American Library, 1963), with occasional modifications of my own. Latin quotations are from the Skutella edition published by A. Solignac, *Oeuvres de Saint Augustin,* vols. 13–14 (Paris: Desclée de Brouwer, 1962). Petrarch's "desire to see" may also be analyzed in terms of "vain curiosity" (see Arnaud Tripet, *Pétrarque ou la connaissance de soi* [Geneva: Librairie Droz, 1967], 62–73), whose ill effects are best illustrated by what happens to Alypius at the gladiatorial games (*Confessions* VI.8). On Augustinian curiosity, see Hans Blumenberg, "Augustins Anteil an der Geschichte des Begriffs der theoretischen Neugierde," *Revue des études Augustiniennes* 7 (1961); André Labhardt, "Curiositas: Notes sur l'histoire d'un mot et d'une notion," *Museum Helveticum* 17 (1960).

9. Thanks to Warren Ginzburg for his help on this point.

10. Compare, in the same passage, *error, peragrare,* and *anfractus.*

11. Petrarch writes: "My brother then sang his song with his mind set upon heaven *[erecto ad celum animo];* I bent toward the earth *[curvatus in terram],* keeping in mind earthly things." And again, while recalling the stormy youth they shared, Petrarch addresses Gherardo: "We walked between such snares, we navigated among such reefs, my dear brother. But why do I speak as if our states were equal? I, a wretch, am still turning *[versor]* among these perils; you, thank God, have already arrived in port *[portum tenes].*" Petrarch, *Rerum Familiarium,* X.3. All citations from the *Rerum Familiarium* are from Petrarca, *Opere,* cited in n.1. The English translation, unless otherwise identified, is from Aldo S. Bernardo, *Rerum familiarium libri* I–VIII (Albany: State University of New York Press, 1975), and *Letters on Familiar Matters: Rerum familiarium libri* IX–XVI (Baltimore: Johns Hopkins University Press, 1982), with occasional modifications of my own.

12. Compare to Augustine, *Confessions* VIII.5, and VIII.12, respectively.

13. See A. B. Chambers, "Goodfriday, 1613. Riding Westward: The Poem and the Tradition," *English Literary History* 28 (1961). Petrarch's *verto me in tergum, ad occidentem respiciens* (literally, "I turned myself around to the back, looking back toward the west"), which marks the passage to reading for conversion, is syntactically a double turning.

14. Petrarch's lifting up of the mind might be read as an example of the "false conversion" (i.e., merely philosophical conversion) that John Freccero discusses in "Dante's Prologue Scene," *Dante Studies* 84 (1966); repr. in *Dante: The Poetics of Conversion*, ed. Rachel Jacoff (Cambridge, Mass.: Harvard University Press, 1986). It also recalls the flight of the mind that Petrarch attempted earlier: "I sat down in a valley. There I leaped in my winged thoughts from things corporeal to what is incorporeal" *(a corporeis ad incorporea volucri cogitatione transiliens)* (p. 39).

15. Augustine, *Confessions* VIII.12.

16. O'Connell, "Authority and the Truth," 509-10.

17. The projects of knowing the self and of knowing God are in every way consonant, because man is in the image of God. See Etienne Gilson, "Self-Knowledge and Christian Socratism," in *The Spirit of Medieval Philosophy*, trans. A. H. C. Downes (New York: Charles Scribner's Sons, 1940); Gérard Verbeke, "Connaissance de soi et connaissance de Dieu chez saint Augustin," *Augustiniana* (1954). On the *nosceteipsum* tradition in which this episode takes part, see Pierre Courcelle, "'Nosceteipsum' du bas-empire au haut moyen-âge: l'héritage profane et les développements chrétiens," *Settimana di studio del Centro italiano di studi sull'alto Medioevo* 9 (1962), 265-95; Tripet, *Pétrarque ou la connaissance*, 62-73.

18. In Livy's account, King Philip V of Macedonia "ascends Mt. Haemus in Thessaly since he believed the rumor that you could *see* two seas from its top" (p. 36).

19. The use of most of these elements is noted by Courcelle, *Les Confessions de Saint Augustin*, 329-51, and Robert M. Durling, "The Ascent of Mont Ventoux and the Crisis of Allegory," *Italian Quarterly* 18 (1974): 7-28. Durling's essay offers an important discussion of the problematic status of Petrarch's allegorical discourse.

20. Augustine, *Confessions* IX.4.

21. That Gherardo does not get an oracle of his own is noted by Durling and O'Connell.

22. First of all, Petrarch invokes a chain of anteriority (Augustine and Anthony) which consists of exemplary conversions. Then, in *Fam.*

XVI.9, he recounts the exemplary legend of the founding of the Carthusian monastery of Montrieux, where Gherardo resided. In brief, it is the story of twin brothers, merchants sailing on a stormy sea. One of them undergoes a conversion and builds a monastery. The other brother, "burning to imitate him," builds a second monastery on a nearby hill. Petrarch says, "Now the twin buildings house a single Christian community, and its appearance seems to reflect that the founders were indeed twins, yet of one mind." In short, Petrarch's implicit reading of this legend in "The Ascent of Mont Ventoux" is antiphrastic and negative.

23. To put this somewhat differently, Petrarch "constates" reading for conversion, yet he does not perform it. In denying his brother an oracle, Petrarch disrupts the performative function of his narrative of conversion.

24. Petrarch is explaining to Gherardo why, in the first eclogue of the *Bucolicum Carmen*—which involves a conversation between sibling shepherds—the Gherardo figure is named Monicus: "the name is appropriate, since one of the Cyclops is named Monicus, as if he were one-eyed" *(quia cum unum ex Cyclopibus Monicum dicant quasi monoculum).* In giving Gherardo the name "Monicus," Petrarch certainly plays on the word *monachus,* "monk" in ecclesiastical Latin. But the dyad blindness and sight, a dominant figure for conversion, finds a somewhat grotesque incarnation here. To compare Gherardo to a Cyclops, even an allegorized Cyclops, is perhaps not without malice. (Of course, if Gherardo at all resembles the Monicus of the *Bucolicum Carmen*—whose "rural ignorance" *[pastoria ruditate]* is quite pronounced—he is so ignorant of literary matters that he is likely to miss the barb altogether.) For a reading of the one-eyed Gherardo in terms of the eclogue as a whole, see Thomas M. Greene, "Petrarch *Viator:* The Displacements of Heroism," *Yearbook of English Studies* 12 (1982).

25. The substance of our argument is unaffected by the critical debate about whether or not Petrarch read aloud (see O'Connell, "Authority and the Truth," 517–19). Even if Petrarch does not read aloud and then grow mute but rather is mute throughout, this does not justify Petrarch's not passing on the book, which is, finally, the kind of muteness we are talking about.

26. Many of Petrarch's biographers seem to have accepted Petrarch's flattened-out version of Gherardo's story. Edward H. R. Tatham uses the fraternal difference as the basis for the periodization of literary history: Gherardo is "a true representative of the Middle Ages. . . . He rejoiced in passivity and routine." Petrarch is "the protagonist of the new spirit of freedom and inquiry." (*Francesco Petrarca: The First*

Modern Man of Letters, vol. 2 [London: The Sheldon Press, 1925], 211). See also Henry Cochin, *Le frère de Pétrarque et le livre du repos des religieux* (Paris: Librairie Émile Bouillon, 1903). However, it is not a question of choosing one version of Gherardo's story over another: both versions are Petrarch's.

27. Augustine, *Confessions* X.8.

28. Augustine, *On Christian Doctrine* III.5–6, trans. D. W. Robertson, Jr. (Indianapolis: Bobbs-Merrill, 1958). The Latin text is from *Oeuvres de Saint Augustin,* vol. 11 (Paris: Desclée de Brouwer, 1949). Marguerite R. Waller also cites this passage in a discussion of Petrarch in relation to Augustine's theory of language (*Petrarch's Poetics and Literary History* [Amherst, Mass.: University of Massachusetts Press, 1980], chap. 1).

29. On the servitude of the signifying function, compare Augustine, *City of God* XV.2, trans. Henry Bettenson (Baltimore: Penguin Books, 1976), where Augustine glosses Galatians 4. See the discussion of this passage in the Introduction to this book.

30. In fact this antiphrastic opacity was already contained within the Livy account that Petrarch imitates. Again, Petrarch's "desire to see" the view from the mountain's peak is an imitation of King Philip V of Macedon's desire to see two seas from the summit of Mt. Haemus. But, as Thomas Greene reminds us, in Livy the legend that two seas can be seen is treated as a joke (*The Light in Troy: Imitation and Discovery in Renaissance Poetry* [New Haven, Conn.: Yale University Press, 1982], 105). If we turn to the Livy text, we find that when Philip and his men reach the summit, "everything was so covered with fog . . . that they were slowed down just as if they were on a night march *[nocturno itinere].* . . . When they came down they said nothing to contradict the general notion—not because the different seas, mountains, and rivers could in fact be seen from one place, but to prevent their futile expedition from providing material for mirth" (*History of Rome* XL.21, trans. Henry Bettenson, slightly modified [Harmondsworth: Penguin Books, 1976]; the Latin text is from the Loeb Classical Library [London: William Heinemann, 1919]). Philip, who climbs to see, does not see but pretends he does. Petrarch, who ostensibly climbs to see but really climbs to blind himself, sees. We might add to this two observations: (1) Petrarch's "carnal" reading of Livy is in fact a reading of a text that describes not physical seeing but physical "blindness"; (2) The Livy account—framed on one end by a rivalry between brothers, Perseus and Demetrius, and on the other by the younger brother's murder— deserves more treatment as an intertext of Petrarch's letter. According to Livy, King Philip made his ascent *in the name of* his elder son, leaving his younger son behind to be murdered.

158   NOTES TO PAGES 64-71

31. See Rosemary Reuther, *Faith and Fratricide: The Theological Roots of Anti-Semitism* (New York: Seabury Press, 1979).

32. John Freccero, "The Fig Tree and the Laurel: Petrarch's Poetics," *Diacritics* 5 (1975).

33. Augustine, *On Christian Doctrine* I.4.

34. Greene, "Petrarch *Viator*," shows that all of Petrarch's work may be organized around the idea of erring.

35. The word *anfractus*, which means "digression" as well as "detour," is one instance of the way physical and locutionary detours may refer to each other.

36. This is borne out by a reading of the *Secretum*, where Petrarch explicitly identifies his spiritual weakness with his desire for poetic immortality. On figurative language and error in St. Augustine, see Margaret Ferguson, "Saint Augustine's Region of Unlikeness: The Crossing of Exile and Language," *Georgia Review* 29 (1975).

37. In what might be a blueprint for a strategic idolatry, Augustine explains use and enjoyment by analogy to a journey: "Suppose we were wanderers *[Quomodo ergo, si essemus peregrini]* who could not live in blessedness except at home *[in patria]*, miserable in our wandering *[perigrinatione]*, and desiring to end it and to return *[redire]* to our native country. We would need vehicles *[vehiculis]* for land and sea which could be used *[utendum]* to help us to reach our homeland, which is to be enjoyed *[fruendum]*. But if the amenities of the journey and the motion of the vehicles *[gestatio vehiculorum]* itself delighted us, and we were led *[conversi]* to enjoy those things which we should use, we should not wish our to end our journey quickly, and, entangled in a perverse *[perversa]* sweetness, we should be alienated from our country, whose sweetness would make us blessed" (*On Christian Doctrine* I.4).

38. J. C. O'Neill's gloss on this passage is instructive: "The contrast is between clothing oneself with the Lord, living entirely with mind fixed on him, and living for the flesh, the outward senses." He adds: "Here it is . . . a moral clothing oneself with the Lord that is in question." *Paul's Letter to the Romans* (Harmondsworth: Penguin Books, 1975), 218–19.

39. Augustine cannot quote Scripture either. See chapter 1.

Toward the Outside

1. Augustine, *The Confessions* II.6, trans. Rex Warner (New York: New American Library, 1963), with occasional modifications of mine. Latin quotations are from the Skutella edition published by A. Solignac, *Oeuvres de Saint Augustin*, vols. 13–14 (Paris: Desclée

de Brouwer, 1962). Subsequent references are given in the text.

2. Emmanuel Levinas, *Quatre lectures talmudiques* (Paris: Minuit, 1968), 73–75. Derrida takes up this theme in "Violence and Metaphysics," in *Writing and Difference* (Chicago: University of Chicago Press, 1978), 82. I discuss both in chapter 4, pp. 112–13, and 116–17.

3. See Mark C. Taylor's discussion of prodigality as a challenge to the dominant logic of "utility and consumption" in *Erring: A Postmodern A/theology* (Chicago: University of Chicago Press, 1984), 25, 143–44, 159; *Altarity* (Chicago: University of Chicago Press, 1987), 31–32.

4. Emmanuel Levinas, *Difficile liberté: Essais sur le judaïsme* (Paris: Albin Michel, 1963; 2d ed. 1967, 1974), 19.

5. Søren Kierkegaard, *Fear and Trembling*, trans. Howard V. Hong and Edna H. Hong (Princeton, N.J.: Princeton University Press, 1983), 28. All subsequent references will be given in the text.

6. Erich Auerbach, "Odysseus' Scar," in *Mimesis: The Representation of Reality in Western Literature*, trans. Willard R. Trask (Princeton, N.J.: Princeton University Press, 1953).

7. Taylor, *Erring*, 55–59. It is Taylor who, more than any other commentator, teaches us to read Kierkegaard, teaches us the extent to which Kierkegaard's writing anticipates poststructuralist insights. See Taylor's brilliant chapter on Kierkegaard in *Altarity* (cited above), which culminates an already distinguished series of readings of Kierkegaard in *Journeys to Selfhood: Hegel and Kierkegaard* (Berkeley: University of California Press, 1980); *De-constructing Theology* (New York: Scholars Press, 1982); and the essay "Sounds of Silence," in *Kierkegaard's Fear and Trembling: Critical Appraisals*, ed. Robert L. Perkins (University, Ala.: University of Alabama Press, 1981).

8. *Genesis Rabbah, Vayera* LVI.7, in *The Midrash Rabbah: Genesis*, trans. and eds. H. Freedman and Maurice Simon (London: Soncino Press, 1977).

9. See Maurice Blanchot, *The Space of Literature*, trans. Ann Smock (Lincoln: University of Nebraska Press, 1982). *L'espace littéraire* (Paris: Gallimard, 1955). Jean Starobinski expresses a very similar thought about Kafka's double exile in "Note sur le judaïsme de Kafka," in *Aspects du génie d'Israël* (Paris: Cahiers du Sud, 1950).

10. Emmanuel Levinas, "The Trace of the Other," trans. Alphonso Lingis, in *Deconstruction in Context*, ed. Mark C. Taylor (Chicago: University of Chicago Press, 1986), 348. "La trace de l'autre," *Tijdscrift voor Filosofie* 3 (1963); repr. in *En découvrant l'existence avec Husserl et Heidegger*, 2d ed. (Paris: Vrin, 1967, 1974), 191.

11. *Genesis Rabbah, Vayera* LV.6, in *The Midrash Rabbah*, vol. 1. Thanks to Daniel Boyarin for his help with this rabbinic passage.

12. See Yochanan Muffs, "Joy and Love as Metaphorical Expressions of Willingness and Spontaneity in Cuneiform, Ancient Hebrew, and Related Literatures," in *Christianity, Judaism and Other Greco-Roman Cults,* vol. 3, ed. Jacob Neusner (Leiden: E. J. Brill, 1975).

13. Emmanuel Levinas, *Otherwise than Being or Beyond Essence,* trans. Alphonso Lingis (The Hague: Nijhoff, 1981), 114. *Autrement qu'être ou au-delà de l'essence* (The Hague: Nijhoff, 1974), 145. Subsequent references to this work are given in the text as (OB).

3/ Kafka's Parables

1. Franz Kafka, *The Castle,* trans. Willa and Edwin Muir, (New York: Modern Library, 1969), with occasional modifications of my own: *Das Schloß* (Frankfurt am Main: Fischer Verlag, 1979). Page citations will refer first to the English, then to the German edition (e.g., 84, 65).

2. Kafka, *Castle,* 4, 7.

3. Kafka, *Castle,* 89, 69.

4. Kafka, *Castle,* 112, 85.

5. This includes Heinz Politzer, *Franz Kafka: Parable and Paradox* (1962; repr. Ithaca, N.Y.: Cornell University Press, 1966); Nahum N. Glatzer, editor of the volume of Kafka's writings entitled (not by Kafka) *Parables and Paradoxes* (New York: Schocken Books, 1971). Therapeutic in this regard are Henry Sussman, *Franz Kafka: Geometrician of Metaphor* (Madison, Wis.: Coda Press, 1979); Jacques Derrida, "Préjugés, devant la loi," in *La faculté de juger,* ed. Jean-François Lyotard (Paris: Minuit, 1985). See also the recent collection of essays edited by Alan Udoff, *Kafka and the Contemporary Critical Performance: Centenary Readings* (Bloomington: Indiana University Press, 1987).

6. Sigmund Freud, *Jokes and Their Relation to the Unconscious,* trans. James Strachey (New York: W. W. Norton, 1963), 62. *Der Witz und seine Beziehung zum Unbewußten* (Frankfurt am Main: Fischer Verlag, 1971), 50.

7. Freud, *Jokes,* 205, 167.

8. Richard A. Lanham, *A Handlist of Rhetorical Terms* (Berkeley: University of California Press, 1969), 71.

9. To use a rhetorical rather than a grammatical term here, one could also say that the logic of the Mayor's discourse is asyndeton (from the Greek "unconnected"), the "omission of conjunctions between words, phrases or clauses," while its rhetoric is polysyndeton, the "use of a conjunction between each clause." Lanham, *Handlist,* 18, 78.

10. Horst Steinmetz, *Suspensive Interpretation: Am Beispiel Franz*

Kafkas (Göttingen: Vandenhoeck und Ruprecht, 1977), 107–19. Uyttersprot's remarks are cited by Steinmetz.

11. See J. Hillis Miller's "Parable and Performative in the Gospels and in Modern Literature," in *Humanizing America's Iconic Book* (Chico, Calif.: Scholars Press, 1980), 57–71.

12. Franz Kafka, *The Trial*, trans. Willa and Edwin Muir (New York: Schocken Books, 1968), 217. *Der Prozeß* (Frankfurt am Main: Fischer Verlag, 1963), 185.

13. Politzer, *Franz Kafka*, 1–22.

14. Stanley Corngold, *The Commentators' Despair* (Port Washington, N.Y.: Kennikat Press, 1973).

15. Politzer, *Franz Kafka*, 21.

16. Corngold, *Commentators' Despair*, 7. That Corngold is aware of this and other necessary risks of reading Kafka is also clear. See Stanley Corngold, *Franz Kafka: The Necessity of Form* (Ithaca, N.Y.: Cornell University Press, 1988).

17. Frank Kermode, *The Genesis of Secrecy: On the Interpretation of Narrative* (Cambridge, Mass.: Harvard University Press, 1979), 20.

18. Kafka, *Parables*, 92. It was published posthumously in *Hochzeitsvorbereitungen auf dem Lande* (Frankfurt am Main: Fischer Verlag, 1980), 31, and is included in the English volume *Dearest Father* (New York: Schocken Books, 1954), 34.

19. See, for example, Geoffrey H. Hartman, "Structuralism: The Anglo-American Adventure," in *Beyond Formalism* (New Haven, Conn.: Yale University Press, 1970), 3–23.

20. Kermode, *Genesis of Secrecy*, 26–7.

21. See Kermode, *Genesis of Secrecy*, chap. 2.

22. Kermode, *Genesis of Secrecy*, 32.

23. Walter Benjamin, "Franz Kafka: On the Tenth Anniversary of His Death," in *Illuminations*, trans. Harry Zohn (New York: Schocken Books, 1969); Maurice Blanchot, "Kafka et l'exigence de l'oeuvre," in *L'espace littéraire* (Paris: Gallimard, 1955); Martin Buber, *Two Types of Faith*, trans. Norman P. Goldhawk (New York: Harper Torchbook, 1961); Politzer, chap. 1.

24. Kafka, *Diaries* 1910–1913, trans. Joseph Kresh, with occasional modifications of my own (New York: Schocken Books, 1965), August 21, 1913. *Diaries* 1914–1923, trans. Martin Greenberg, with occasional modifications of my own (New York: Schocken Books, 1965). *Tagebücher* 1910–1923 (Frankfurt am Main: Fischer Verlag, 1973).

25. Kafka, *Diaries* 1914–23, August 27, 1916. *Tagebücher* 1910–1923.

26. Letter to Max Brod, Zürau, middle or end of January 1918, in

Letters to Friends, Family, and Editors, trans. Richard and Clara Winston (New York: Schocken Books, 1977). *Briefe* 1902–1924 (Frankfurt am Main: Fischer Verlag, 1975).

27. Kafka frequently claims to be getting away from Kierkegaard, despite the fact that he seems to be unable to get away from him. In 1918, Kafka writes to Max Brod about Kierkegaard's concern with the problem of finding a true marriage: "But *[aber]* I have, in spite of *[trotzdem]* the fact that Kierkegaard is always in some way present to me, truly forgotten this concern, so much am I roaming about elsewhere, yet *[allerdings]* without ever fully coming out of contact with it" (*Letters,* Zürau, mid-March 1918). And again to Brod, Kafka writes: "Kierkegaard is no longer so present to me, since I have not read his old books for some time. . . . You evidently feel as I do that one cannot withdraw from the power of his terminology" (*Letters,* Zürau, end of March 1918).

28. Jean Wahl, "Kafka et Kierkegaard," in *Esquisse pour une histoire de "l'existentialisme"* (Paris: L'Arche, 1949), trans. Lienhard Bergel, in *The Kafka Problem,* ed. Angel Flores (New York: Octagon Books, 1963). The fragments Wahl discusses were published posthumously in *Hochzeitsvorbereitungen auf dem Lande* (Fourth Octavo Notebook).

29. Søren Kierkegaard, *Fear and Trembling,* trans. Howard V. Hong and Edna H. Hong (Princeton, N.J.: Princeton University Press, 1983), 9.

30. *The Pentateuch and Haftorahs: Hebrew Text, English Translation, and Commentary,* ed. J. H. Hertz, 2d. ed. (London: Soncino Press, 1978), translation slightly modified.

31. In one version, for example, Abraham "seized Isaac by the chest, threw him to the ground, and said, 'Stupid boy, do you think I am your father? I am an idolator. Do you think it is God's command? No, it is my desire.' Then Isaac trembled and cried out in his anguish: 'God in heaven, have mercy on me, God of Abraham, have mercy on me; if I have no father on earth, then you be my father!' But Abraham said softly to himself, 'Lord God in heaven, I thank you; it is better that he believes me a monster than that he should lose faith in you'" (Kierkegaard, *Fear,* 10–11).

32. Kierkegaard, *Fear,* 30.

33. Kierkegaard, *Fear,* 118. Against Kierkegaard's conclusions one midrashic reading settles the question of how to read Abraham's answer differently. The grammatical ambiguity of "my son" in Hebrew (in the vocative case or in apposition to "the lamb," in the accusative case) allows two possible readings: "God will provide for Himself the lamb for the burnt offering, O my son" or "God will provide for Himself the lamb for the burnt offering, namely, my son." See *Genesis Rabbah,*

Vayera LVI.4, in *Midrash Rabbah,* trans. H. Freedman and Maurice Simon (London: Soncino Press, 1977). Geoffrey H. Hartman plays on this grammatical ambiguity with a difference in "The Sacrifice: A New Biblical Narrative," *A Jewish Journal at Yale* 2 (Fall 1984).

34. Kierkegaard, *Fear,* 27–53.

35. Kafka, *Letters,* Zürau, mid-March 1918.

36. Kierkegaard, *Fear,* 74.

37. The substitution of Cain (murderer) for Abraham goes back to Augustine (*City of God* XV.7–8, trans. Henry Bettenson [Baltimore: Penguin Books, 1976]). It is closely linked, as an exegetical gesture, to typological readings of the Old Testament. The Old Testament, read without reference to the Gospel, is a dead or killing letter. Read spiritually it bears witness to "the prophecies that were given beforehand concerning Christ" (XVIII.46). Kierkegaard's emphasis on Abraham's getting Isaac *back* is not unlike Augustine's: "Abraham is to be praised in that he believed without hesitation that his son would rise again [*resurrecturum*] when he had been sacrificed" (XVI.32).

38. Kafka, *Letters,* Matliary, June 1921. Translation (modified) from *Parables and Paradoxes.*

39. Kierkegaard, *Fear,* 38–41.

40. According to Walter Lowrie, Kierkegaard broke his engagement with Regina Olsen for the last time and fled to Berlin, where he wrote *Fear and Trembling* and *Repetition.* Lowrie writes: "We know that while he was writing these two works the struggle to attain resignation was complicated by the hope that he might yet make Regina his wife. This was so evident in *Repetition,* that the text had to be altered when, on his return to Copenhagen, S.K. learned that Regina was already engaged to another." But in *Fear and Trembling,* Lowrie continues, the truth is "so thoroughly refracted" that "the reader . . . may need to be told that Abraham's sacrifice of Isaac is a symbol of S.K.'s sacrifice of the dearest thing he had on earth, and that in order to liberate Regina from her attachment and to 'set her afloat' S.K. felt obliged to be cruel enough to make her believe he was a scoundrel who had merely been trifling with her affections." See the introduction to *Fear and Trembling,* trans. Walter Lowrie (Princeton, N.J.: Princeton University Press, 1954), 9–10.

41. Kenneth Burke correctly points out that "this story, as told in the Bible, does not quite serve the purpose. For there is nothing in it to parallel the very important point about Kierkegaard's 'acting like a scoundrel.' The Bible does not say that Abraham lied to Isaac for Isaac's good. However: Kierkegaard, writing in a highly psychologistic century, improvises a 'psychology' for Abraham. And *this improvised psychology, not the Biblical story,* is the element that helps him solve the

most crucial problem in the redeeming of his conduct. For it is the part that parallels, in Biblical ennoblement, Kierkegaard's depicting of himself as a scoundrel who had trifled with Regina's affections" (*A Rhetoric of Motives* [Berkeley: University of California Press, 1950], 246).

42. Kafka, *Letters to Felice,* trans. James Stern and Elisabeth Duckworth (New York: Schocken Books, 1973), 288. *Briefe an Felice* (Frankfurt am Main: Fischer Verlag, 1976), 426.

43. Kafka to Robert Klopstock, Matliary, June 1921, in *Letters.*

44. Kafka to Robert Klopstock, Matliary, June 1921, in *Letters.*

45. Cited by Rashi, in ed. and trans. M. Rosenbaum and A. M. Silbermann, *Pentateuch with Targum Onkelos, Haphtaroth and Rashi's Commentary* (Jerusalem, 5733).

46. On this, and on a wide range of rabbinic interpretations of the *Akedah,* see the important study by Shalom Spiegel, *The Last Trial: On the Legends and Lore of the Command to Abraham to Offer Isaac as a Sacrifice: The Akedah,* trans. and introd. by Judah Goldin (New York: Behrman House, 1979).

47. Dan Via, Jr., *The Parables: Their Literary and Existential Dimension* (Philadelphia: Fortress Press, 1967), 147–54.

48. Joachim Jeremias, *The Parables of Jesus* (1954; repr. New York: Charles Scribner's Sons, 1972), 34.

49. Jeremias, *The Parables,* 38.

50. *The Interpreter's Bible,* vol. 7 (New York: Abingdon Press, 1951).

51. Kafka, *Castle,* 14, 15.

4 / Alterity and the Judaic

1. For Levinas's own account of his philosophical and biographical itinerary, see "Signature," ed. and annotated by Adriaan Peperzak, trans. M. E. Petrisko, *Research in Phenomenology* 8 (1978): 175–89.

The following abbreviations to works by Emmanuel Levinas are used in references in the text and in the notes:

ADDV   *L'au-delà du verset: Lectures et discours talmudiques* (Paris: Minuit, 1982).

DEHH   *En découvrant l'existence avec Husserl et Heidegger,* 2d ed. (Paris: Vrin, 1967, 1974).

DL   *Difficile liberté: Essais sur le judaïsme* (Paris: Albin Michel, 1963; 2d ed. 1967, 1974).

EE   *Existence and Existents,* trans. Alphonso Lingis (The Hague: Nijhoff, 1978). *De l'existence à l'existant* (Paris: Fontaine, 1947; Vrin, 1973, 1978).

EI   *Ethics and Infinity,* trans. Richard A. Cohen (Pittsburgh: Duquesne University Press, 1985). *Ethique et infini* (Paris: Fayard, 1982).

HAH   *Humanisme de l'autre homme* (Montpellier: Fata Morgana, 1972).

OB   *Otherwise than Being or Beyond Essence,* trans. Alphonso Lingis (The Hague: Nijhoff, 1981). *Autrement qu'être ou au-delà de l'essence* (The Hague: Nijhoff, 1974).

QLT   *Quatre lectures talmudiques* (Paris: Minuit, 1968). Translations from this work are my own. Just as the present volume was going to press, a new English translation appeared: *Nine Talmudic Readings,* trans. and introd. by Annette Aronowicz (Bloomington: Indiana University Press, 1990).

T   "The Trace of the Other," trans. Alphonso Lingis, in *Deconstruction in Context,* ed. Mark C. Taylor (Chicago: University of Chicago Press, 1986). "La trace de l'autre," *Tijdscrift voor Filosofie* 3 (1963); repr. in *En découvrant l'existence.*

TI   *Totality and Infinity,* trans. Alphonso Lingis (Pittsburgh: Duquesne University Press, 1969, 1979). *Totalité et infini* (The Hague: Nijhoff, 1961, 1965, 1968, 1971, 1974).

TO   *Time and the Other,* trans. Richard A. Cohen (Pittsburgh: Duquesne University Press, 1987). *Le temps et l'autre* (Paris: Presses Universitaires de France, 1979).

TrH   "Transcendance et hauteur," *Bulletin de la Société Française de Philosophie* 118 (1962).

TrI   *Transcendance et intelligibilité* (Geneva: Labor et Fides, 1984).

2. Jacques Derrida, "Comment ne pas parler: Dénégations," in *Psyché: Inventions de l'autre* (Paris: Galillée, 1987). My reading of Levinas is indebted to Derrida's two major essays on Levinas, "Violence and Metaphysics: An Essay on the Thought of Emmanuel Levinas" (hereafter cited with page references as VM in the text), in *Writing and Difference* (Chicago: University of Chicago Press, 1978) and "En ce moment même dans cet ouvrage me voici," in *Textes pour Emmanuel Levinas,* ed. François Laruelle (Paris: Jean-Michel Place, 1980); to his "Of an Apocalyptic Tone Recently Adopted in Philosophy," trans. John P. Leavey, Jr., *Oxford Literary Review* 6 (1984): 3–37; and to the seminar he gave on "Political Theology of Language" at the Institute for Semiotic and Structural Studies, University of Toronto, June 1987. The formulation "Judaism and alterity" alludes to the fine book by

Catherine Chalier, *Judaïsme et alterité* (Paris: Verdier, 1982), which registers the impact of Levinas's philosophy by reading the question of the other in the Hebrew Bible.

3. His later work also contains a terminology of election, prophecy, and responsibility that seems biblical.

4. "I always make a clear distinction in what I write, between philosophical and confessional texts. I do not deny that they may ultimately have a common source of inspiration. I simply state that it is necessary to draw a line of demarcation between them as distinct methods of exegesis, as separate languages. I would never, for example, introduce a talmudic or biblical verse into one of my philosophical texts, to try to prove or justify a phenomenological argument" (Interview with Richard Kearney in *Face to Face with Levinas,* ed. Richard A. Cohen [Albany: State University of New York Press, 1986], 18). Levinas also writes, "The word God . . . expresses religiously the clearest notion, philosophically the most obscure one. A notion that could become clear for philosophers starting from the human ethical situations that talmudic texts describe. The inverse procedure would certainly be more edifying and pious; it would not be at all philosophical" (QLT, 70–71).

5. For readers familiar with the Talmud this is not an unusual assertion. The Talmud is not a theology, in the sense of a discourse on the attributes of God. It does not emphasize a *credo* but a primary *doing* for the other. Its open-ended debate that thrives on contradiction indicates a nondogmatic orientation.

6. "The whole [of talmudic discourse] is tied around the prescriptive" (ADDV, 165).

7. Interview with Richard Kearney, *Face to Face,* 19. My conflation of biblical and talmudic wisdom here is deliberate, since in the Jewish tradition the Bible is always read with its talmudic and midrashic commentary.

8. As Mark C. Taylor points out, Levinas's opposition between Odysseus and Abraham is an opposition between "speculative work and ethical works" and thus between, on the one hand, "the utilitarian calculation of the speculator who requires a profitable return on every investment" and, on the other hand, "self-less" "works undertaken in response to the appeal of the Good." See Taylor's chapter on Levinas in *Altarity* (Chicago: University of Chicago Press, 1987), 212–13.

9. In rabbinic literature, these two episodes are traditionally read together, specifically the "Get thee *[lech lecha]* out of thy country" of Gen. 12:1 and the "Get thee *[lech lecha]* into the land of Moriah" of Gen. 22:2. We wonder at Levinas's particular exegetical emphasis on not bringing the son of Abraham's servant Eliezer to the point of departure—whose son is at issue here? Kierkegaard had also given Eliezer

("Abraham's faithful servant") a prominent role in his iteration of the story.

10. Matthew Arnold, "Hebraism and Hellenism," in *Culture and Anarchy* (London: Cambridge University Press, 1932, 1971), 130.

11. "The God of the philosophers from Aristotle to Leibnitz by way of the God of the scholastics is a god adequate to reason, a comprehended god who could not trouble the *autonomy* of consciousness, which finds itself again in all its adventures, returning home to itself like Odysseus, who throughout all his peregrinations is only on the way to his native land" (T, 346). "As a stage the separated being traverses on the way of its return to its metaphysical source, metaphysics would be an Odyssey and its disquietude nostalgia" (TI, 102). "If 'know thyself' could have become the fundamental precept of all Western philosophy, that is because ultimately the West rediscovers the universe in itself. As it is for Odysseus, its periplus is but the accident of a return. In this sense, *The Odyssey* dominates literature" (DL, 24).

12. If the reader's getting or not getting the allusion depends on the rhetorical dimension of language, the hermeneutic model for text understanding will break down. See Paul de Man's introduction to Hans Robert Jauss, *Toward an Aesthetic of Reception* (Minneapolis: University of Minnesota Press, 1982).

13. See, for example, the account of discourse as the fundamental, nontotalizing relationship to the other in *Totality and Infinity,* section 1. In Levinas's later work, the distinction between *le dire* and *le dit* should perhaps be understood as a speech situation in which the asymmetrical addresser-addressee relationship has precedence over the message (i.e., should be understood performatively). For a helpful discussion of Levinas's difficult later work, especially the role of language there, see Taylor, *Altarity.*

14. Jean-François Lyotard, "Levinas' Logic," trans. Ian McLeod, in *Face to Face with Levinas,* ed. Richard A. Cohen (Albany: State University of New York Press, 1986), 118.

15. Derrida, "En ce moment même," 24 (see note 2 above). All translations from this essay are mine.

16. Derrida, "En ce moment même," 25.

17. Lyotard, "Levinas' Logic," 117–18.

18. Derrida, "En ce moment même," 24.

19. For deconstruction as "reversal and reinscription" see Rodolphe Gasché, "Deconstruction as Criticism," *Glyph* 6 (1979). I have also benefited from Gasché's account of Derrida's philosophy in *The Tain of the Mirror: Derrida and the Philosophy of Reflection* (Cambridge, Mass.: Harvard University Press, 1986).

20. See the exchange of letters between Franz Rosenzweig and

Eugen Rosenstock-Huessy, in *Judaism despite Christianity*, ed. Eugen Rosenstock-Huessy (University, Ala.: University of Alabama Press, 1969).

21. Bernhard Blumenkranz, "Augustin et les juifs," *Recherches Augustiniennes* 1 (1958).

22. We say "not primarily" historical in order not to close off other senses in which these oppositions are historical. For example, how are we to read the place of the Judaic in the economy of Augustine's Christian philosophy of history and, in turn, its relation to the anti-Judaic legislation in North Africa that Augustine instituted in his capacity of Bishop of Hippo? How is one to read the triumph of Christianity as positive religion over Judaism? The task of mediating between the non-historicist sense of these oppositions and other, historical senses is as important as it is difficult.

23. In an interview with Philip Nemo, when asked if his intention is to "harmonize" the biblical and the philosophical traditions, Levinas says: "If the two traditions happen to be in harmony, it is probably because every philosophical thought rests on prephilosophical experiences, and because for me reading the Bible has belonged to those founding experiences" (EI, 24). At the close of "Violence and Metaphysics," Derrida suggests that the other name for the experience of the infinitely other in Levinas's work is empiricism. On the role of empiricism in Jewish philosophy, see Emil Fackenheim, *Encounters between Judaism and Modern Philosophy: A Preface to Future Jewish Thought* (New York: Schocken Books, 1980).

24. Translated by Nahum H. Glatzer in *Franz Rosenzweig: His Life and Thought* (New York: Schocken Books, 1953, 1961), 282. From Franz Rosenzweig, *Jehuda Halevi* (Berlin: Lambert Schneider, 1927), 191; repr. in Franz Rosenzweig, *Der Mensch und sein Werk*, vol. I.4 (The Hague: Nijhoff, 1983), 73.

25. Rosenzweig, *Jehuda Halevi*, 191.

26. Julius Guttmann, *Philosophies of Judaism: The History of Jewish Philosophy from Biblical Times to Franz Rosenzweig*, trans. David W. Silverman (New York: Holt, Rinehart and Winston, 1964), 361.

27. When we say that there is, properly speaking, no speaking Hebrew, we do not, of course, refer to an empirical possibility. Nor would we want to reduce this empirical level of speaking a language to something of no importance. But this level may be more complicated than it first appears. Does the pious Jew's speech figure the purity of a language, of the Hebrew language? We do not really know what language the pious Jew speaks; it may be Yiddish. Moreover, this anecdote is recounted by Rosenzweig in German in a note to his translation of Jehuda Halevi's poetry from Hebrew into German. Within the context

of the anecdote as it is glossed by Rosenzweig, the pious Jew's speech figures one discursive pole of a dialectic of God as "near" or "far."

28. Both of Derrida's essays on Levinas are concerned with this question. Bernasconi has devoted several articles to it, and his work offers an important reading of the relationship between Derrida, Levinas, and Heidegger. See his "Deconstruction and the Possibility of Ethics," in *Deconstruction and Philosophy: The Texts of Jacques Derrida,* ed. John Sallis (Chicago: University of Chicago Press, 1987), 122–39; "Levinas and Derrida: The Question of the Closure of Metaphysics," in *Face to Face,* 181–202; "The Trace of Levinas in Derrida," in *Derrida and Différance,* ed. David Wood and Robert Bernasconi (Evanston, Ill.: Northwestern University Press, 1988), 13–30; "Fundamental Ontology, Metontology, and the Ethics of Ethics," *Irish Philosophical Journal* 4 (1987), 76–93.

29. "Existent" is Levinas's translation of the Heideggerian *Seiendes,* which Macquarrie renders as "entity." On this problematic translation, see Derrida (VM, 89). There is also the question as to whether Levinas's or Heidegger's claims should be described as "transcendental." In *The Tain of the Mirror,* Gasché suggests that the ontological structures with which Heidegger characterizes *Dasein* are to be understood as "finite or immanent transcendentals" (a contradiction in terms) because they indicate a prereflexive relationship to the world and because they are conditions of possibility that may or may not be taken up by *Dasein,* that allow for error. Thanks to Rodolphe Gasché for expanding on this notion in conversation.

30. "The presentation and the development of the notions employed [here] owe everything to the phenomenological method" (TI, 28) even if "the intentionality of transcendence is unique in its kind" (TI, 49). "The relationship with the Other can be sought as an irreducible intentionality, even if one must end by seeing that it ruptures intentionality" (EI, 32). "These lines, and those that follow, owe much to Heidegger. Deformed and ill-understood? Perhaps. At least this deformation will not have been a way to deny the debt. Nor this debt a reason to forget" (OB, 189).

31. First of all, to the extent that he does not accept the resemblance of his inquiry to any theology, it is unlikely that Heidegger would accept this characterization. On the question of Judaic nonontotheological theology, see Jean-Luc Marion, *Dieu sans l'être* (Paris: Fayard, 1982), and *L'idole et la distance* (Paris: Grasset, 1977); Rodolphe Gasché, "God for Example," in *Phenomenology and the Numinous,* Fifth Annual Symposium of the Simon Silverman Phenomenology Center (Pittsburgh: Duquesne University Press, 1988); Derrida, "Comment ne pas parler." Paul Ricoeur also suggests that the tradi-

tional interpretation of God's self-revelation in Exodus 3 ("I am that I am") "in the sense of a positive, ontological assertion" may be an illegitimate imposition of a "Neo-Platonic and Augustinian ontology" onto this biblical verse (*Essays on Biblical Interpretation* [Philadelphia: Fortress Press, 1980], 94). After all, God's answer to Moses' question—"who?"—can be interpreted as the refusal of an answer to a question that asks after essence. The lack of the verb "to be" in Hebrew contributes to this enormous question.

32. On how it makes no sense to talk about the "primacy" of ontology or, as Levinas also tries to argue, "the priority of Being over the existent," see Derrida (VM, 135–36). On not misunderstanding Derrida's reading of Levinas's "misreading" of Husserl and Heidegger, on not mistaking Derrida's double gesture of deconstruction for a critique, see Bernasconi, "Deconstruction," and "Levinas and Derrida." Bernasconi's important discussion of the relationship between ethics and ontology in "Fundamental Ontology, Metontology, and the Ethics of Ethics" significantly complicates the question as we have posed it above.

33. The following exposition of Heidegger on which we base this extended analogy is strongly indebted to Rodolphe Gasché's explication of the Heideggerian "as-structure" in *The Tain of the Mirror* and in "God for example" (both cited above) and as it was developed in a graduate seminar that he delivered on Heidegger at the State University of New York at Buffalo in spring 1987. We look forward to the publication of the reading that was developed in seminar, along with other important essays on Heidegger, Derrida, and de Man, in Gasché's next book, *Inventions of Difference*.

34. Gasché, Heidegger seminar.

35. Martin Heidegger, "What Is Metaphysics?" in *Basic Writings*, ed. and trans. David Farrel Krell (New York: Harper and Row, 1977). This problem was treated by Gasché in his Heidegger seminar and by Derrida in his seminar on "Political Theology of Language."

36. Is the name for this rhetorical trope litotes or diminutio—denial of the contrary, an understatement that intensifies? Levinas's "use" of these and other rhetorical figures, including hysteron proteron ("first, last"), hyperbole, and what he has referred to as "insinuation" (TrI, 44), would merit a much longer discussion. Such a discussion would have to deal with Levinas's negative views on rhetoric, which he conceives in the sense of persuasion, and with the incommensurability between these rhetorical terms, which belong to a (derivative) science of figures and the more originary level of Levinas's description. Derrida has also given attention to the question of style and syntax in his two essays on Levinas.

37. They recall the unobtrusiveness of the imperative to be responsible, despite the violence of this originary assignation, as it is described in *Otherwise than Being*.

38. In "Enigme et phénomène" Levinas glosses the "maybe" *(peut-être)* as "the modality of the enigma, irreducible to the modalities of being and of certitude" (DEHH, 214). On the Levinasian *peut-être*, see Derrida, "En ce moment même," 35.

39. *Un pacte neuf,* trans. and introd. by André Chouraqui (Paris: Desclée de Brouwer, 1977). Derrida discusses this work in "Of an Apocalyptic Tone" (see note 2).

40. Chouraqui, *Un pacte,* 9-19.

41. On this double bind, see Derrida, "Des tours de Babel," in *Difference in Translation,* ed. Joseph F. Graham (Ithaca, N.Y.: Cornell University Press, 1985). Here we might signal some of our disagreements with Chouraqui's underlying assumptions about text interpretation, translation, and language. For example, Chouraqui understands "the disappearance of the traces" of the Hebraic substratum of the New Testament as the result of a "Judeo-Christian schism": "If the Judeo-Christian *schism* has been one of the causes of the total or partial *effacement* of the semitic substratum of the New Testament, the Judeo-Christian *reconciliation* will repair the consequences of this break" (*Un pacte,* 10-11). In keeping with the ecumenical inspiration for his project, "the grand ecumenical current since Vatican II" (p. 15) that leads him to "resuscitate the historical realities of the New Testament" (p. 10), Chouraqui hopes that his translation can help effect a Judeo-Christian reconciliation. But is not the "effacement" of the Judaic the very condition of a (unitary) conception of a Judeo-Christian schism *or* reconciliation? Could a consensus, even if it were arrived at miraculously by 72 translators secluded in 72 separate cells, respect the alterity that is marked (and effaced) as a trace?

Chouraqui not only hopes that his translation will effect a dialogue between persons, he conceives of the biblical text itself as such a dialogue. The "exceptional beauty" of the New Testament is due to the fact that it "weds in a unique synthesis, two universes, that of the Hebrews and that of the Greeks" (p. 9). Not wanting to privilege the semitic substratum over the Greek and wanting "to reflect the meeting, in a moment that was tragically privileged in their history, of the east and the west" (p. 12), Chouraqui aims at a "subtle mixture, harmonious and *living(!)* of the two essential components of this work, Hebraicism and Hellenism" (p. 13). This dialogical ecumenicalism is not only complicit with an aesthetic conception of the biblical text (its "exceptional beauty," "harmonious mixture"), it relies on an opposition proper to Christian hermeneutics in aiming at a "living" mixture.

Moreover, Chouraqui's use of a terminology of layers to describe his project—searching out "the Hebraic *substratum*" *"under"* the Greek text (p. 9)—implies that the text has a buried meaning that can be uncovered or dug up. Chouraqui's assumptions about text interpretation are thus hermeneutic in a derived sense, insofar as they rely on a dialectic of veiling and unveiling and on a model of intersubjective dialogue. Chouraqui's explicit theory of translation, in its privileging the semantic pole of language over the syntactic, is also hermeneutic, that is, oriented toward the determination of a transcendental signified. (How can a biblical translation be otherwise?) But Chouraqui's translation is, in a sense, otherwise. His explicit pronouncements about his project are often belied by its aporetic rigor, its internal tensions, and the hermeneutical radicality of his retroversion of biblical names and what he calls "defigured usages" (p. 14). His translation procedure, as opposed to his theory, ultimately suggests a conception of the New Testament text as a differential constitution of traces.

42. Caution is in order here that we not understand this hermeneutic sense of "first" in terms of mere succession. This "first" belongs to an irreversible past that cannot be assembled into the present. There is thus an incommensurability between the sense of the metaleptic reversals we explore in this chapter and those we explore in terms of the prodigal son paradigm in the preceding chapters. See the discussion of this in the Introduction.

43. Martin Heidegger, *The Basic Problems of Phenomenology*, trans. A. Hofstadter (Bloomington: Indiana University Press, 1982), 21. Cited by Gasché, *The Tain of the Mirror*, 113.

44. In his seminar on "Political Theology of Language" Derrida alluded to the Heideggerian nothing in an analogously incongruous context.

45. Franz Rosenzweig, *Briefe* (Berlin: Schocken Verlag, 1935), 70–71.

46. I return to Levinas's discourse on the face in the Conclusion.

47. *Pentateuch with Targum Onkelos, Haphtaroth and Rashi's Commentary*, trans. M. Rosenbaum and A. M. Silbermann (Jerusalem, 5733).

48. *Mekilta de-Rabbi Ishmael*, trans. Jacob Z. Lauterbach (Philadelphia: Jewish Publication Society, 1933), Tractate *Bahodesh*, chap. IX.

49. Of Abraham's piety, Geoffrey H. Hartman writes, "Even his voice he veiled." See "The Sacrifice: A New Biblical Narrative," *A Jewish Journal at Yale* 2 (Fall 1984).

50. Lyotard, "Oedipe juif," *Critique* 277 (1970). "Jewish Oedipus," trans. Susan Hanson, *Genre* 10 (1977).

51. Derrida analyzes the always possible becoming-theological of the deconstructionist discourse in "Comment ne pas parler." See Rodolphe Gasché's discussion of the law of this exchange in "God for Example."

Conclusion: Versions of the Other

1. Peter Brown, *Augustine of Hippo* (Berkeley: University of California Press, 1967), 180.

2. Brown, *Augustine,* 161, 201. See also Marie Aquinas McNamara, *Friendship in Saint Augustine* (Fribourg, Switzerland: University Press, 1958). John Gibb and William Montgomery refer to Augustine's "genius for friendship" in their edition of *The Confessions of Augustine* (London: Cambridge University Press, 1927), xvii.

3. Brown, *Augustine,* 161; McNamara, *Friendship,* chap. 4.

4. Brown, *Augustine,* 161.

5. *dimidium animae suae, Confessions* IV.6, also cited by Brown, *Augustine,* and McNamara, *Friendship.*

6. Jacques Derrida, "The Politics of Friendship," *Journal of Philosophy* 85 (1988): 632–44.

7. Augustine, *The Confessions* IV. English translation (modified) by Rex Warner (New York: New American Library, 1963). This passage—cited by Brown, *Augustine;* McNamara, *Friendship;* and Gibb and Montgomery, *Confessions*—is considered to be an unsurpassed depiction of a friendly intellectual circle and of the satisfactions of (male) friendships. Derrida remarks the virile exclusion of women that characterizes many discourses on friendship; Augustine would be no exception here ("Politics," 642). Brown is aware of this in a recent discussion of Augustine, *The Body and Society: Men, Women, and Sexual Renunciation in Early Christianity* (New York: Columbia University Press, 1988), 389.

8. See McNamara, *Friendship,* 4–7, 193–95.

9. In this passage, the sign is described as if it had the properties of a symbol, as Paul de Man differentiates them in "The Rhetoric of Temporality," in *Blindness and Insight,* 2d ed. (Minneapolis: University of Minnesota, 1971, 1983). On the distinctive way in which the face signifies, see also Augustine's discussion in *On Christian Doctrine* II.1–2, trans. D. W. Robertson, Jr. (Indianapolis: Bobbs-Merrill, 1958), where the example of the face is a borderline case between the two types of signs, natural and conventional.

10. Augustine, *Confessions* IV.4.

11. Etienne Gilson, *The Christian Philosophy of Saint Augustine,* trans. L. E. M. Lynch (New York: Vintage Books, 1967), 140–42.

12. Brown, *Augustine,* 201n. See also McNamara's discussion of Christian friendship in *Friendship,* 193–225.

13. Augustine, *On Christian Doctrine* I.22.

14. Augustine, *On Christian Doctrine* I.3–4.

15. See McNamara, *Friendship,* 205.

16. Søren Kierkegaard, *Fear and Trembling,* trans. Howard V. Hong and Edna H. Hong (Princeton, N.J.: Princeton University Press, 1983), 68.

17. Emphasis mine. Emil Fackenheim, *Encounters between Judaism and Modern Philosophy: A Preface to Future Jewish Thought* (New York: Schocken Books, 1980), 48–49.

18. Interview with Richard Kearney in *Face to Face with Levinas,* ed. Richard A. Cohen (Albany: State University of New York Press, 1986), 23.

19. The phrase is Pierre de Labriolle's, used as a subtitle for his translation of book VIII. *Confessions* (Paris: Société d'Édition 'Les Belles Lettres,' 1947).

20. Romano Guardini, *The Conversion of Augustine* (Westminster, Md.: Newman Press, 1960), 229–30.

21. John Freccero, "The Fig Tree and the Laurel: Petrarch's Poetics," *Diacritics* 5 (1975), 37.

22. Jean Starobinski, "The Struggle with Legion: A Literary Analysis of Mark 5:1–20," trans. Dan Via, Jr., *New Literary History* 4 (1973), 346. "Le combat avec Légion," in *Trois fureurs* (Paris: Gallimard, 1974).

23. Would this also be the case with the Christian community "welded together in love" *(caritate),* to which Augustine refers in the *Confessions* and which he elaborates in the *City of God?* Here the matter is certainly more complex. But a reading of the *City of God,* particularly chap. XV.21, which describes the relationship between the two cities, would show the essential continuity between this description of community and the others I have analyzed, particularly as Augustine's chapter, which is in the form of an exegesis of Gal. 4:21–31, is founded on exactly the kind of problematic fraternal difference on which this book has focused. Such a reading is advanced in a preliminary way in this book's Introduction, where I discuss Augustine's gloss on Paul's allegory of Abraham's two wives, Sarah and Hagar, and two sons, Isaac and Ishmael.

24. Emmanuel Levinas, *Totality and Infinity,* trans. Alphonso Lingis (Pittsburgh: Duquesne University Press, 1969, 1979), 35. *Totalité et infini* (The Hague: Nijhoff, 1961, 1965, 1968, 1971, 1974). All subsequent references to this work will be given in the text as TI.

25. Interview with Richard Kearney, *Face to Face*, 25. Robert Bernasconi discusses this movement as an intentionality in reverse in "Levinas and Derrida: The Question of the Closure of Metaphysics," in *Face to Face*, 188.

26. See Maurice Blanchot's reading of Levinas in *L'Entretien infini* (Paris: Gallimard, 1969).

27. Emmanuel Levinas, *Difficile liberté: Essais sur le judaïsme* (Paris: Albin Michel, 1963; 2d ed. 1967, 1974), 20–21.

28. Maurice Blanchot, *The Writing of the Disaster*, trans. Ann Smock (Lincoln: University of Nebraska, 1986), 19. *L'écriture du désastre* (Paris: Gallimard, 1980), 36–37.

29. Derrida is referring implicitly to Levinas in his discussion in "Politics," 640–41.

30. For a discussion of the *in*ability in responsibility, see Ann Smock, "Disastrous Responsibility," *L'Esprit Créateur* 24 (1984), 5–20.

31. Emmanuel Levinas, *Ethics and Infinity*, trans. Richard A. Cohen (Pittsburgh: Duquesne University Press, 1985), 100–101. *Ethique et infini* (Paris: Fayard, 1982), 107–8.

Index

178   INDEX

Blanchot, Maurice, 15, 77, 89, 100,
    142, 143
Blindness, 104, 113–14; double, 7,
    31; of the Jews, 6–7, 11, 40–41,
    42, 114, 139; and sight, 3, 24, 32,
    43–44, 46, 51, 52, 54, 57, 60, 85,
    113
Bloch, Renée, 147n.24
Bloom, Harold, 1
Blumenkranz, Bernhard, 7, 41, 114
Boccaccio, Giovanni, 50
Bowker, John, 147n.24
Boyarin, Daniel, 148n.28
Brod, Max, 91
Brown, Peter, 133, 136, 173n.7
Bruns, Gerald L., 148n.28
Buber, Martin, 17, 89
Budick, Sanford, 15
Burke, Kenneth, 25, 26, 163n.41

Cain, 37, 38, 39, 41, 42, 43, 44, 73,
    91, 163n.37
Caritas, 135, 174n.23
Carnal and spiritual, 3, 5, 9, 11–12,
    39–41, 43–44, 62–64, 66–68, 86,
    87–88
Catechresis, 131
Chalier, Catherine, 165n.2
Chiasmus, 8, 32, 40, 57, 132
Chouraqui, André, 126, 128,
    171n.41
Cohen, Hermann, 105, 118–19, 125
Conversion, 3, 21, 25–26, 49, 85,
    141; exegetical, 40, 42, 43–44;
    false, 26–27, 32; narrative of, 10,
    21–22, 24, 26, 32, 43, 49, 51, 67,
    71, 73, 129, 138; by reading, 27–
    29, 45–46, 49, 51, 55–58, 66–67,
    138
Corngold, Stanley, 84, 85, 161n.16

Dead Letter, 12, 18, 40–41, 46, 63,
    69, 70, 73; that kills, 38, 42, 76–77
Deconstruction, 114, 132
de Labriolle, Pierre, 27
de Man, Paul, 167n.12, 173n.9
Derrida, Jacques, 17, 100, 101, 134,

143, 160n.5, 169n.31, 173n.7;
    reading of Levinas, 102, 109–111,
    114, 115–18, 119–20, 122–23,
    168n.23, 169nn. 28, 29,
    170nn.32, 36, 171n.38
—Works: "Comment ne pas parler,"
    101, 169n.31, 173n.51; "Des
    tours de Babel," 171n.41; "En ce
    moment même dans cet ouvrage
    me voici," 109–11, 169n.28,
    170n.36; "Of an Apocalyptic Tone
    Recently Adopted in Philosophy,"
    171n.39; "Violence and Metaphys-
    ics," 102, 114, 115–18, 119–20,
    122–23, 168n.23, 169n.28
Dionigi da Borgo San Sepolcro, 49,
    50
Dissimulation, 103, 105, 111, 118–
    19, 120, 122–25, 127–29, 130,
    142, 143
Dodd, C. H., 151n.24
Double bind, 10, 67–68, 109–11,
    171n.41
Durling, Robert M., 155n.19

Economy, 25, 86, 107, 113, 139; in
    Luke's parables, 34–35; of recipro-
    cal exchange, 37, 109; of salvation,
    3, 10, 23–24, 35, 51, 72; of the
    selfsame, 72, 141
Elder brother, 4–5, 10–11, 17, 18,
    33–34, 36–43, 64, 73, 139,
    152n.39
Erring, 24, 53, 65, 70, 71, 88
Error, 26, 53–54, 62, 70, 80–81, 82–
    83, 84, 104; of reading, 68; of vi-
    sion, 68; of hearing, 94–95, 97, 98
Esau, 4
Ethical, 90–91, 110–11, 124, 129,
    130, 143; question of, 101, 105,
    120–23
Ethics, 17–18, 77–78, 100, 102,
    105, 106, 120, 127, 132, 137,
    141; as a problem of language,
    117, 119, 122
Exile, 72, 77, 88
Exteriority, 108, 117, 118, 130

Date Due

MAY - 8 1995	

HENRY FORD COMMUNITY COLLEGE LIBRARY
Form 9004 - Rev. 4/82